*C*hinese *B*reakthrough

LEARNING CHINESE LANGUAGE THROUGH TV AND NEWSPAPERS

*C*hinese *B*reakthrough
中文突破

LEARNING CHINESE LANGUAGE THROUGH TV AND NEWSPAPERS
電視報紙綜合教材

TEXTBOOK
TRADITIONAL AND SIMPLIFIED CHARACTERS

HONG GANG JIN

靳洪剛

DE BAO XU

許德寶

JOHN BERNINGHAUSEN

白志昂

CHENG & TSUI COMPANY

Cheng & Tsui Company
25 West Street
Boston, MA 02111-1268 USA

Library of Congress Catalog Number: 93-74517

ISBN 0-88727-194-4

Companion workbook, video tape, and audio cassettes are also available from the publisher.

Printed in the United States of America

PUBLISHER'S NOTE

The Cheng & Tsui Company is pleased to announce the most recent volume of its Asian Language Series, *Chinese Breakthrough*. This intermediate-to-advanced-level multimedia course uses live news broadcasts to enable students to bridge the gap between purely academic learning and the real world of native speakers. It is our hope that, with the help of the accompanying workbook, audio tapes, and video tape, the student will increase his/her listening and speaking abilities along with reading and writings skills through this very enjoyable format.

The C&T Asian Language Series is designed to publish and widely distribute quality language texts as they are completed by such leading institutions as the Beijing Language Institute, as well as other significant works in the field of Asian languages developed in the United States and elsewhere.

We welcome readers' comments and suggestions concerning the publications in this series. Please contact the following members of the Editorial Board:

Professor Shou-hsin Teng, Chief Editor
3 Coach Lane, Amherst, MA 01002

Dana Scott Bourgerie
Asian and Near Eastern Languages Brigham Young University, Provo, UT 84602

Professor Samuel Cheung
Dept. of Oriental Languages, University of California, Berkeley, CA 94720

Professor Ying-che Li
Dept. of East Asian Languages, University of Hawaii, Honolulu, HI 96822

Professor Timothy Light
Office of the Provost, Western Michigan University, Kalamazoo, MI 49008

TABLE OF CONTENTS

目錄

目录

Preface

In today's global linkup of electronic mass media, daily **televised news broadcasts** are a pervasive, influential and highly popular medium of mass communication. Among the various large-scale televised news broadcasting systems providing local, national and international news are Mandarin language news programs; these programs constitute a compelling and valuable source of information for a large percentage of the viewing public in China, Taiwan, Singapore, Hong Kong and the Chinese-speaking populations of Southeast Asia and the rest of the world.

News broadcasts in Mandarin originating in China and in Taiwan are now widely disseminated across the globe via cable stations and satellite linkups. Just as Chinese newspapers from the Far East are supplemented in other parts of the world by locally published Chinese language newspapers, nowadays TV news broadcasts from China and Taiwan relayed by satellite and rebroadcast abroad are augmented by locally produced Chinese (Mandarin) language television news programming. For the high-intermediate to advanced student of spoken Mandarin and written Chinese,[1] becoming more adept and comfortable at comprehending news items presented in Mandarin language TV news broadcasts is both an important skill and a natural desire.

The vocabulary and stylistic conventions of Chinese broadcast and print journalism, as is true of other modes of formal written language in Chinese, often diverge significantly from more colloquial forms of spoken and written Chinese. Acquiring greater proficiency in the actual language of Chinese broadcast and print journalism can be quite a challenging process for non-native learners. The learner must acquire familiarity with the somewhat specialized vocabulary, idioms, syntax, stylistic conventions including *shumianyu*,[2] abbreviations, etc. As always there is a lot of background information for the student to absorb as well as gaining greater familiarity with the implicit cultural values which various Chinese news shows assume to be shared by its intended audience. Then there is the fact that the learner is faced with the extra and formidable challenge of adjusting to the "rapid fire delivery" typical of most TV and radio news broadcasters the world over.

To date, there is little available in the way of structured pedagogic materials specifically designed to introduce students to *television* news programming in Mandarin and to carry them through their early adjustment to the vocabulary as well as the speed of news reporting on television.[3] A *structured* introduction to the specific medium and format of Chinese TV news broadcasts can be and doubtless should be one of several components in a well-balanced instructional program in Mandarin Chinese. Becoming *truly proficient* at reading Chinese newspapers or at the closely related but distinct skill of viewing and comprehending news programming broadcast in Mandarin may entail greater frustration and take longer than anticipated by the neophyte. Nonetheless non-native learners can markedly increase their familiarity with much of the necessary vocabulary and syntax, enhance their self-confidence and improve their capacity to follow rapidly delivered news items.

---

[1] This set of materials anticipate prior mastery of approximately 1200 to 1500 *hanzi* and a *high intermediate* level of vocabulary, syntax and grammar. For many Western students at the college level, this generally equates to 250 to 300 hours of rigorous formal classroom instruction in spoken and written Mandarin Chinese or its equivalent.

[2] *"Shumianyu,"* an important register involving more formal or erudite vocabulary and syntax characteristic of written Chinese (e.g., academic, ceremonial, epistolary or *belles lettristic*) is also a prominent feature of Chinese journalistic language, whether printed in newspapers or broadcast over the airwaves.

[3] To be sure, there are several textbooks aimed at the non-native learner, some quite good, which introduce "newspaper Chinese." However, these previously published pedagogic materials do not address themselves directly to the special problems learners will experience in attempting to view televised news reports in Mandarin.

Basic Aims

A. To enable those learners of Chinese who have reached *high intermediate* or *advanced* level of proficiency to "break through" the initial frustrations and seeming incomprehensibility of television news programs in Mandarin to a significantly greater facility in *comprehending* and enjoying this important form of mass communication.[4]

B. To create a structured yet flexible multi-media course format based on authentic examples of journalistic Chinese, supported by extensive examples and exercises, appropriate for high school, college, or adult learners in government, business, journalism, education, etc. **ZHONGWEN TUPO** should also prove readily adaptable for use in other learning contexts including self-study.

C. To promote the learner's continuing progress in all five skill areas: listening comprehension with an emphasis on the particular challenges posed by the rapid pace of radio and TV news broadcasters, speaking, reading comprehension, writing, and control of the necessary background information (cultural competency). This course of study seeks to present a series of news items, moving sequentially from the easier to the more difficult, and suitable for increasing the learner's competence and self-confidence. It attempts to do this by providing extensive vocabulary glosses, grammatical explanations including considerable attention to *shumianyu*, necessary background information and ample oral and written exercises.

D. To provide integrated and fully annotated audiovisual materials including video tapes, audio tapes, text book and exercise workbook which can be used both during classroom instruction as well as outside of class in the language lab, at home, etc.

Special Features of ZHONGWEN TUPO

A. Content divided among four main units

The textbook consists of a total of fifteen lessons divided among four basic units, each unit consisting of three or four separate lessons centered on authentic People's Republic of China (PRC) TV news items recorded on video tape and their written transcription combined with one or two short articles on the same topic chosen from the Chinese press:

Unit 1	DAILY NEWS & CURRENT EVENTS[5]
Unit 2	BUSINESS & ECONOMIC NEWS
Unit 3	NEWS OF CULTURAL AFFAIRS
Unit 4	NEWS FROM THE WORLD OF SPORTS

Within each unit one or two televised "public service messages" and a popular folk song have been included as distinct and optional "mini lessons" so as to provide a change of pace, increased cultural insights and some relatively colloquial, or perhaps more "entertaining" examples.

---

[4] It goes with saying that no single course nor set of introductory materials, no matter how successful, should be expected to carry a high intermediate or advanced student from the initial stages of competency in viewing Mandarin TV news broadcasts all the way to a truly high-level proficiency in this area. The *tupo* or "breakthrough" implicitly promised in our title refers to helping the student get over the initial but nonetheless formidable hurdle of incomprehensibility and lack of self-confidence to a moderate level of understanding.

[5] Including news coverage of stories dealing with international, diplomatic, political or military topics.

B. Four-part organization of each lesson

1. Texts: From 400 to 600 characters in length and including approximately 45 to 70 new vocabulary items, the texts of all fifteen lessons include a short introduction, dialogues, the transcription of the TV news item(s) along with one or two corresponding newspaper articles and a humorous snippet at the end. The brief introductory passage and the relatively short dialogues have been designed to introduce the learner to relevant new vocabulary and background information; these first two sections and the audio tapes should help prepare the student to listen to and view with greater comprehension the authentic, videotaped TV news story that follows.

2. Grammar Points: There are also several points of grammar emphasized in each lesson including numerous examples and explication of the usage of frequently encountered classical Chinese words, abbreviations, idioms, phrases, etc. which have appeared in the lesson's texts.

3. Classroom Exercises: Several different types of exercises, written and oral, designed to be completed in class are coordinated with the televised news items and will assist in sharpening the student's listening skills.

4. Homework Assignments: Exercises such as translating short phrases, sentence completion, language application, newspaper reading and translating sentences are provided to help the student reinforce what has been studied in class.

C. Authenticity and Contextualization

This course of study has been designed to capitalize on the authenticity and the visual appeal and reinforcement provided by short recorded segments of actual Chinese television news broadcasts. In following the format of highly episodic or "fragmented" broadcast news programming, it would be both difficult and artificial to attempt to link together the various news stories with any common thread.[6] A significant and generally usable range of vocabulary and grammatical structures is, nonetheless, presented and often highlighted in a journalistic *context* within each segment or news item.

The accompanying exercises as well as the various activities, discussion topics, and suggested writing assignments included are intended to reinforce the mastery of the newly contextualized vocabulary and grammar. Along with the copious vocabulary glosses and grammatical explanations provided, in principle (and we hope in practice) these exercises will serve to reduce the amount of time the instructor or tutor needs to spend in devising supplementary reinforcement exercises.

D. Vocabulary Glosses

Due to the inability to predict exactly which vocabulary items various learners will have already mastered prior to using this textbook, we have intentionally provided rather "generous" vocabulary glosses. In many instances, we have provided at least two or three separate examples (contextualized at least up to the level of a sentence) of how various words or grammatical patterns are used. It has been our conscious purpose to restrict to a minimum the amount of time learners will spend with dictionaries looking up unknown or forgotten compounds or *hanzi*. [7]

---

[6] There is also the inevitable problem of *topicality*. In selecting representative items, it is virtually impossible to avoid including news reports that are already "dated" or "unfamiliar" by the time the text is published. About all one can do is to guess which "old news items" will introduce or reinforce vocabulary and similar topics still frequently encountered in the news stories of a later period.

[7] It might be argued that we have been excessively generous in the amount of vocabulary definitions and English translation for the examples, thereby "spoon-feeding" (depriving the learner of sufficient opportunities to practice "guessing strategies"). Such choices in pedagogical strategies, as always, proved rather difficult and we spent considerable

While not attempting to include comprehensive listings of all possible "parts of speech" (grammatical function) which the glossed vocabulary items might fulfil, we have tried to indicate the grammatical function for the glossed word in its context. When we thought it sufficiently important to do so, we have sometimes chosen to alert the learner to one or more other grammatical functions (nominal, adverbial, verbal, adjectival, etc.) in which a certain Chinese word could be used.

E. Active utilization by learner

Wherever possible, we have designed the accompanying dialogues, readings, grammatical or idiomatic examples, classroom activities, written exercises, etc. to encourage and to expand the capacity of the learner to actively utilize in culturally appropriate ways and thus to better "internalize" a fairly broad range of vocabulary and background information relevant to contemporary China and Chinese language news broadcasts.

F. Multi-media resources

There can be many opportunities for creative interaction between watching the authentic video tape segments and using the textbook. It is our hope that in the not too distant future, these materials may become even more interactive by means of greater interaction by the student with digitalized images and a more computer-based format including computer-assisted-learning and exercises.

ZHONGWEN TUPO comes into two volumes, a textbook and a workbook each with both traditional and simplified Chinese characters (on the left-hand pages are traditional characters and on the right-hand pages are simplified characters).

Finally, we would like to express our thanks to Christine Ingersoll for designing the cover page, Jeff Inui for creating the illustrations for the book, and China Central Television, Beijing Television, and Shanxi Television Stations for providing the news programs.

---

time and effort wrestling with them. While conceding the validity and utility of a pedagogical strategy that emphasizes guessing, after polling the preferences of several experienced teachers, we opted to provide extensive vocabulary glosses and translations of the sentence-based examples in what we hope are accurate and contextually colloquial English equivalents. Needless to say, we would appreciate any suggestions for improving or refining any of our examples, explanations or definitions.

.

前言

　　中國的電視新聞，跟其他語種的電視新聞一樣，是一種影響極其廣泛的大眾傳播媒介。同樣，每日印發的中文報紙也跟其他世界性刊物一樣，具有相當大的影響力。然而這種電視報紙所用的新聞語言卻與日常口語區別很大，有其獨特的詞彙、句法結構以及文體。要看懂中國電視新聞、讀懂中文報紙，非得學習這種新聞語言不可。

　　要想順利無誤地聽懂以及讀懂這種電視報紙特有的新聞語言，不但需要很熟悉牠的詞彙、句法、文體以及觀眾所具備的背景知識，而且必須對中文書面語的詞彙以及語法特徵有相當的了解，例如：成語、縮略語、固定短語、諺語、常用結構以及具有高度文化特色的比喻等。這些都很難掌握。只有真正接觸了這種新聞語言，才能在實踐中慢慢地學會牠們。因此，利用電視以及報紙新聞語言就成了中文教學中必不可少的一部分。

　　為了使學生有效地掌握這種新聞語言，我們特別編排了這套多媒體並用（錄像、錄音、課本、練習本）的中文電視、報紙綜合教材。

　　這套教材的特點可以歸納如下：

　　一、利用真實的現代新聞媒體為學生提供一個材料真實，聽、說、讀、寫以及文化背景兼顧的高級中文教材，使學生能在學習新聞語言的同時熟悉當代中國的各種文化現象，為以後獨立看電視、讀報紙打下基礎。

　　二、利用多種媒介設計各種練習，視聽並舉，同時強調詞彙以及句子結構的特殊語用環境以及重複使用率，使學生能在短時期內掌握新聞體中的各種詞彙、句子結構以及文體特點。

　　三、課程安排由易至難，循序漸進。不但適用於高中、大學以及成人自學，也適用於政府外交以及職業培訓。

　　四、提供充分有效的課堂活動以及相應的課下練習，能節省教師背課時間。

　　五、學生程度宜在二年級以上，學過一千二百至一千五百中國字。

　　這套教材共包括四個單元十五課課文，分別介紹四種常見的新聞文體：

前言

　　中国的电视新闻，跟其他语种的电视新闻一样，是一种影响极其广泛的大众传播媒介。同样，每日印发的中文报纸也跟其他世界性刊物一样，具有相当大的影响力。然而这种电视报纸所用的新闻语言却与日常口语区别很大，有其独特的词汇、句法结构以及文体。要看懂中国电视新闻、读懂中文报纸，非得学习这种新闻语言不可。

　　要想顺利无误地听懂以及读懂这种电视报纸特有的新闻语言，不但需要很熟悉它的词汇、句法、文体以及观众所具备的背景知识，而且必须对中文书面语的词汇以及语法特徵有相当的了解，例如：成语、缩略语、固定短语、谚语、常用结构以及具有高度文化特色的比喻等。这些都很难掌握。只有真正接触了这种新闻语言，才能在实践中慢慢地学会它们。因此，利用电视以及报纸新闻语言就成了中文教学中必不可少的一部分。

　　为了使学生有效地掌握这种新闻语言，我们特别编排了这套多媒体并用（录像、录音、课本、练习本）的中文电视、报纸综合教材。

　　这套教材的特点可以归纳如下：
　　一、利用真实的现代新闻媒体为学生提供一个材料真实，听、说、读、写以及文化背景兼顾的高级中文教材，使学生能在学习新闻语言的同时熟悉当代中国的各种文化现象，为以後独立看电视、读报纸打下基础。
　　二、利用多种媒介设计各种练习，视听并举，同时强调词汇以及句子结构的特殊语用环境以及重复使用率，使学生能在短时期内掌握新闻体中的各种词汇、句子结构以及文体特点。
　　三、课程安排由易至难，循序渐进。不但适用於高中、大学以及成人自学，也适用於政府外交以及职业培训。
　　四、提供充分有效的课堂活动以及相应的课下练习，能节省教师背课时间。
　　五、学生程度宜在二年级以上，学过一千二百至一千五百中国字。

　　这套教材共包括四个单元十五课课文，分别介绍四种常见的新闻文体：

第一單元：每日新聞

第二單元：經濟新聞

第三單元：文化新聞

第四單元：體育新聞

每單元包括三至四課。每課均配備真實電視新聞錄像以及相應內容的報紙新聞。除此以外，各單元均穿插一至兩則常見廣告及一個流行歌曲，以使學生熟悉理解中國文化，同時也用以調節學習節奏。

每課由四個部分組成：

一、課文：

包括簡介、對話、電視新聞、報紙新聞及小幽默等約四到六百字。生詞量在45到70之間。

二、語法要點：

著重歸納、舉例講解新聞體中常見的文言詞、縮略語、慣用語、常用短語結構等用法。

三、課堂練習：

配合錄像帶用關鍵詞填空以及回答問題等形式訓練學生對電視新聞的視聽能力。

四、課下練習：

用短語翻譯、完成句子、語言實踐、報紙閱讀以及句子翻譯等協助學生復習課堂所學內容。

本教材備有繁簡兩體的課本与練習本（左頁為繁體、右頁為簡體），並配有錄像帶、錄音帶，還將配備電腦輔助練習材料等。教師可以根據學生的實際需要有選擇地使用。

在本教材的編寫過程中，多承Christine Ingersoll設計封面，Jeff Inui（乾真）繪製插圖，中國中央電視台、北京電視台以及山西電視台提供新聞節目，在此一並致以誠摯的謝意。

第一单元: 每日新闻

第二单元: 经济新闻

第三单元: 文化新闻

第四单元: 体育新闻

每单元包括三至四课。每课均配备真实电视新闻录像以及相应内容的报纸新闻。除此以外，各单元均穿插一至两则常见广告及一个流行歌曲，以使学生熟悉理解中国文化，同时也用以调节学习节奏。

每课由四个部分组成:

一、课文:

包括简介、对话、电视新闻、报纸新闻及小幽默等约四到六百字。生词量在45到70之间。

二、语法要点:

着重归纳、举例讲解新闻体中常见的文言词、缩略语、惯用语、常用短语结构等用法。

三、课堂练习:

配合录像带用关键词填空以及回答问题等形式训练学生对电视新闻的视听能力。

四、课下练习:

用短语翻译、完成句子、语言实践、报纸阅读以及句子翻译等协助学生复习课堂所学内容。

本教材备有繁简两体的课本与练习本（左页为繁体、右页为简体），并配有录像带、录音带，还将配备电脑辅助练习材料等。教师可以根据学生的实际需要有选择地使用。

在本教材的编写过程度中，多承Christine Ingersoll设计封面，Jeff Inui（乾真）绘制插图，中国中央电视台、北京电视台以及山西电视台提供新闻节目，在此一并致以诚挚的谢意。

Unit 1: News Kaleidoscope

第一單元 每日新聞

第一課

新聞提要

課文

一、簡介 (Introduction)

中國電視新聞的開始都有新聞提要。提要的目的就是先把當天的新聞用簡單明白的話報告給觀眾。報告新聞提要之前和之後都有一定的電視新聞套語，很少有變化。下面介紹的就是中國電視新聞聯播中的新聞提要。

生詞

新聞	(xīn wén)	N.	news
提要	(tí yào)	N.	highlight, synopsis, summary of main points
簡介	(jiǎn jiè)	N.	introduction
目的	(mù dì)	N.	purpose, goal, aim
報告	(bào gào)	N/V.	report; to report
觀眾	(guān zhòng)	N.	spectators, (the) audience, the public, the listener
之前/後	(zhī qián/hòu)	Prep.	before/after
套語	(tào yǔ)	N.	set phrase, fixed expressions
聯播	(lián bō)	N.	broadcast over a network; i.e., national news broadcast hookup

第一单元 每日新闻

第一课

新闻提要

课文

一、简介 (Introduction)

　　中国电视新闻的开始都有新闻提要。提要的目的就是先把当天的新闻用简单明白的话报告给观众。报告新闻提要之前和之后都有一定的电视新闻套语，很少有变化。下面介绍的就是中国电视新闻联播中的新闻提要。

生词

新闻	(xīn wén)	*N.*	news
提要	(tí yào)	*N.*	highlight, synopsis, summary of main points
简介	(jiǎn jiè)	*N.*	introduction
目的	(mù dì)	*N.*	purpose, goal, aim
报告	(bào gào)	*N/V.*	report; to report
观众	(guān zhòng)	*N.*	spectators, (the) audience, the public, the listener
之前/后	(zhī qián/hòu)	*Prep.*	before/after
套语	(tào yǔ)	*N.*	set phrase, fixed expressions
联播	(lián bō)	*N.*	broadcast over a network; i.e., national news broadcast hookup

二、對話 (Dialogues)

（一）

鄧平：江敏，你知道今天的新聞聯播節目是幾點嗎？

江敏：對不起，鄧平，你可問錯人了。我不是一個電視觀眾，我家連電視都
沒有。

問題：鄧平想知道甚麼事情？ 江敏是怎麼回答的？

生詞

節目	(jié mù)	N.	program (TV)
電視觀眾	(diàn shì guān zhòng)	NP.	TV viewers, the viewing public, the viewers

（二）

鄧平：江敏，你知道嗎，奧運會上，中國體育健兒取得矚目成就。

江敏：鄧平，這已經是舊聞了，你還在說呢。前天的新聞聯播節目已經報告
過了，這些奧運健兒都將分別回北京了。首都各界都在做準備，歡迎
他們回來。

問題：前天的新聞聯播報告了一條甚麼消息？

生詞

奧運	(ào yùn)	Abbrev.	the Olympic Games＝奧運會＝奧林匹克運動會
健兒	(jiàn ér)	N.	top athletes; valiant warriors
分別	(fēn bié)	Adv.	respectively, separately
獲得	(huò dé)	V.	to achieve; to attain, to earn, to gain

二、对话 (Dialogues)

（一）

邓平：　江敏，你知道今天的新闻联播节目是几点吗？

江敏：　对不起，邓平，你可问错人了。我不是一个电视观众，我家连电视都
　　　　没有。

问题：邓平想知道什么事情？江敏是怎么回答的？

生词

节目	(jié mù)	*N.*	program (TV)
电视观众	(diàn shì guān zhòng)	*NP.*	TV viewers, the viewing public, the viewers

（二）

邓平：　江敏，你知道吗，奥运会上，中国体育健儿取得瞩目成就。

江敏：　邓平，这已经是旧闻了，你还在说呢。前天的新闻联播节目已经报告
　　　　过了，这些奥运健儿都将分别回北京了。首都各界都在做准备，欢迎
　　　　他们回来。

问题：前天的新闻联播报告了一条什么消息？

生词

奥运	(ào yùn)	*Abbrev.*	the Olympic Games = 奥运会 = 奥林匹克运动会
健儿	(jiàn ér)	*N.*	top athletes; valiant warriors
分别	(fēn bié)	*Adv.*	respectively, separately
获得	(huò dé)	*V.*	to achieve; to attain, to earn, to gain

取得	(qǔ dé)	V.	to achieve; to obtain
矚目	(zhǔ mù)	Adj.	amazing, remarkable, eye-opening
成就	(chéng jìu)	N.	achievement (s) ; accomplishment (s)
舊聞	(jìu wén)	N.	old news, out-of-date news
首都各界	(shǒu dū gè jiè)	NP.	people from all walks of life in the capital city (here: 北京)
歡迎	(huān yíng)	V/N.	to welcome; welcome

（三）

江敏：鄧平，你這個電視迷，能不能告訴我最近國內外發生了甚麼事情？

鄧平：行啊。現在我可以向你報告兩條新聞：泰國和印度尼西亞客人今天分別到達北京對中國進行訪問。中國海南經濟開發區取得矚目成就。

問題：鄧平報告的兩條新聞是甚麼？

生詞

電視迷	(diàn shì mí)	N.	TV fan, "TV junkie"
國內外	(guó nèi wài)	NP.	domestic and international
泰國	(tài guó)	Place N.	Thailand
印度尼西亞	(yìn dù ní xī yà)	Place N.	Indonesia
到達	(dào dá)	V.	to arrive
海南	(hǎi nán)	Place N.	Hainan, an island province off the coast of South China
開發	(kāi fā)	V.	to develop; to open up
區	(qū)	N.	area; district; zone
開發區	(kāi fā qū)	N.	(the) development zone; a district or a region slated for concentrated industrial, commercial and/or agribusiness development

3

取得	(qǔ dé)	*V.*	to achieve; to obtain
瞩目	(zhǔ mù)	*Adj.*	amazing, remarkable, eye-opening
成就	(chéng jìu)	*N.*	achievement (s) ; accomplishment (s)
旧闻	(jìu wén)	*N.*	old news, out-of-date news
首都各界	(shǒu dū gè jiè)	*NP.*	people from all walks of life in the capital city (here: 北京)
欢迎	(huān yíng)	*V/N.*	to welcome; welcome

（三）

江敏： 邓平，你这个电视迷，能不能告诉我最近国内外发生了什么事情？

邓平： 行啊。现在我可以向你报告两条新闻：泰国和印度尼西亚客人今天分别到达北京对中国进行访问。中国海南经济开发区取得瞩目成就。

问题: 邓平报告的两条新闻是什么？

生词

电视迷	(diàn shì mí)	*N.*	TV fan, "TV junkie"
国内外	(guó nèi wài)	*NP.*	domestic and international
泰国	(tài guó)	*Place N.*	Thailand
印度尼西亚	(yìn dù ní xī yà)	*Place N.*	Indonesia
到达	(dào dá)	*V.*	to arrive
海南	(hǎi nán)	*Place N.*	Hainan, an island province off the coast of South China
开发	(kāi fā)	*V.*	to develop; to open up
区	(qū)	*N.*	area; district; zone
开发区	(kāi fā qū)	*N.*	(the) development zone; a district or a region slated for concentrated industrial, commercial and/or agribusiness development

（四）

江敏：這是甚麼？

鄧平：這是美國錢，叫美元。

江敏：這是甚麼錢？

鄧平：這是中國錢，叫人民幣。

江敏：現在美元對人民幣的匯率是多少？

鄧平：1 比 8.55。

江敏：看來人民幣對美元的匯率已經漲到歷史最高水平了。

問題：美元對人民幣的匯率是多少？

生詞

美元	(měi yuán)	*N.*	U.S. dollar
人民幣	(rén mín bì)	*N.*	Chinese Yuan (dollar), RMB
匯率	(huì lǜ)	*N.*	exchange rate
漲到	(zhǎng dào)	*V.*	to go up, to rise
歷史最高水平	(lì shǐ zuì gāo shuǐ píng)	*NP.*	record high, all time high

三、電視新聞 (The TV news)

新聞提要

觀眾同志們晚上好，這次新聞聯播節目的主要內容有：

天津經濟技術開發區取得矚目成就

中共中央總書記江澤民會見印度尼西亞客人

李鵬和萬里分別會見泰國客人

澳星發射試驗隊凱旋

（四）

江敏: 这是什么？

邓平: 这是美国钱，叫美元。

江敏: 这是什么钱？

邓平: 这是中国钱，叫人民币。

江敏: 现在美元对人民币的汇率是多少？

邓平: 1 比 8.55。

江敏: 看来人民币对美元的汇率已经涨到历史最高水平了。

问题: 美元对人民币的汇率是多少？

生词

美元	(měi yuán)	N.	U.S. dollar
人民币	(rén mín bì)	N.	Chinese Yuan (dollar), RMB
汇率	(huì lǜ)	N.	exchange rate
涨到	(zhǎng dào)	V.	to go up, to rise
历史最高水平	(lì shǐ zuì gāo shuǐ píng)	NP.	record high, all time high

三、电视新闻 (The TV news)

新闻提要

观众同志们晚上好，这次新闻联播节目的主要内容有：

天津经济技术开发区取得瞩目成就

中共中央总书记江泽民会见印度尼西亚客人

李鹏和万里分别会见泰国客人

澳星发射试验队凯旋

奧運健兒為首都各界做報告

伊拉克斷然拒絕在其領空建立空中禁區

美元匯率降低到歷史最低水平

下面請看詳細內容

生詞

內容	(nèi róng)	*N.*	content
技術	(jì shù)	*N.*	technology; technique
中共中央	(zhōng gòng zhōng yāng)	*Abbrev.*	Central Committee of the Chinese Communist Party (CCCCP)＝中國共產黨中央委員會
總書記	(zǒng shū jì)	*Title/rank.*	General Secretary
江澤民	(jiāng zé mín)	*Personal N.*	Jiang Zemin
李鵬	(lǐ péng)	*Personal N.*	Li Peng, Chinese Premier
萬里	(wàn lǐ)	*Personal N.*	Wan Li, an important Chinese government official
澳星	(ào xīng)	*Abbrev.*	澳大利亞的衛星, the Australian satellite (a communications satellite launched by China for Australia)
發射	(fā shè)	*V/N.*	to launch; the launching of
試驗隊	(shì yàn duì)	*N.*	"test crew"
發射試驗隊	(fā shè shì yàn duì)	*NP.*	"launch crew"
凱旋	(kǎi xuán)	*V.*	triumphant return; returning in triumph
伊拉克	(yī lā kè)	*Place N.*	Iraq
斷然	(duàn rán)	*Adv.*	flatly, categorically
拒絕	(jù jué)	*V/N.*	to refuse; refusal
在其	(zài qí)	*Prep P.*	at its, on its
領空	(lǐng kōng)	*N.*	territorial airspace (i.e., airspace over sovereign territory)
空中禁區	(kōng zhōng jìn qū)	*NP.*	a no-fly zone; restricted airspace
降低	(jiàng dī)	*V.*	to drop, to reduce
詳細	(xiáng xì)	*Adv/Adj.*	in detail, detailed

5

奥运健儿为首都各界做报告

伊拉克断然拒绝在其领空建立空中禁区

美元汇率降低到历史最低水平

下面请看详细内容

生词

内容	(nèi róng)	*N.*	content
技术	(jì shù)	*N.*	technology; technique
中共中央	(zhōng gòng zhōng yāng)	*Abbrev.*	Central Committee of the Chinese Communist Party (CCCCP) = 中国共产党中央委员会
总书记	(zǒng shū jì)	*Title/rank.*	General Secretary
江泽民	(jiāng zé mín)	*Personal N.*	Jiang Zemin
李鹏	(lǐ péng)	*Personal N.*	Li Peng, Chinese Premier
万里	(wàn lǐ)	*Personal N.*	Wan Li, an important Chinese government official
澳星	(ào xīng)	*Abbrev.*	澳大利亚的卫星, the Australian satellite (a communications satellite launched by China for Australia)
发射	(fā shè)	*V/N.*	to launch; the launching of
试验队	(shì yàn duì)	*N.*	"test crew"
发射试验队	(fā shè shì yàn duì)	*NP.*	"launch crew"
凯旋	(kǎi xuán)	*V.*	triumphant return; returning in triumph
伊拉克	(yī lā kè)	*Place N.*	Iraq
断然	(duàn rán)	*Adv.*	flatly, categorically
拒绝	(jù jué)	*V/N.*	to refuse; refusal
在其	(zài qí)	*Prep P.*	at its, on its
领空	(lǐng kōng)	*N.*	territorial airspace (i.e., airspace over sovereign territory)
空中禁区	(kōng zhōng jìn qū)	*NP.*	a no-fly zone; restricted airspace
降低	(jiàng dī)	*V.*	to drop, to reduce
详细	(xiáng xì)	*Adv/Adj.*	in detail, detailed

四、報紙閱讀 (Newspaper reading)

1. 楊尚昆祝賀"澳星"發射成功

杨尚昆祝贺"澳星"发射成功

2. 外商在天津經濟開發區投資的三種主要形式

外商在天津经济开发区
投资的三种主要形式

3. 萬里會見泰國上院議長

万里会见泰国上院议长

4. 天津經濟技術開發區專版

天津经济技术开发区专版
天津市经济技术开发区管委会供稿

5. 美元對馬克匯價緣何暴跌

美元对马克汇价缘何暴跌

四、报纸阅读 (Newspaper reading)

1. 杨尚昆祝贺"澳星"发射成功

杨尚昆祝贺"澳星"发射成功

2. 外商在天津经济开发区投资的三种主要形式

外商在天津经济开发区
投资的三种主要形式

3. 万里会见泰国上院议长

万里会见泰国上院议长

4. 天津经济技术开发区专版

天津经济技术开发区专版
天津市经济技术开发区管委会供稿

5. 美元对马克汇价缘何暴跌

美元对马克汇价缘何暴跌

生詞

楊尚昆	(yáng shàng kūn)	*Personal N.*	Yang Shangkun, a very senior Chinese military and government official
祝賀	(zhù hè)	*V.*	to congratulate
外商	(wài shāng)	*Abbrev.*	外國商人 foreign business people
投資	(tóu zī)	*VO/N.*	to invest; investment
形式	(xíng shì)	*N.*	form, style
上院議長	(shàng yì yuàn zhǎng)	*Title/rank.*	the leader (speaker) of the upper house (of a congress, parliament)
專版	(zhuān bǎn)	*N.*	special issue; special edition; special section (separate section of periodical or journal)
緣何	(yuán hé)	*QW.*	why
馬克	(mǎ kè)	*N.*	the Deutsche Mark, the German Mark
暴跌	(bào diē)	*VP.*	to drop sharply, to plunge, to plummet

生词

杨尚昆	(yáng shàng kūn)	*Personal N.*	Yang Shangkun, a very senior Chinese military and government official
祝贺	(zhù hè)	*V.*	to congratulate
外商	(wài shāng)	*Abbrev.*	外国商人 foreign business people
投资	(tóu zī)	*VO/N.*	to invest; investment
形式	(xíng shì)	*N.*	form, style
上院议长	(shàng yì yuàn zhǎng)	*Title/rank.*	the leader (speaker) of the upper house (of a congress, parliament)
专版	(zhuān bǎn)	*N.*	special issue; special edition; special section (separate section of periodical or journal)
缘何	(yuán hé)	*QW.*	why
马克	(mǎ kè)	*N.*	the Deutsche Mark, the German Mark
暴跌	(bào diē)	*VP.*	to drop sharply, to plunge, to plummet

五、幽默小品 (Humor)

誠實孩子

兒子：“我今天拾了五十元，結果還給了失主。”

父親：“好孩子，真誠實，你是怎麼還的？”

兒子：“丟錢的人揪住了我的耳朵，痛得受不了，只好還給他了。”

生詞

拾	(shí)	V.	to pick up (from ground/floor)
失主	(shī zhǔ)	N.	person who lost the thing (or something)
誠實	(chéng shí)	Adj.	honest
揪住	(jīu zhù)	V.	to grab firmly, to take a firm grip on, to seize tightly

五、幽默小品 (Humor)

诚实孩子

儿子："我今天拾了五十元，结果还给了失主。"

父亲："好孩子，真诚实，你是怎么还的？"

儿子："丢钱的人揪住了我的耳朵，痛得受不了，只好还给他了。"

生词

拾	(shí)	V.	to pick up (from ground/floor)
失主	(shī zhǔ)	N.	person who lost the thing (or something)
诚实	(chéng shí)	Adj.	honest
揪住	(jīu zhù)	V.	to grab firmly, to take a firm grip on, to seize tightly

課文要點 (Key Points)

一、常用文言詞、縮略語與慣用語 (Frequently used classical Chinese phrases, abbreviations, and fixed expressions)

1. 奧運＝奧林匹克運動會 (the Olympic Games)

例： 他去看過三次奧運會。
He has gone to see the Olympics three times.

2. 緣何＝為甚麼 (why)

例：伊拉克緣何斷然拒絕在其領空建立空中禁區？
Why did Iraq flatly refuse to establish a no-fly zone in its territory?

3. 觀眾同志們 (our viewers, comrade televiewers, dear viewers)

例：這個節目受到觀眾同志們的歡迎。
This program is very well received by the television audience.

4. 經濟技術開發區 (economic and technology development zone)

例：廣州共有十個經濟技術開發區。
Altogether there are ten economic and technology development zones in Guangzhou.

5. 其 ＝ 他（她、它、他們、她們）的

例：泰國歡迎其他國家在其領土開發經濟。
Thailand welcomes other countries to develop its economy within its own (Thai) territory.

课文要点 (Key Points)

一、常用文言词、缩略语与惯用语 (Frequently used classical Chinese phrases, abbreviations, and fixed expressions)

1. 奥运 = 奥林匹克运动会 (the Olympic Games)

　例: 他去看过三次奥运会。
　　　He has gone to see the Olympics three times.

2. 缘何 = 为什么 (why)

　例: 伊拉克缘何断然拒绝在其领空建立空中禁区？
　　　Why did Iraq flatly refuse to establish a no-fly zone in its territory?

3. 观众同志们 (our viewers, comrade televiewers, dear viewers)

　例: 这个节目受到观众同志们的欢迎。
　　　This program is very well received by the television audience.

4. 经济技术开发区 (economic and technology development zone)

　例: 广州共有十个经济技术开发区。
　　　Altogether there are ten economic and technology development zones in Guangzhou.

5. 其 = 他（她、它、他们、她们）的

　例: 泰国欢迎其他国家在其领土开发经济。
　　　Thailand welcomes other countries to develop its economy within its own (Thai) territory.

6. 空中禁區 (no-fly zone)

例：這是空中禁區，不准入內。

This is a no-fly zone, no one is allowed to enter.

7. 匯率 (the exchange rate)

例：現在美元對人民幣的匯率是多少？

What is the exchange rate for U.S. dollars against RMB?

8. 首都各界 (people from all walks of life in the capital city)

例：今天，中共中央總書記江澤民會見了首都各界人士。

Today the general secretary of the CCP, Jiang Zemin, met with people from all walks of life in the capital.

9. 中共中央總書記 (the General Secretary of the Central Committee of the Chinese Communist Party)

例：現在中共中央總書記不是江澤民嗎？

Isn't the General Secretary of Central Committee of the Chinese Communist Party (CCCCP) Jiang Zemin?

10.新聞聯播 (news broadcasting)

例：中國的新聞聯播節目時間是每天下午六點。

China's national network news broadcast is at 6 p.m. everyday.

6. 空中禁区 (no-fly zone)

例：这是空中禁区，不准入内。
This is a no-fly zone, no one is allowed to enter.

7. 汇率 (the exchange rate)

例：现在美元对人民币的汇率是多少？
What is the exchange rate for U.S. dollars against RMB?

8. 首都各界 (people from all walks of life in the capital city)

例：今天，中共中央总书记江泽民会见了首都各界人士。
Today the general secretary of the CCP, Jiang Zemin, met with people from all walks of life in the capital.

9. 中共中央总书记 (the General Secretary of the Central Committee of the Chinese Communist Party)

例：现在中共中央总书记不是江泽民吗？
Isn't the General Secretary of Central Committee of the Chinese Communist Party (CCCCP) Jiang Zemin?

10. 新闻联播 (news broadcasting)

例：中国的新闻联播节目时间是每天下午六点。
China's national network news broadcast is at 6 p.m. everyday.

二、常用短語 (Frequently used structures)

1. A 會見 B (A meets with B)

例：昨天紐約市長會見了中國經濟代表團。
Yesterday, the mayor of New York City met with an economic delegation from China.

上個月天津經濟技術開發區的總書記會見了美國經濟代表團。
Last month the secretary general of Tianjin's economic and technology development zone met with an American economic delegation.

2. 取得…成就 (to achieve accomplishments)

例：幾十年來，美國在民權運動上取得了很大的成就。
During the last few decades, the U.S. has achieved major accomplishments in its civil rights movement.

首都各界人民努力工作，在北京城市建設上取得了巨大的成就。
People from all walks of life in the capital worked extremely hard and achieved a great deal in the construction of Beijing.

3. 分別 (separately, respectively)

例：我跟我的同學分別去圖書館借書，可是誰都沒借到所要借的書。
My classmates and I went separately to the library to borrow books. None of us, however, succeeded in getting the books we wanted.

奧運會健兒分別乘飛機回到首都北京。
The top athletes attending the Olympic Games arrived on different flights (separately) in Beijing.

4. 凱旋 (to return in victory)

例：我校籃球隊昨日凱旋，他們跟印第安那大學球隊的比分是 103:90。
Our school's basketball team returned in triumph yesterday with a score of 103 to Indiana University's 90.

二、常用短语 (Frequently used structures)

1. A 会见 B (A meets with B)

例: 昨天纽约市长会见了中国经济代表团。
Yesterday, the mayor of New York City met with an economic delegation from China.

上个月天津经济技术开发区的总书记会见了美国经济代表团。
Last month the secretary general of Tianjin's economic and technology development zone met with an American economic delegation.

2. 取得…成就 (to achieve accomplishments)

例: 几十年来，美国在民权运动上取得了很大的成就。
During the last few decades, the U.S. has achieved major accomplishments in its civil rights movement.

首都各界人民努力工作，在北京城市建设上取得了巨大的成就。
People from all walks of life in the capital worked extremely hard and achieved a great deal in the construction of Beijing.

3. 分别 (separately, respectively)

例: 我跟我的同学分别去图书馆借书，可是谁都没借到所要借的书。
My classmates and I went separately to the library to borrow books. None of us, however, succeeded in getting the books we wanted.

奥运会健儿分别乘飞机回到首都北京。
The top athletes attending the Olympic Games arrived on different flights (separately) in Beijing.

4. 凯旋 (to return in victory)

例: 我校篮球队昨日凯旋，他们跟印第安那大学球队的比分是 103:90。
Our school's basketball team returned in triumph yesterday with a score of 103 to Indiana University's 90.

11

《人民日報》昨天報道：東亞運動會健兒今天下午從日本凱旋。

It was reported in yesterday's People's Daily that our top athletes at the East Asian Games will return in triumph from Japan this afternoon.

5. 為…做報告 (to give a talk for/to)

例：上星期從中國回來的同學為我們做了一個關於他在中國學習和生活的報告。

Last week, the student who just came back from China gave us a talk about his study and life in China.

從日本回來後，他已經為開發區的技術人員作了幾次報告。

Since returning from Japan, he has given several reports to (for the benefit of) the technical personnel in the economic development zone(s).

6. …拒絕… (to refuse)

例：我的母親拒絕跟我大姐見面，因為她還沒畢業就跟她的男朋友同居了。

My mother refuses to see my eldest sister because she lived with her boyfriend before she graduated.

泰國斷然拒絕跟伊拉克建立外交關係。

Thailand flatly refuses to establish diplomatic relations with Iraq.

《人民日报》昨天报道： 东亚运动会健儿今天下午从日本凯旋。
It was reported in yesterday's People's Daily that our top athletes at the East Asian Games will return in triumph from Japan this afternoon.

5. 为…做报告 (to give a talk for/to)

例： 上星期从中国回来的同学为我们做了一个关于他在中国学习和生活的报告。
Last week, the student who just came back from China gave us a talk about his study and life in China.

从日本回来后， 他已经为开发区的技术人员作了几次报告。
Since returning from Japan, he has given several reports to (for the benefit of) the technical personnel in the economic development zone(s).

6. …拒绝… (to refuse)

例： 我的母亲拒绝跟我大姐见面，因为她还没毕业就跟她的男朋友同居了。
My mother refuses to see my eldest sister because she lived with her boyfriend before she graduated.

泰国断然拒绝跟伊拉克建立外交关系。
Thailand flatly refuses to establish diplomatic relations with Iraq.

第一單元　每日新聞

第二課

江澤民會見印尼客人

課文

一、簡介 (Introduction)

中南海是中共中央要人生活和工作的地方。中共中央的官員每天都要在中南海會見各國來訪的代表團。這類新聞也常在電視和報紙上報道。

生詞

中南海	(zhōng nán hǎi)	*Place N.*	Zhongnanhai, the name of the walled compound in Beijing near the Imperial Palaces in which the highest Chinese officials and their families reside.
要人	(yào rén)	*N.*	VIP (s), important figure(s), important person/people
官員	(guān yuán)	*N.*	officials
來訪	(lái fǎng)	*VP.*	to visit, to pay a visit; to come and visit
代表團	(dài biǎo tuán)	*N.*	delegation
報道	(bào dào)	*V/N.*	to report; report

13

第一单元 每日新闻

第二课

江泽民会见印尼客人

课文

一、简介 (Introduction)

中南海是中共中央要人生活和工作的地方。中共中央的官员每天都要在中南海会见各国来访的代表团。这类新闻也常在电视和报纸上报道。

生词

中南海	(zhōng nán hǎi)	*Place N.*	Zhongnanhai, the name of the walled compound in Beijing near the Imperial Palaces in which the highest Chinese officials and their families reside.
要人	(yào rén)	*N.*	VIP(s), important figure(s), important person/people
官员	(guān yuán)	*N.*	officials
来访	(lái fǎng)	*VP.*	to visit, to pay a visit; to come and visit
代表团	(dài biǎo tuán)	*N.*	delegation
报道	(bào dào)	*V/N.*	to report; report

13

二、對話 (Dialogues)

（一）

大衛： 小紅，問你一個問題，看新聞聯播時，常常聽到"中南海"這三個字，這是甚麼地方？

小紅： 你怎麼連中南海都不知道？中南海是中共中央要人工作和生活的地方，所以常在那里會見或歡迎外國客人。

問題： 中南海是一個甚麼地方？ 它的作用是甚麼？

（二）

小紅： 大衛，你認為美國總統應該怎麼處理美日關係？

大衛： 這還用問，美國和日本在世界上都是經濟大國，這兩個國家必須友好相處，加強合作。不然的話，這兩個國家的衝突會對亞洲乃至世界和平和穩定都有影響。

問題： 美國總統的美日關係政策應該是甚麼？

生詞

總統	(zǒng tǒng)	*Title/rank .*	president
處理	(chǔ lǐ)	*V.*	to handle, to deal with
相處	(xiāng chǔ)	*V.*	get along with
加強	(jiā qiáng)	*V.*	to strengthen
合作	(hé zuò)	*V/N.*	to cooperate; cooperation
衝突	(chōng tū)	*N/V.*	conflict; to conflict
亞洲	(yà zhōu)	*Place N.*	Asia

14

二、对话 (Dialogues)

（一）

大卫： 小红，问你一个问题，看新闻联播时，常常听到"中南海"这三个字，这是什么地方？

小红： 你怎么连中南海都不知道？中南海是中共中央要人工作和生活的地方，所以常在那里会见或欢迎外国客人。

问题： 中南海是一个什么地方？ 它的作用是什么？

（二）

小红： 大卫，你认为美国总统应该怎么处理美日关系？

大卫： 这还用问，美国和日本在世界上都是经济大国，这两个国家必须友好相处，加强合作。不然的话，这两个国家的冲突会对亚洲乃至世界和平和稳定都有影响。

问题： 美国总统的美日关系政策应该是什么？

生词

总统	(zǒng tǒng)	*Title/rank.*	president
处理	(chǔ lǐ)	*V.*	to handle, to deal with
相处	(xiāng chǔ)	*V.*	get along with
加强	(jiā qiáng)	*V.*	to strengthen
合作	(hé zuò)	*V/N.*	to cooperate; cooperation
冲突	(chōng tū)	*N/V.*	conflict; to conflict
亚洲	(yà zhōu)	*PlaceN.*	Asia

乃至	(nǎi zhì)	*Conj.*	and (up to; including, to the extent of)＝以至
和平	(hé píng)	*N.*	peace
穩定	(wěn dìng)	*N/Adj/V.*	stability; stable, firm; to stabilize
政策	(zhèng cè)	*N.*	policy

（三）

小紅： 大衛，今天學校的報紙上有甚麼新聞？

大衛： 沒有甚麼有意思的。哦，對了，有一條也許你會感興趣。你知道，我們學校要跟中國人民大學建立姐妹學校關係，以便促進兩校的友好往來，增進學校之間的交流。應人民大學的邀請，我們學校的學生會主席將在下個月首次訪問人民大學。

問題： 校報的新聞是甚麼？

生詞

增進	(zēng jìn)	*V.*	to promote, to enhance
交流	(jiāo líu)	*V/N.*	to exchange, exchange
以便	(yǐ biàn)	*Prep.*	so that, for the sake of, in order to
促進	(cù jìn)	*V.*	to promote
往來	(wǎng lái)	*V/N.*	to have dealings with each other; contact(s)
應	(yìng)	*Prep.*	in response to
邀請	(yāo qǐng)	*V.*	to invite
首次	(shǒu cì)	*N.*	first time

乃至	(nǎi zhì)	*Conj.*	and (up to; including, to the extent of) = 以至
和平	(hé píng)	*N.*	peace
稳定	(wěn dìng)	*N/Adj/V.*	stability; stable, firm; to stabilize
政策	(zhèng cè)	*N.*	policy

（三）

小红： 大卫，今天学校的报纸上有什么新闻？

大卫： 没有什么有意思的。哦，对了，有一条也许你会感兴趣。你知道，我们学校要跟中国人民大学建立姐妹学校关系，以便促进两校的友好往来，增进学校之间的交流。应人民大学的邀请，我们学校的学生会主席将在下个月首次访问人民大学。

问题: 校报的新闻是什么？

生词

增进	(zēng jìn)	*V.*	to promote, to enhance
交流	(jiāo líu)	*V/N.*	to exchange, exchange
以便	(yǐ biàn)	*Prep.*	so that, for the sake of, in order to
促进	(cù jìn)	*V.*	to promote
往来	(wǎng lái)	*V/N.*	to have dealings with each other; contact(s)
应	(yìng)	*Prep.*	in response to
邀请	(yāo qǐng)	*V.*	to invite
首次	(shǒu cì)	*N.*	first time

三、電視新聞 (The TV news)

江澤民會見印尼客人

中共中央總書記江澤民今天下午在中南海會見了印尼專業集團總主席瓦霍諾一行。江澤民對瓦霍諾的來訪表示熱烈歡迎。他說："中國和印尼友好相處，加強合作，對亞洲乃至世界和平與穩定都具有重要意義。我相信，總主席這次訪問必將促進兩國關係的發展和增進兩國人民的友好往來。"江澤民請瓦霍諾回國後轉達他對蘇哈托總統的問候。印尼專業集團是印尼最大的政黨。瓦霍諾是應中國全國政協的邀請首次率團訪華。這是本台報道的。

生詞

印尼	(yìn ní)	Abbrev.	Indonesia＝印度尼西亞
專業	(zhuān yè)	N.	specialization; specialized trade
集團	(jí tuán)	N.	group
總主席	(zǒng zhǔ xí)	Title/rank.	the chairperson
瓦霍諾	(wǎ huò nuò)	Personal N.	personal name
一行	(yī xíng)	N.	and accompanying party, and his/her group
熱烈	(rè liè)	Adj/Adv.	warm, warmly, ardent
轉達	(zhuǎn dá)	V.	to pass on to; to convey
蘇哈托	(sū hā tuō)	Personal N.	Suharto, the president of Indonesia
問候	(wèn hòu)	N/V.	greetings; to send one's best wishes to
政黨	(zhèng dǎng)	N.	political party
政協	(zhèng xié)	Abbrev.	the Chinese People's Political Consultative Conference
率團	(shuài tuán)	VO.	to lead a delegation
華	(huá)	Abbrev.	the People's Republic of China＝中國，中華人民共和國
本台	(běn tái)	N.	one's own station; our own broadcasting station; this station

三、电视新闻 (The TV news)

江泽民会见印尼客人

中共中央总书记江泽民今天下午在中南海会见了印尼专业集团总主席瓦霍诺一行。江泽民对瓦霍诺的来访表示热烈欢迎。他说："中国和印尼友好相处，加强合作，对亚洲乃至世界和平与稳定都具有重要意义。我相信，总主席这次访问必将促进两国关系的发展和增进两国人民的友好往来。"江泽民请瓦霍诺回国后转达他对苏哈托总统的问候。印尼专业集团是印尼最大的政党。瓦霍诺是应中国全国政协的邀请首次率团访华。这是本台报道的。

生词

印尼	(yìn ní)	Abbrev.	Indonesia = 印度尼西亚
专业	(zhuān yè)	N.	specialization; specialized trade
集团	(jí tuán)	N.	group
总主席	(zǒng zhǔ xí)	Title/rank.	the chairperson
瓦霍诺	(wǎ huò nuò)	Personal N.	personal name
一行	(yī xíng)	N.	and accompanying party, and his/her group
热烈	(rè liè)	Adj/Adv.	warm, warmly, ardent
转达	(zhuǎn dá)	V.	to pass on to; to convey
苏哈托	(sū hā tuō)	Personal N.	Suharto, the president of Indonesia
问候	(wèn hòu)	N/V.	greetings; to send one's best wishes to
政党	(zhèng dǎng)	N.	political party
政协	(zhèng xié)	Abbrev.	the Chinese People's Political Consultative Conference
率团	(shuài tuán)	VO.	to lead a delegation
华	(huá)	Abbrev.	the People's Republic of China = 中国、中华人民共和国
本台	(běn tái)	N.	one's own station; our own broadcasting station; this station

四、報紙閱讀 (Newspaper reading)

江泽民会见瓦霍诺一行

新华社北京8月22日电（记者卢劲）中共中央总书记江泽民今天下午在中南海会见了印度尼西亚专业集团总主席瓦霍诺一行，对他率代表团来访表示欢迎。

据中国官员介绍，江泽民在会见中说，中国和印尼友好相处、加强合作对亚洲以至世界的和平与稳定都具有重要意义。他说，相信瓦霍诺总主席这次访问必将进一步促进两国关系的发展和增进两国人民的友好往来。

江泽民还请瓦霍诺转达他对印尼总统苏哈托的问候。

全国政协副主席谷牧、秘书长宋德敏等参加了会见。

江澤民會見瓦霍諾一行

新華社北京8月22日電（記者盧勁）中共中央總書記江澤民今天下午在中南海會見了印度尼西亞專業集團總主席瓦霍諾一行，對他率代表團來訪表示歡迎。

據中國官員介紹，江澤民在會見中說，中國和印尼友好相處、加強合作對亞洲以至世界的和平與穩定都具有重要意義。他說，相信瓦霍諾總主席這次訪問必將進一步促進兩國關係的發展和增進兩國人民的友好往來。

江澤民還請瓦霍諾轉達他對印尼總統蘇哈托的問候。

全國政協副主席谷牧、秘書長宋德敏等參加了會見。

四、报纸阅读 (Newspaper reading)

江泽民会见瓦霍诺一行

新华社北京8月22日电（记者卢劲）中共中央总书记江泽民今天下午在中南海会见了印度尼西亚专业集团总主席瓦霍诺一行，对他率代表团来访表示欢迎。

据中国官员介绍，江泽民在会见中说，中国和印尼友好相处、加强合作对亚洲以至世界的和平与稳定都具有重要意义。他说，相信瓦霍诺总主席这次访问必将进一步促进两国关系的发展和增进两国人民的友好往来。

江泽民还请瓦霍诺转达他对印尼总统苏哈托的问候。

全国政协副主席谷牧、秘书长宋德敏等参加了会见。

江泽民会见瓦霍诺一行

新华社北京8月22日电（记者卢劲）中共中央总书记江泽民今天下午在中南海会见了印度尼西亚专业集团总主席瓦霍诺一行，对他率代表团来访表示欢迎。

据中国官员介绍，江泽民在会见中说，中国和印尼友好相处、加强合作对亚洲以至世界的和平与稳定都具有重要意义。他说，相信瓦霍诺总主席这次访问必将进一步促进两国关系的发展和增进两国人民的友好往来。

江泽民还请瓦霍诺转达他对印尼总统苏哈托的问候。

全国政协副主席谷牧、秘书长宋德敏等参加了会见。

生詞

新華社	(xīn huá shè)	N.	Xin Hua News Agency
記者	(jì zhě)	N.	reporter, journalist,
以至	(yǐ zhì)	Conj.	and (up to; including, to the extent of) ＝乃至
副主席	(fù zhǔ xí)	Title/rank.	the vice chairman
谷牧	(gǔ mù)	Personal N.	Gu Mu, an important Chinese government official
秘書長	(mì shū zhǎng)	N.	the secretary-general; head of the secretariat
宋德敏	(sòng dé mǐn)	Personal N.	Song Demin, an important Chinese government official

五、幽默小品 (Humor)

露出馬腳

　　十歲的小明打電話給他的老師："小明病得很厲害，他今天不能上學了。"

　　"哎呀，這怎麼好呢？"老師說："請問你是誰？"

　　"是我的父親。"

生詞

露出馬腳	(lòu chū mǎ jiǎo)	VO.	to let the cat out of the bag; to give oneself away

生词

新华社	(xīn huá shè)	*N.*	Xin Hua News Agency
记者	(jì zhě)	*N.*	reporter, journalist,
以至	(yǐ zhì)	*Conj.*	and (up to; including, to the extent of) = 乃至
副主席	(fù zhǔ xí)	*Title/rank*	.the vice chairman
谷牧	(gǔ mù)	*Personal N.*	Gu Mu, an important Chinese government official
秘书长	(mì shū zhǎng)	*N.*	the secretary-general; head of the secretariat
宋德敏	(sòng dé mǐn)	*Personal N.*	Song Demin, an important Chinese government official

五、幽默小品 (Humor)

露出马脚

十岁的小明打电话给他的老师：
"小明病得很厉害，他今天不能上学了。"

"哎呀，这怎么好呢？"老师说："请问你是谁？"

"是我的父亲。"

生词

露出马脚	(lòu chū mǎ jiǎo)	*VO.*	to let the cat out of the bag; to give oneself away

課文要點 (Key Points)

一、常用文言詞、縮略語與慣用語 (Frequently used classical Chinese phrases, abbreviations, and fixed expressions)

1. 乃至＝以至、以及、跟、和 (as well as; along with; and)

   例：這是有關中國乃至世界的大事。
   This is a weighty issue concerning China and even the whole world.

2. 必將＝一定會 (certainly will, will surely)

   例：這次訪問必將促進兩國關係的發展。
   This visit will surely enhance the relationship between the two countries.

3. 應＝接受、答應 (in response to)

   例：他應我的邀請參加我們的婚禮。
   In response to my invitation, he attended our wedding.

4. 一行＝以…為首的一組（人）(as a group or delegation; an accompanying group or party)
   例：印尼代表團一行在中南海跟中共中央總書記見面。
   The Indonesian delegation as a group met with the General Secretary at Zhongnanhai.

5. 來訪＝來訪問 (to visit, visiting)

   例：小李的來訪給了我很大的希望。
   Xiao Li's visit gave me great hope.

课文要点 (Key Points)

一、常用文言词、缩略语与惯用语 (Frequently used classical Chinese phrases, abbreviations, and fixed expressions)

1. 乃至 = 以至、以及、跟、和 (as well as; along with; and)

   例： 这是有关中国乃至世界的大事。
       This is a weighty issue concerning China and even the whole world.

2. 必将 = 一定会 (certainly will, will surely)

   例： 这次访问必将促进两国关系的发展。
       This visit will surely enhance the relationship between the two countries.

3. 应 = 接受、答应 (in response to)

   例： 他应我的邀情参加我们的婚礼。
       In response to my invitation, he attended our wedding.

4. 一行 = 以…为首的一组（人）(as a group or delegation; an accompanying group or party)

   例： 印尼代表团一行在中南海跟中共中央总书记见面。
       The Indonesian delegation as a group met with the General Secretary at Zhongnanhai.

5. 来访 = 来访问 (to visit, visiting)

   例： 小李的来访给了我很大的希望。
       Xiao Li's visit gave me great hope.

19

6. 首次＝第一次 (the first time)

例：這是李明首次訪澳。
This is the first time that Li Ming is visiting Australia.

7. 率團＝帶領一個代表團 (to lead a delegation)

例：是誰率團去日訪問的？
Who led the delegation on a visit to Japan ?

8. 訪華＝訪問中國 (to visit China)

例：最近訪華的人很多。
Recently a great many people are traveling to China.

9. 印尼＝印度尼西亞 (Indonesia)

10. 本台＝（包括説話人在內的）我們的電視台(this station, one's own station)

二、常用短語 (Frequently used structures)

1. ⋯會見了⋯一行 (to meet with someone and his/her accompanying group, delegation, party)

例：鄧小平會見了香港貿易集團主席一行。
Deng Xiaoping met with the chairperson of the Hong Kong Trade Group and his accompanying delegation.

克林頓 (Clinton) 總統昨天在白宮會見了英國代表團一行。
President Clinton received the delegation from Great Britain at the White House yesterday.

6. 首次 = 第一次 (the first time)

  例： 这是李明首次访澳。
      This is the first time that Li Ming is visiting Australia.

7. 率团 = 带领一个代表团 (to lead a delegation)

  例： 是谁率团去日访问的？
      Who led the delegation on a visit to Japan ?

8. 访华 = 访问中国 (to visit China)

  例： 最近访华的人很多。
      Recently a great many people are traveling to China.

9. 印尼 = 印度尼西亚 (Indonesia)

10. 本台 = （包括说话人在内的）我们的电视台(this station, one's own station)

二、 常用短语 (Frequently used structures)

1. …会见了…一行 (to meet with someone and his/her accompanying group, delegation, party)

  例： 邓小平会见了香港贸易集团主席一行。
      Deng Xiaoping met with the chairperson of the Hong Kong Trade Group and his accompanying delegation.

      克林顿 (Clinton) 总统昨天在白宫会见了英国代表团一行。
      President Clinton received the delegation from Great Britain at the White House yesterday.

2. …對…表示（熱烈）歡迎 (to express [a warm] welcome to)

例：紐約市長對中國貿易代表團表示熱烈歡迎。
The mayor of New York City extended a cordial welcome to the Chinese trade delegation.

上海各界人士對建立經濟開發區表示歡迎。
People from all walks of life in Shanghai welcome the establishment of economic development zones in the area.

3. …對…具有重要（很大）意義 (to have [profound] significance for)

例：印尼總統訪華對兩國的貿易發展具有重大意義。
The visit of the Indonesian president to China has profound significance for the development of trade between the two countries.

學習電視和報紙新聞對提高中文水平具有很大的意義。
Studying TV and newspaper news in Chinese is highly important in enhancing one's level of proficiency in Chinese.

4. …促進…的發展 (to promote the development of)

例：學中文的美國學生可以做很多事情促進中美關係的發展。
American students learning Chinese language can do a lot to promote Sino-American relations.

中美建立外交關係可以促進世界和平事業的發展。
The normalization of diplomatic relations between China and the U.S. may well promote the cause of world peace.

2. …对…表示（热烈）欢迎 (to express [a warm] welcome to)

例: 纽约市长对中国贸易代表团表示热烈欢迎。
The mayor of New York City extended a cordial welcome to the Chinese trade delegation.

上海各界人士对建立经济开发区表示欢迎。
People from all walks of life in Shanghai welcome the establishment of economic development zones in the area.

3. …对…具有重要（很大）意义 (to have [profound] significance for)

例: 印尼总统访华对两国的贸易发展具有重大意义。
The visit of the Indonesian president to China has profound significance for the development of trade between the two countries.

学习电视和报纸新闻对提高中文水平具有很大的意义。
Studying TV and newspaper news in Chinese is highly important in enhancing one's level of proficiency in Chinese.

4. …促进…的发展 (to promote the development of)

例: 学中文的美国学生可以做很多事情促进中美关系的发展。
American students learning Chinese language can do a lot to promote Sino-American relations.

中美建立外交关系可以促进世界和平事业的发展。
The normalization of diplomatic relations between China and the U.S. may well promote the cause of world peace.

5. …增進…的友好往來（了解、友誼）(to enhance the friendly exchange [understanding, friendship...])

　　例：克林頓總統訪日可以增進美日人民的友好往來。
　　President Clinton's visit to Japan may well increase friendly interaction between the U.S. and Japan.

　　我們公司經理希望不同人種的人能有機會在一起工作，進一步增進他們之間的了解。
　　The manager of our company hopes that the people from different ethnic backgrounds will have the opportunity to work together and further enhance their mutual understanding.

6. …轉達對…的問候 (to pass greetings on to)

　　例：請（你）轉達我對同學們的問候。
　　Please send my regards to our classmates.

　　中國外交部部長請法國駐華大使轉達他對法國總統的問候。
　　China's Minister of Foreign Affairs asked the French ambassador to China to send his regards to the president of France.

7. …應…的邀請 (in response to the invitation of)

　　例：鄧小平應日本政府的邀請去日本訪問。
　　Deng Xiao Ping visited Japan in response to the invitation of the Japanese government.

　　應中華人民共和國的邀請，西班牙外交部長將在下個月來華訪問。
　　In response to the invitation from the People's Republic of China, the foreign minister of Spain will visit China next month.

5. …增进…的友好往来（了解、友谊）(to enhance the friendly exchange [understanding, friendship...])

例：克林顿总统访日可以增进美日人民的友好往来。

President Clinton's visit to Japan may well increase friendly interaction between the U.S. and Japan.

我们公司经理希望不同人种的人能有机会在一起工作，进一步增进他们之间的了解。

The manager of our company hopes that the people from different ethnic backgrounds will have the opportunity to work together and further enhance their mutual understanding.

6. …转达对…的问候 (to pass greetings on to)

例：请（你）转达我对同学们的问候。

Please send my regards to our classmates.

中国外交部部长请法国驻华大使转达他对法国总统的问候。

China's Minister of Foreign Affairs asked the French ambassador to China to send his regards to the president of France.

7. …应…的邀请 (in response to the invitation of)

例：邓小平应日本政府的邀请去日本访问。

Deng Xiao Ping visited Japan in response to the invitation of the Japanese government.

应中华人民共和国的邀请，西班牙外交部长将在下个月来华访问。

In response to the invitation from the People's Republic of China, the foreign minister of Spain will visit China next month.

22

小課文

公民公益靠公德

一、看電視小課文、回答問題

    1. 電視中的老人為甚麼非常難過？她說了些甚麼？

    2. 這個廣告反映了甚麼社會問題？

    3. 看完這個廣告以後，你懂甚麼叫"公民公益"嗎？在美國這樣的問題怎麼解決？

生詞

公民	(gōng mín)	citizen
公益	(gōng yì)	public interest

二、用你自己的話把廣告中的這個故事講給大家聽 (Tell the story in your own words to your classmates)

23

小课文

公民公益靠公德

一、看电视小课文、回答问题

1. 电视中的老人为什么非常难过？她说了些什么？

2. 这个广告反映了什么社会问题？

3. 看完这个广告以后，你懂什么叫"公民公益"吗？在美国这样的问题怎么解决？

生词

| 公民 | (gōng mín) | citizen |
| 公益 | (gōng yì) | public interest |

二、用你自己的话把广告中的这个故事讲给大家听 (Tell the story in your own words to your classmates)

第一單元 每日新聞

第三課

聯合國武器核查小組完成在伊檢查工作

課文

一、簡介 (Introduction)

　　聯合國是一個世界組織。它的使命是促進世界和平、增進和加強國家與國家之間的友好往來與合作。聯合國有權對任何破壞和平的國家採取行動。例如，武器核查、經濟懲罰、或者軍事行動。本課的新聞就是有關 1992年海灣戰爭以後聯合國在伊拉克核查武器的報道。

生詞

聯合國	(lián hé guó)	N.	the United Nations
組織	(zǔ zhī)	N/V.	organization; to organize
使命	(shǐ mìng)	N.	mission
有權	(yǒu quán)	VO.	to have a right (to ...)
破壞	(pò huài)	V.	to break; to undermine
採取	(cǎi qǔ)	V.	to adopt (a plan), to take (action)
行動	(xíng dòng)	N.	action
武器	(wǔ qì)	N.	weapon
核查	(hé chá)	V.	to check up on, to inspect
懲罰	(chéng fá)	V.	to punish

第一单元 每日新闻

第三课

联合国武器核查小组完成在伊检查工作

课文

一、简介 (Introduction)

　　联合国是一个世界组织。它的使命是促进世界和平，增进和加强国家与国家之间的友好往来与合作。联合国有权对任何破坏和平的国家采取行动。例如，武器核查、经济惩罚、或者军事行动。本课的新闻就是有关 1992年海湾战争以后联合国在伊拉克核查武器的报道。

生词

联合国	(lián hé guó)	N.	the United Nations
组织	(zǔ zhī)	N/V.	organization; to organize
使命	(shǐ mìng)	N.	mission
有权	(yǒu quán)	VO.	to have a right (to ...)
破坏	(pò huài)	V.	to break; to undermine
采取	(cǎi qǔ)	V.	to adopt (a plan), to take (action)
行动	(xíng dòng)	N.	action
武器	(wǔ qì)	N.	weapon
核查	(hé chá)	V.	to check up on, to inspect
惩罚	(chéng fá)	V.	to punish

| 軍事行動 | (jūn shì xíng dòng) | NP. | military action(s) |
| 海灣戰爭 | (hǎi wān zhàn zhēng) | N. | Gulf War (Persian Gulf War, first half of 1992) |

二、對話 (Dialogues)

(一)

方寶蘭：你看昨天中國外交部部長接受外國記者採訪的消息了嗎？

李慶生：沒有。

方寶蘭：聽說上個月中國政府官員和伊拉克方面的代表進行了秘密會談，討論出售武器的問題，是真的嗎？

李慶生：我哪里知道。據中國外交部長說他們雖然和伊拉克方面舉行了會談，但從未出售過武器給他們。另外，外交部長也沒有透露會談的內容。所以，對中國和伊拉克的關係很難做出正確的猜測。

問題：為甚麼李慶生說對中國和伊拉克的關係問題很難做出猜測？

生詞

外交部	(wài jiāo bù)	N.	Foreign Ministry, Department (or Ministry) of External Affairs [in USA=Department of State]
部長	(bù zhǎng)	Title/rank.	minister
採訪	(cǎi fǎng)	V.	to gather information, to cover the story
秘密	(mì mì)	Adj.	secret
出售	(chū shòu)	V.	to sell
從未	(cóng wèi)	Adv.	never
透露	(tòu lù)	V.	to divulge; to leak out; to reveal

| 军事行动 | (jūn shì xíng dòng) | NP. | military action(s) |
| 海湾战争 | (hǎi wān zhàn zhēng) | N. | Gulf War (Persian Gulf War, first half of 1992) |

二、对话 (Dialogues)

（一）

方宝兰： 你看昨天中国外交部部长接受外国记者采访的消息了吗？

李庆生： 没有。

方宝兰： 听说上个月中国政府官员和伊拉克方面的代表进行了秘密会谈，讨论出售武器的问题，是真的吗？

李庆生： 我哪里知道。据中国外交部长说他们虽然和伊拉克方面举行了会谈，但从未出售过武器给他们。另外，外交部长也没有透露会谈的内容。所以，对中国和伊拉克的关系很难做出正确的猜测。

问题: 为什么李庆生说对中国和伊拉克的关系问题很难做出猜测？

生词

外交部	(wài jiāo bù)	N.	Foreign Ministry, Department (or Ministry) of External Affairs [in USA=Department of State]
部长	(bù zhǎng)	Title/rank.	minister
采访	(cǎi fǎng)	V.	to gather information, to cover the story
秘密	(mì mì)	Adj.	secret
出售	(chū shòu)	V.	to sell
从未	(cóng wèi)	Adv.	never
透露	(tòu lù)	V.	to divulge; to leak out; to reveal

| 猜測 | （cāi cè） | *V/N.* | to speculate about; to guess; speculation; conjecture(s), guesses |

（二）

方寶蘭：聽説昨天晚上在希爾頓飯店又發生了一起殺人案。

李慶生：是嗎？是怎麼回事？

方寶蘭：據警方透露，一位日本官員昨天晚上八點住進了飯店。按原訂計劃，他要在當天晚上十點與一位伊拉克官員秘密會談。但到九點他已被人殺死了。

李慶生：現在怎麼樣呢？

方寶蘭：現在警方正在尋找與殺人有關的證據及武器。真可怕啊。

問題： 昨天晚上在希爾頓飯店發生了甚麼事情？

生詞

希爾頓飯店	（xī ěr dùn fàn diàn）	*NP.*	Hilton Hotel
警方	（jǐng fāng）	*N.*	the police (the police authorities)
按	（àn）	*Prep.*	according to
原訂計劃	（yuán dìng jì huà）	*NP.*	original plan
尋找	（xún zhǎo）	*V.*	to look for, to search for
證據	（zhèng jù）	*N.*	evidence; proof of; testimony

（三）

方寶蘭：你常看《紐約時報》嗎？

李慶生：常看，這家報紙也算是西方規模最大的新聞媒介之一。

| 猜测 | (cāi cè) | *V/N.* | to speculate about; to guess; speculation; conjecture(s), guesses |

（二）

方宝兰： 听说昨天晚上在希尔顿饭店又发生了一起杀人案。

李庆生： 是吗？是怎么回事？

方宝兰： 据警方透露，一位日本官员昨天晚上八点住进了饭店。按原订计划，他要在当天晚上十点与一位伊拉克官员秘密会谈。但到九点他已被人杀死了。

李庆生： 现在怎么样呢？

方宝兰： 现在警方正在寻找与杀人有关的证据及武器。真可怕啊。

问题: 昨天晚上在希尔顿饭店发生了什么事情？

生词

希尔顿饭店	(xī ěr dùn fàn diàn)	*NP.*	Hilton Hotel
警方	(jǐng fāng)	*N.*	the police (the police authorities)
按	(àn)	*Prep.*	according to
原订计划	(yuán dìng jì huà)	*NP.*	original plan
寻找	(xún zhǎo)	*V.*	to look for, to search for
证据	(zhèng jù)	*N.*	evidence; proof of; testimony

（三）

方宝兰： 你常看《纽约时报》吗？

李庆生： 常看，这家报纸也算是西方规模最大的新闻媒介之一。

方寶蘭： 看這樣的報紙有助於英文學習嗎？

李慶生： 據一個科學家透露，看《紐約時報》可以在一年內增加百分之二十
的詞彙量，也能提高閱讀速度。

問題：《紐約時報》對學英文有甚麼幫助？

生詞

《紐約時報》	(nǐu yuē shí bào)	*N.*	New York Times
規模	(guī mó)	*N.*	scale, scope
新聞媒介	(xīn wén méi jìe)	*N.*	the news media
有助（於）	(yǒu zhù)	*Adj.*	to be helpful
於	(yú)	*Prep.*	to
詞彙量	(cí huì liàng)	*N.*	quantity of vocabulary, vocabulary range
閱讀	(yuè dú)	*N/V.*	reading; to read
速度	(sù dù)	*N.*	speed, rate of speed, velocity

三、電視新聞 (The TV news)

聯合國武器核查小組完成在伊檢查工作

聯合國武器核查小組負責人斯米多維奇昨天在巴格達說這個小組已完成
了在伊拉克的使命，將按原定計劃於今天離開巴格達。斯米多維奇對記者
說：“核查小組昨天平靜地完成了任務，從未遇到伊拉克方面的對抗。”核
查小組前天晚上在巴格達的希爾頓飯店與伊拉克官員舉行了秘密會議，但是
雙方都拒絕透露會議內容。斯米多維奇昨天在一份聲明中說核查小組學到了
一些有益和有助於今後核查工作的東西。但是他沒透露他的小組檢查了哪些

方宝兰: 看这样的报纸有助于英文学习吗？

李庆生: 据一个科学家透露，看《纽约时报》可以在一年内增加百分之二十
的词汇量，也能提高阅读速度。

问题: 《纽约时报》对学英文有什么帮助？

生词

《纽约时报》	(niǔ yuē shí bào)	*N.*	New York Times
规模	(guī mó)	*N.*	scale, scope
新闻媒介	(xīn wén méi jìe)	*N.*	the news media
有助（于）	(yǒu zhù)	*Adj.*	to be helpful
于	(yú)	*Prep.*	to
词汇量	(cí huì liàng)	*N.*	quantity of vocabulary, vocabulary range
阅读	(yuè dú)	*N/V.*	reading; to read
速度	(sù dù)	*N.*	speed, rate of speed, velocity

三、电视新闻 (The TV news)

联合国武器核查小组完成在伊检查工作

联合国武器核查小组负责人斯米多维奇昨天在巴格达说这个小组已完成
了在伊拉克的使命，将按原定计划于今天离开巴格达。斯米多维奇对记者
说："核查小组昨天平静地完成了任务，从未遇到伊拉克方面的对抗。"核
查小组前天晚上在巴格达的希尔顿饭店与伊拉克官员举行了秘密会议，但是
双方都拒绝透露会议内容。斯米多维奇昨天在一份声明中说核查小组学到了
一些有益和有助于今后核查工作的东西。但是他没透露他的小组检查了哪些

地點和發現了甚麼。這個小組由 22 人組成，在異乎尋常的保密情況下工作了
10天，尋找與伊拉克大規模殺傷武器有關的證據。在《紐約時報》上周末報
道美國準備採取軍事行動懲罰伊拉克之後，西方新聞媒介對這個核查小組在
伊拉克的調查結果進行了種種猜測。

生詞

小組	(xiǎo zǔ)	*N.*	team, small group
核查小組	(hé chá xiǎo zǔ)	*NP.*	inspection team
伊	(yī)	*Abbrev.*	Iraq＝伊拉克
檢查	(jiǎn chá)	*V/N.*	to examine, to inspect; inspection
負責人	(fù zé rén)	*N.*	responsible person; person in charge
斯米多維奇	(sī mǐ duō wéi qí)	*Personal N.*	the name of a person
巴格達	(bā gé dá)	*Place N.*	Bagdad (Baghdad)
平靜地	(píng jìng de)	*Adv.*	peacefully; calmly
遇到	(yù dào)	*V.*	to encounter, to run into, to come across
對抗	(duì kàng)	*V/N.*	to resist, to oppose, to confront; resistance, confrontation
聲明	(shēng míng)	*V/N.*	to announce, to declare; announcement, declaration
有益（於）	(yǒu yì)	*Adj.*	beneficial (to); advantageous (to)
異乎尋常	(yì hū xún cháng)	*Idiom.*	extraordinary; very unusual
保密	(bǎo mì)	*Adj/Adv.*	secretive; secretively
殺傷	(shā shāng)	*Adj/V.*	to kill and wound; to inflict severe casualities (including death) upon
大規模	(dà guī mó)	*Adj/Adv.*	on a large scale
大規模殺傷武器	(dà guī mó shā shāng wǔ qì)	*NP.*	weapons of mass destruction

地点和发现了什么。这个小组由22人组成，在异乎寻常的保密情况下工作了10天，寻找与伊拉克大规模杀伤武器有关的证据。在《纽约时报》上周末报道美国准备采取军事行动惩罚伊拉克之后，西方新闻媒介对这个核查小组在伊拉克的调查结果进行了种种猜测。

生词

小组	(xiǎo zǔ)	N.	team, small group
核查小组	(hé chá xiǎo zǔ)	NP.	inspection team
伊	(yī)	Abbrev.	Iraq= 伊拉克
检查	(jiǎn chá)	V/N.	to examine, to inspect; inspection
负责人	(fù zé rén)	N.	responsible person; person in charge
斯米多维奇	(sī mǐ duō wéi qí)	Personal N.	the name of a person
巴格达	(bā gé dá)	Place N.	Bagdad (Baghdad)
平静地	(píng jìng de)	Adv.	peacefully; calmly
遇到	(yù dào)	V.	to encounter, to run into, to come across
对抗	(duì kàng)	V/N.	to resist, to oppose, to confront; resistance, confrontation
声明	(shēng míng)	V/N.	to announce, to declare; announcement, declaration
有益（于）	(yǒu yì)	Adj.	beneficial (to); advantageous (to)
异乎寻常	(yì hū xún cháng)	Idiom.	extraordinary; very unusual
保密	(bǎo mì)	Adj/Adv.	secretive; secretively
杀伤	(shā shāng)	Adj/V.	to kill and wound; to inflict severe casualities (including death) upon
大规模	(dà guī mó)	Adj/Adv.	on a large scale
大规模杀伤武器	(dà guī mó shā shāng wǔ qì)	NP.	weapons of mass destruction

四、報紙閱讀 (Newspaper Reading)

联合国武器核查小组完成在伊检查工作

联合国武器核查小组负责人斯米多维奇8月17日在巴格达说，该小组已完成在伊拉克的使命，将按预定计划于18日离开巴格达。斯米多维奇17日在一份声明中说，核查小组学到了一些有益和有助于今后核查工作的东西。但他没有透露他的小组检查了哪些地点和发现了什么。

聯合國武器核查小組完成在伊檢查工作

聯合國武器核查小組負責人斯米多維奇8月17日在巴格達説，該小組已完成在伊拉克的使命，將按預訂計劃於 18日離開巴格達。斯米多維奇 17日在一份聲明中説，核查小組學到了一些有益和有助於今後核查工作的東西。但他沒有透露他的小組檢查了哪些地點和發現了甚麼。

五、幽默小品 (Humor)

閉眼睛寫字

兒子問父親：“爸爸，你能閉上眼睛，在紙上寫字嗎？”父親：“這有甚麼難的，寫幾行也行。”兒子：“幾行沒有必要，只要你閉著眼睛在我的成績表上簽個名就行了。”

四、报纸阅读 (Newspaper Reading)

联合国武器核查小组完成在伊检查工作

联合国武器核查小组负责人斯米多维奇8月17日在巴格达说，该小组已完成在伊拉克的使命，将按预定计划于18日离开巴格达。斯米多维奇17日在一份声明中说，核查小组学到了一些有益和有助于今后核查工作的东西。但他没有透露他的小组检查了哪些地点和发现了什么。

联合国武器核查小组完成在伊检查工作

联合国武器核查小组负责人斯米多维奇8月17日在巴格达说，该小组已完成在伊拉克的使命，将按预订计划于18日离开巴格达。斯米多维奇17日在一份声明中说，核查小组学到了一些有益和有助于今后核查工作的东西。但他没有透露他的小组检查了哪些地点和发现了什么。

五、 幽默小品 (Humor)

闭眼睛写字

儿子问父亲："爸爸，你能闭上眼睛，在纸上写字吗？"父亲："这有什么难的，写几行也行。"儿子："几行没有必要，只要你闭著眼睛在我的成绩表上签个名就行了。"

生詞

閉	（bì）	*V.*	to close (eyes, mouth, gate, etc.),
成績表	（chéng jì biǎo）	*N.*	report card, grade booklet
簽名	（qiān míng）	*VO.*	to sign (one's signature)

生词

闭	（bì）	*V.*	to close (eyes, mouth, gate, etc.),
成绩表	（chéng jì biǎo）	*N.*	report card, grade booklet
签名	（qiān míng）	*VO.*	to sign (one's signature)

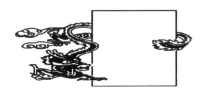

課文要點 (Key Points)

一、常用文言詞、縮略語與專用名詞 (Frequently used classical Chinese phrases, abbreviations, and proper nouns)

1. 與＝跟 (with)

　　例：上周中國與美國就貿易問題舉行了會談。
　　　　China and the U.S. held talks on trade issues last week.

2. 之後＝以後 (after)

　　例：採取軍事行動之後，這幾個國家就停止出售武器了。
　　　　After taking military measures, these several countries suspended selling weapons to other countries.

3. 從未＝從來沒有 (never)

　　例：核查團在檢查中從未遇到任何困難。
　　　　The inspection team never ran into any difficulties during its inspection.

4. 伊＝伊拉克 (Iraq)

　　例：這個小組完成了在伊的兩輪會談。
　　　　This group completed their two rounds of talk held in Iraq.

5. 於＝對（常常用在動詞後面）

　　例：有益於我們的學習＝對我們的學習有益
　　　　It is beneficial to our study.

31

课文要点 (Key Points)

一、常用文言词、缩略语与专用名词 (Frequently used classical Chinese phrases, abbreviations and proper nouns)

1. 与 = 跟 (with)

例: 上周中国与美国就贸易问题举行了会谈。
China and the U.S. held talks on trade issues last week.

2. 之后 = 以后 (after)

例: 采取军事行动之后，这几个国家就停止出售武器了。
After taking military measures, these several countries suspended selling weapons to other countries.

3. 从未 = 从来没有 (never)

例: 核查团在检查中从未遇到任何困难。
The inspection team never ran into any difficulties during its inspection.

4. 伊 = 伊拉克 (Iraq)

例: 这个小组完成了在伊的两轮会谈。
This group completed their two rounds of talk held in Iraq.

5. 于 = 对（常常用在动词后面）

例: 有益于我们的学习 = 对我们的学习有益
It is beneficial to our study.

6. 西方新聞媒介 (Western news media)

7. 紐約時報 (New York Times)

二、常用短語 (Frequently used structures)

1. 完成…使命 (to complete the mission of...)

例：昨天江蘇專業集團一行完成了在香港的使命回到南京。
Yesterday the special trade delegation from Jiangsu wound up its mission in Hong Kong and returned to Nanjing.

聯合國主席完成了觀察南非政府選舉的使命，按原訂計劃將於明天離開南非。
The Secretary General of the U.N. fulfilled his mission of observing the South African election and in accordance with the original plan will leave South Africa tomorrow.

2. 按原訂計劃 (according to the original plan)

例：他將按原訂計劃提前一個學期畢業。
Following his original plan, he will graduate a semester ahead of (the normal) schedule.

按原訂計劃，中英雙方將在希爾頓飯店舉行第十次會談。
According to the original plan, China and Great Britain will hold the tenth round of talks at the Hilton Hotel.

3. 遇到…的對抗 (to encounter resistance from...)

例：事實上，聯合國武器核查小組遇到了一些伊拉克政府的對抗。
In fact, the U.N. weapons inspection team encountered some resistance from the Iraqi government.

6. 西方新闻媒介 (Western news media)

7. 纽约时报 (New York Times)

二、 常用短语 (Frequently used structures)

1. 完成…使命 (to complete the mission of...)

例： 昨天江苏专业集团一行完成了在香港的使命回到南京。
Yesterday the special trade delegation from Jiangsu wound up its mission in Hong Kong and returned to Nanjing.

联合国主席完成了观查南非政府选举的使命，按原订计划将於明天离开南非。
The Secretary General of the U.N. fulfilled his mission of observing the South African election and in accordance with the original plan will leave South Africa tomorrow.

2. 按原订计划 (according to the original plan)

例： 他将按原订计划提前一个学期毕业。
Following his original plan, he will graduate a semester ahead of (the normal) schedule.

按原订计划，中英双方将在希尔顿饭店举行第十次会谈。
According to the original plan, China and Great Britain will hold the tenth round of talks at the Hilton Hotel.

3. 遇到…的对抗 (to encounter resistance from...)

例： 事实上，联合国武器核查小组遇到了一些伊拉克政府的对抗。
In fact, the U.N. weapons inspection team encountered some resistance from the Iraqi government.

昨天警方透露，他們已尋找到殺人犯，而且在逮捕時並沒有遇到殺人犯的對抗。

According to what was divulged by the police yesterday, they have apprehended the murderer and when arresting him encountered no resistance whatsoever.

4. 由…組成 (to be composed of)

例：這個代表團是由十二個人組成的。

This delegation is composed of 12 members.

聯合國是由世界各國的代表組成的。

The United Nations is composed of representatives from different countries.

5. 尋找與…有關的證據 (to look for evidence of)

例：警察正在尋找與他們開秘密會議有關的證據。

The police are looking for evidence pertaining to their secret meetings.

據《紐約時報》報道，記者和警察們正在尋找那兩個澳大利亞政府官員被打傷的證據。

According to a report in New York Times, many journalists and policemen are searching for evidence involving assault upon the two Australian government officials.

6. （對）…採取…行動 (to take action against)

例：對南斯拉夫的情形，聯合國準備採取軍事行動。

The U.N. prepared to take military action to deal with the situation in Yugoslavia.

由於這個政府官員秘密出售武器的證據已定，政府決定採取行動，懲罰此人。

Because evidence of secretly selling weapons by this government official has been established, the government has decided to take action and punish this person.

昨天警方透露，他们已寻找到杀人犯，而且在逮捕时并没有遇到杀人犯的对抗。

According to what was divulged by the police yesterday, they have apprehended the murderer and when arresting him encountered no resistance whatsoever.

4. 由…组成 (to be composed of)

例: 这个代表团是由十二个人组成的。

This delegation is composed of 12 members.

联合国是由世界各国的代表组成的。

The United Nations is composed of representatives from different countries.

5. 寻找与…有关的证据 (to look for evidence of)

例: 警察正在寻找与他们开秘密会议有关的证据。

The police are looking for evidence pertaining to their secret meetings.

据《纽约时报》报道，记者和警察们正在寻找那两个澳大利亚政府官员被打伤的证据。

According to a report in New York Times, many journalists and policemen are searching for evidence involving assault upon the two Australian government officials.

6.（对）…采取…行动 (to take action against)

例: 对南斯拉夫的情形，联合国准备采取军事行动。

The U.N. prepared to take military action to deal with the situation in Yugoslavia.

由于这个政府官员秘密售武器的证据已定，政府决定采取行动，惩罚此人。

Because evidence of secretly selling weapons by this government official has been established, the government has decided to take action and punish this person.

7. 對…進行（種種）猜測 (to entertain various speculations about, to come up with conjectures concerning)

例：昨天老師沒來上課，同學們對此進行了種種猜測。

The teacher did not come to class yesterday; so the students indulged in various conjectures about her absence.

對於1997年香港回歸大陸的問題， 西方媒介不斷地進行種種猜測。

The western news media has speculated endlessly about the reversion of Hong Kong to China in 1997.

8. 在…情況下 (under the condition of)

例：在雙方都同意的情況下，代表團團長接受了記者的採訪。

Upon agreement by both sides, the head of the delegation accepted an interview by journalists.

在異常困難的情況下，警察找到了與武器有關的證據。

Under the extremely difficult circumstances, the police found evidence linking to the murder weapon.

7. 对…进行（种种）猜测 (to entertain various speculations about, to come up with conjectures concerning)

例: 昨天老师没来上课，同学们对此进行了种种猜测。
The teacher did not come to class yesterday; so the students indulged in various conjectures about her absence.

对于1997年香港回归大陆的问题，西方媒介不断地进行种种猜测。
The western news media has speculated endlessly about the reversion of Hong Kong to China in 1997.

8. 在…情况下 (under the condition of)

例: 在双方都同意的情况下，代表团团长接受了记者的采访。
Upon agreement by both sides, the head of the delegation accepted an interview by journalists.

在异常困难的情况下，警察找到了与武器有关的证据。
Under the extremely difficult circumstances, the police found evidence linking to the murder weapon.

第一單元　每日新聞

第四課

中英就香港問題舉行第六輪會談

課文

一、簡介 (Introduction)

　　香港將要在1997年回歸大陸。由於香港與大陸的政治和經濟制度完全不同，所以香港平穩過渡問題一直是一個關係到世界和平與穩定的大問題。到現在為止，中國和英國已經舉行了很多輪會談，就香港的選舉問題和今後的政治和經濟體制問題進行討論。下面的這條新聞就是報道中英的第六輪會談。

生詞

回歸	(huí guī)	V/N.	to revert to; reversion
大陸	(dà lù)	N.	Mainland China
制度	(zhì dù)	N.	system
平穩	(píng wěn)	Adj.	smooth, stable, smooth and stable
過渡	(guò dù)	Adj/N.	transitional; transition
舉行	(jǔ xíng)	V.	to hold
輪	(lún)	Classifier.	the/a round (of talks, sports)
會談	(huì tán)	N.	talks, face to face discussions
就	(jìu)	Prep.	on, about, with regard to (certain issues)

第一单元　每日新闻

第四课

中英就香港问题举行第六轮会谈

课文

一、简介 (Introduction)

　　香港将要在1997年回归大陆。由于香港与大陆的政治和经济制度完全不同，所以香港平稳过渡问题一直是一个关系到世界和平与稳定的大问题。到现在为止，中国和英国已经举行了很多轮会谈，就香港的选举问题和今后的政治和经济体制问题进行讨论。下面的这条新闻就是报道中英的第六轮会谈。

生词

回归	(huí guī)	*V/N.*	to revert to; reversion
大陆	(dà lù)	*N.*	Mainland China
制度	(zhì dù)	*N.*	system
平稳	(píng wěn)	*Adj.*	smooth, stable, smooth and stable
过渡	(guò dù)	*Adj/N.*	transitional; transition
举行	(jǔ xíng)	*V.*	to hold
轮	(lún)	*Classifier.*	the/a round (of talks, sports)
会谈	(huì tán)	*N.*	talks, face to face discussions
就	(jiù)	*Prep.*	on, about, with regard to (certain

| 選舉 | （xuǎn jǔ） | *V/N.* | to hold an election, to elect; election |
| 體制 | （tǐ zhì） | *N.* | (political/economic) form(s), system |

二、對話 (Dialogues)

（一）

許賓： 小高，最近香港問題有甚麼新發展？

小高： 據昨天的報紙報道，中英正在舉行第十輪會談。

許賓： 就甚麼問題會談呢？

小高： 我想還是就香港將來的選舉問題。已經談了很多次了，但進展還不夠快，可見這不是一件輕而易舉的事情。

問題： *最近，香港問題有甚麼新發展？*

生詞

據	（jù）	*Prep.*	according to
進展	（jìn zhǎn）	*N.*	progress
輕而易舉	（qīng ér yì jǔ）	*Idiom.*	without effort, easily

（二）

小高： 許賓，你是美國人，考你幾個政治問題。

許賓： 好吧。我試試看。

小高： 現在誰是美國駐華大使？誰是英國駐華大使？誰是中國外交部部長？

issues)

| 选举 | （xuǎn jǔ） | V./N. | to hold an election, to elect; election |
| 体制 | （tǐ zhì） | N. | (political/economic) form(s), system |

二、对话 (Dialogues)

（一）

许宾： 小高，最近香港问题有什么新发展？

小高： 据昨天的报纸报道，中英正在举行第十轮会谈。

许宾： 就什么问题会谈呢？

小高： 我想还是就香港将来的选举问题。已经谈了很多次了，但进展还不够快，可见这不是一件轻而易举的事情。

问题： *最近，香港问题有什么新发展？*

生词

据	（jù）	*Prep.*	according to
进展	（jìn zhǎn）	*N.*	progress
轻而易举	（qīng ér yì jǔ）	*Idiom.*	without effort, easily

（二）

小高： 许宾，你是美国人，考你几个政治问题。

许宾： 好吧。我试试看。

小高： 现在谁是美国驻华大使？谁是英国驻华大使？谁是中国外交部部长？

誰是美國駐英大使？

問題：請你回答小高的四個問題。

生詞

| 駐 | (zhù) | *V.* | to be stationed in/at |
| 駐華大使 | (zhù huá dà shǐ) | *NP.* | the/an ambassador accredited to China |

（三）

許賓：小高，你對香港97年回歸中國大陸有甚麼看法？這一回歸會不會影響香港的繁榮和穩定。

小高：我想這個問題主要要看中共對香港的態度以及這幾年中國的經濟發展。如果中共仍然在政治上和經濟上採取開放合作態度，這一政策必將促進香港的繁榮和穩定。

許賓：我基本上贊同你的意見。希望雙方都努力工作，使會談取得很大進展。

問題：小高對97年香港回歸大陸的看法是甚麼？

生詞

| 繁榮 | (fán róng) | *N/Adj.* | prosperity; to be flourishing, booming (of economy, city, etc.) |
| 贊同 | (zàn tóng) | *V/N.* | to agree, to approve of; agreement |

谁是美国驻英大使？

问题：请你回答小高的四个问题。

生词

驻	(zhù)	*V.*	to be stationed in/at
驻华大使	(zhù huá dà shǐ)	*NP.*	the/an ambassador accredited to China

（三）

许宾： 小高，你对香港97年回归中国大陆有什么看法？这一回归会不会影响香港的繁荣和稳定。

小高： 我想这个问题主要要看中共对香港的态度以及这几年中国的经济发展。如果中共仍然在政治上和经济上采取开放合作态度，这一政策必将促进香港的繁荣和稳定。

许宾： 我基本上赞同你的意见。希望双方都努力工作，使会谈取得很大进展。

问题：小高对97年香港回归大陆的看法是什么？

生词

繁荣	(fán róng)	*N/Adj.*	prosperity; to be flourishing, booming (of economy, city, etc.)
赞同	(zàn tóng)	*V/N.*	to agree, to approve of; agreement

三、電視新聞 (The TV news)

中英就香港問題舉行第六輪會談

　　中國政府代表、外交部副部長姜恩柱和英國政府代表、駐華大使麥若彬6月23號在北京開始就香港1994、1995年選舉安排問題舉行第六輪會談。

　　會談正式開始前，姜恩柱和麥若彬接受了記者五分鐘的採訪。姜恩柱說，現在我們雙方的會談正在正常進行，我們的會談像攀登一座高峰一樣，當然不是一件輕而易舉的事情。但是我們雙方都在努力工作，我相信只要我們雙方都有決心和毅力共同努力，我們就能加快前進的步伐，最終成功地達到頂峰。

　　麥若彬對姜恩柱的講話表示贊同。他說，他期待著本次會談取得進展，以完成兩國政府賦予的重要任務。

生詞

副部長	(fù bù zhǎng)	*Title/rank*	Deputy Minister, (the) deputy minister
姜恩柱	(jiāng ēn zhù)	*Personal N.*	Jiang Enzhu
麥若彬	(mài ruò bīn)	*Personal N.*	Mai Ruobin
正式	(zhèng shì)	*Adj.*	formal
雙方	(shuāng fāng)	*NP.*	both sides
攀登	(pān dēng)	*V.*	to climb, to scale (a height, a mountain)
高峰	(gāo fēng)	*N.*	peak, summit; pinnacle＝頂峰
毅力	(yì lì)	*N.*	persistence, will power, stamina
加快	(jiā kuài)	*V.*	to speed up, to accelerate
前進	(qián jìn)	*N.*	progress
步伐	(bù fá)	*N.*	steps, pace, speed

三、电视新闻 (The TV news)

中英就香港问题举行第六轮会谈

中国政府代表、外交部副部长姜恩柱和英国政府代表、驻华大使麦若彬6月23号在北京开始就香港1994、1995年选举安排问题举行第六轮会谈。

会谈正式开始前，姜恩柱和麦若彬接受了记者五分钟的采访。姜恩柱说，现在我们双方的会谈正在正常进行，我们的会谈象攀登一座高峰一样，当然不是一件轻而易举的事情。但是我们双方都在努力工作，我相信只要我们双方都有决心和毅力共同努力，我们就能加快前进的步伐，最终成功地达到顶峰。

麦若彬对姜恩柱的讲话表示赞同。他说，他期待著本次会谈取得进展，以完成两国政府赋予的重要任务。

生词

副部长	(fù bù zhǎng)	*Title/rank.*	Deputy Minister, (the) deputy minister
姜恩柱	(jiāng ēn zhù)	*Personal N.*	Jiang Enzhu
麦若彬	(mài ruò bīn)	*Personal N.*	Mai Ruobin
正式	(zhèng shì)	*Adj.*	formal
双方	(shuāng fāng)	*NP.*	both sides
攀登	(pān dēng)	*V.*	to climb, to scale (a height, a mountain)
高峰	(gāo fēng)	*N.*	peak, summit; pinnacle = 顶峰
毅力	(yì lì)	*N.*	persistence, will power, stamina
加快	(jiā kuài)	*V.*	to speed up, to accelerate
前进	(qián jìn)	*N.*	progress
步伐	(bù fá)	*N.*	steps, pace, speed

最終	(zuì zhōng)	*Adv.*	finally, eventually
達到	(dá dào)	*V.*	to arrive, to reach
頂峰	(dǐng fēng)	*N.*	peak, summit, pinnacle
次	(cì)	*Classifier.*	(this) time, (this) round, (this) session
期待	(qī dài)	*V.*	to expect, to anticipate; to look forward to, to await
賦予	(fù yǔ)	*V.*	to entrust to, to bestow on, to endow with
任務	(rèn wù)	*N.*	task, mission

四、報紙閱讀 (Newspaper Reading)

中英就香港问题举行第六轮会谈

新华社北京6月23日电（记者冯秀菊） 中国政府代表、外交部副部长姜恩柱和英国政府代表、驻华大使麦若彬今天上午开始就香港1994／1995年选举安排问题举行第六轮会谈。

会谈在钓鱼台国宾馆10号楼举行。如同前五轮会谈一样，在本次会谈正式开始前，姜恩柱和麦若彬接受了记者5分钟的采访。

姜恩柱说，"我们中方一贯致力于维持香港的繁荣和稳定，实现香港1997年的平稳过渡。现在我们双方的会谈正在正常进行。我们的会谈像攀登一座高峰一样，当然不是一件轻而易举的事情。但是我们双方都在努力工作。我相信，只要我们双方都有决心和毅力，共同努力，我们就能加快前进的步伐，最终成功地到达顶峰。"麦若彬说，他对姜恩柱说的那番话表示赞同。他说，他期待着本次会谈取得进展，以完成两国政府赋予的重要任务。

当记者问到会谈的进展情况时，姜恩柱强调说，"双方有协议，都不向外泄露会谈的具体内容。我们将严守这一协议。"

中英双方商定，为期3天的本轮会谈仍将根据中英联合声明、与基本法衔接的原则以及中英已达成的有关协议和谅解进行。

最终	(zuì zhōng)	Adv.	finally, eventually
达到	(dá dào)	V.	to arrive, to reach
顶峰	(dǐng fēng)	N.	peak, summit, pinnacle
次	(cì)	Classifier.	(this) time, (this) round, (this) session
期待	(qī dài)	V.	to expect, to anticipate; to look forward to, to await
赋予	(fù yǔ)	V.	to entrust to, to bestow on, to endow with
任务	(rèn wù)	N.	task, mission

四、报纸阅读 (Newspaper Reading)

中英就香港问题
举行第六轮会谈

新华社北京 6 月 23 日电（记者冯秀菊）中国政府代表、外交部副部长姜恩柱和英国政府代表、驻华大使麦若彬今天上午开始就香港 1994／1995 年选举安排问题举行第六轮会谈。

会谈在钓鱼台国宾馆 10 号楼举行。如同前五轮会谈一样，在本次会谈正式开始前，姜恩柱和麦若彬接受了记者 5 分钟的采访。

姜恩柱说，"我们中方一贯致力于维持香港的繁荣和稳定，实现香港 1997 年的平稳过渡。现在我们双方的会谈正在正常进行。我们的会谈像攀登一座高峰一样，当然不是一件轻而易举的事情。但是我们双方都在努力工作。我相信，只要我们双方都有决心和毅力，共同努力，我们就能加快前进的步伐，最终成功地到达顶峰。"麦若彬说，他对姜恩柱说的那番话表示赞同。他说，他期待着本次会谈取得进展，以完成两国政府赋予的重要任务。

当记者问到会谈的进展情况时，姜恩柱强调说，"双方有协议，都不向外泄露会谈的具体内容。我们将严守这一协议。"

中英双方商定，为期 3 天的本轮会谈仍将根据中英联合声明、与基本法衔接的原则以及中英已达成的有关协议和谅解进行。

中英就香港問題舉行第六輪會談

　　新華社北京6月23日電（記者馮秀菊）中國政府代表、外交部副部長姜恩柱和英國政府代表、駐華大使麥若彬今天上午開始就香港 1994/1995年選舉安排問題舉行第六輪會談。

　　會談在釣魚台國賓館10號樓舉行。如同前五輪會談一樣，在本次會談開始前，姜恩柱和麥若彬接受了記者5分鐘的採訪。

　　姜恩柱説，"我們中方一貫致力於維持香港的繁榮和穩定，實現香港1997年的平穩過渡。現在我們雙方的會談正在正常進行。我們的會談像攀登一座高峰一樣，當然不是一件輕而易舉的事情。但是我們雙方都在努力工作。我相信，只要我們雙方都有決心和毅力，共同努力，我們就能加快前進的步伐，最終成功地到達頂峰。"麥若彬説，他對姜恩柱説的那番話表示贊同。他説，他期待著本次會談取得進展，以完成兩國政府賦予的重要任務。

　　當記者問到會談的進展情況時，姜恩柱強調説，"雙方有協議，都不向外洩露會談的具體內容。我們將嚴守這一協議。"

　　中英雙方商定，為期 3天的本輪會談仍將根據中英聯合聲明、與基本法銜接的原則以及中英已達成的有關協議和諒解進行。

生詞

釣魚台	(diào yú tái)	*Place N.*	the most prestigious complex of VIP state guest residences in Beijing
致力	(zhì lì)	*V.*	to engage in, to strive for, to devote one's energies to
一貫	(yī guàn)	*Adv.*	all along
維持	(wéi chí)	*V.*	to maintain
番	(fān)	*Classifier.*	＝(here) 些

中英就香港问题举行第六轮会谈

新华社北京6月23日电（记者冯秀菊）中国政府代表、外交部副部长姜恩柱和英国政府代表、驻华大使麦若彬今天上午开始就香港1994/1995年选举安排问题举行第六轮会谈。

会谈在钓鱼台国宾馆10号楼举行。如同前五轮会谈一样，在本次会谈开始前，姜恩柱和麦若彬接受了记者5分钟的采访。

姜恩柱说，"我们中方一贯致力于维持香港的繁荣和稳定，实现香港1997年的平稳过渡。现在我们双方的会谈正在正常进行。我们的会谈象攀登一座高峰一样，当然不是一件轻而易举的事情。但是我们双方都在努力工作。我相信，只要我们双方都有决心和毅力，共同努力，我们就能加快前进的步伐，最终成功地到达顶峰。"麦若彬说，他对姜恩柱说的那番话表示赞同。他说，他期待著本次会谈取得进展，以完成两国政府赋予的重要任务。

当记者问到会谈的进展情况时，姜恩柱强调说，"双方有协议，都不向外泄露会谈的具体内容。我们将严守这一协议。"

中英双方商定，为期3天的本轮会谈仍将根据中英联合声明、与基本法衔接的原则以及中英已达成的有关协议和谅解进行。

生词

钓鱼台	(diào yú tái)	*Place N.*	the most prestigious complex of VIP state guest residences in Beijing
致力	(zhì lì)	*V.*	to engage in, to strive for, to devote one's energies to
一贯	(yī guàn)	*Adv.*	all along
维持	(wéi chí)	*V.*	to maintain
番	(fān)	*Classifier.*	= (here) 些

強調	(qiáng diào)	*V.*	to emphasize
協議	(xié yì)	*N.*	agreement
洩露	(xiè lù)	*V.*	to divulge, to leak out, to reveal (a secret)
具體	(jù tǐ)	*Adj.*	in detail, specific, concrete, detailed
嚴守	(yán shǒu)	*VP.*	to strictly observe or follow
商定	(shāng dìng)	*V.*	to agree upon after consultation
為期	(wéi qī)	*VO.*	not to exceed (a set of time); to be in effect, to last for (a certain period of time), to be completed by such and such a date
聯合聲明	(lián hé shēng míng)	*NP.*	joint communique
銜接	(xián jiē)	*V.*	to connect, to link up with, to dovetail with
諒解	(liàng jiě)	*N.*	understanding

五、幽默小品 (Humor)

"你為什么前天不來吃呢？"

顧客：“夥計，今天的牛肉不新鮮呀！”

夥計：“你為甚麼前天不來吃呢？”

生詞

夥計	(huǒ jì)	*N.*	waiter; servant

强调	(qiáng diào)	*V.*	to emphasize
协议	(xié yì)	*N.*	agreement
泄露	(xiè lù)	*V.*	to divulge, to leak out, to reveal (a secret)
具体	(jù tǐ)	*Adj.*	in detail, specific, concrete, detailed
严守	(yán shǒu)	*VP.*	to strictly observe or follow
商定	(shāng dìng)	*V.*	to agree upon after consultation
为期	(wéi qī)	*VO.*	not to exceed (a set of time); to be in effect, to last for (a certain period of time), to be completed by such and such a date
联合声明	(lián hé shēng míng)	*NP.*	joint communique
衔接	(xián jiē)	*V.*	to connect, to link up with, to dovetail with
谅解	(liàng jiě)	*N.*	understanding

五、 幽默小品 (Humor)

"你为什么前天不来吃呢？"

顾客： "伙计，今天的牛肉不新鲜呀！"

伙计： "你为什么前天不来吃呢？"

生词

| 伙计 | (huǒ jì) | *N.* | waiter; servant |

41

課文要點 (Key Points)

一、常用文言詞、縮略語與慣用語 (Frequently used classical Chinese phrases, abbreviations, and fixed expressions)

1. 就＝關於 (on, about, concerning)

　　例：兩國就香港選舉問題舉行會談。

　　The two countries held talks concerning the issue of elections in Hong Kong.

2. 以＝以便 (so as to)

　　例：他努力工作，以完成政府賦予的重要任務。

　　He worked hard so as to carry out the important mission entrusted to him by his government.

3. 賦予＝給 (to entrust, to give)

　　例：這是歷史賦予我們年青人的責任。

　　This is the mission which history has entrusted to us young people.

4. 輪＝次 (round)

　　例：第八輪中英談判已經結束。

　　The eighth round of talks between China and Great Britain has come to an end.

5. 駐＝停留、住在 (to be stationed at, to reside in, to be quartered at)

　　例：布什 (Bush) 總統曾是駐華大使。

　　President Bush used to be the ambassador to China.

课文要点 (Key Points)

一、常用文言词、缩略语与惯用语 (Frequently used classical Chinese phrases, abbreviations, and fixed expressions)

1. 就 = 关于 (on, about, concerning)

　例: 两国就香港选举问题举行会谈。

　　The two countries held talks concerning the issue of elections in Hong Kong.

2. 以 = 以便 (so as to)

　例: 他努力工作，以完成政府赋予的重要任务。

　　He worked hard so as to carry out the important mission entrusted to him by his government.

3. 赋予 = 给 (to entrust, to give)

　例: 这是历史赋予我们年青人的责任。

　　This is the mission which history has entrusted to us young people.

4. 轮 = 次 (round)

　例: 第八轮中英谈判已经结束。

　　The eighth round of talks between China and Great Britain has come to an end.

5. 驻 = 停留、住在 (to be stationed at, to reside in, to be quartered at)

　例: 布什 (Bush) 总统曾是驻华大使。

　　President Bush used to be the ambassador to China.

6. 如同＝像…一樣 (as if)

例：學中文如同攀登高峰一樣要有自信心。

Studying Chinese is just like scaling a high peak--it requires self-confidence.

7. 番＝些 (some)

例：對我說的那番話，他表示同意。

He expressed his agreement with what I said.

8. 這一＝這一個（項）(this one)

例：這一決定對北美的經濟發展十分重要。

This decision is vitally important to North America's economic development.

9. 中英＝中國跟英國 (China and Britain, Sino-Anglo)

例：中英舉行了很多輪會談。

Many rounds of talks between China and Great Britain have already been held.

10. 將＝要、會 (will, to be going to)

例：香港將在1997年發生很大變化。

Great changes will take place in Hong Kong in 1997.

11. 以及＝跟、和 (and, as well as, along with)

例：香港問題對亞洲以及世界和平都有影響。

The issue of Hong Kong will have an impact on peace in Asia as well as peace in the world.

6. 如同 = 象…一样 (as if)

　　例: 学中文如同攀登高峰一样要有自信心。
　　　　Studying Chinese is just like scaling a high peak--it requires self-confidence.

7. 番 = 些 (some)

　　例: 对我说的那番话，他表示同意。
　　　　He expressed his agreement with what I said.

8. 这一 = 这一个（项）(this one)

　　例: 这一决定对北美的经济发展十分重要。
　　　　This decision is vitally important to North America's economic development.

9. 中英 = 中国跟英国 (China and Britain, Sino-Anglo)

　　例: 中英举行了很多轮会谈。
　　　　Many rounds of talks between China and Great Britain have already been held.

10. 将 = 要、会 (will, to be going to)

　　例: 香港将在1997年发生很大变化。
　　　　Great changes will take place in Hong Kong in 1997.

11. 以及 = 跟、和 (and, as well as, along with)

　　例: 香港问题对亚洲以及世界和平都有影响。
　　　　The issue of Hong Kong will have an impact on peace in Asia as well as peace in the world.

12. 已＝已經 (already)

例：中共中央總書記及其一行現已到美。
The General Secretary of CC, CCP and his delegation have now arrived in the U.S.

13. 仍＝還、還是 (still)

例：中日會談仍在進行。
The talks between China and Japan are still in progress.

14. 於＝在 (on, in, at)

例：奧運健兒於3日回到北京。
The athletes of the Olympic Games returned to Beijing on the third.

二、常用短語 (Frequently used structures)

1. 就…問題 (concerning the question of, on the issue of)

例：雙方就美國和中國共同關心的問題進行了會談。
Both sides discussed the issues concerning both the U.S. and China.

就記者提出的問題，外交部部長作了一個十分鐘的講話。
The foreign minister spoke for 10 minutes in response to questions raised by reporters.

2. 接受…的採訪 (to accept an interview with; to be interviewed by)

例：美國駐中國大使高興地接受《人民日報》記者的採訪。
The U.S. ambassador to China gladly granted an interview to the reporter from the People's Daily.

44

12. 已 = 已经 (already)

例: 中共中央总书记及其一行现已到美。

The General Secretary of CC, CCP and his delegation have now arrived in the U.S.

13. 仍 = 还、还是 (still)

例: 中日会谈仍在进行。

The talks between China and Japan are still in progress.

14. 于 = 在 (on, in, at)

例: 奥运健儿于3日回到北京。

The athletes of the Olympic Games returned to Beijing on the third.

二、常用短语 (Frequently used structures)

1. 就…问题 (concerning the question of, on the issue of)

例: 双方就美国和中国共同关心的问题进行了会谈。

Both sides discussed the issues concerning both the U.S. and China.

就记者提出的问题，外交部部长作了一个十分钟的讲话。

The foreign minister spoke for 10 minutes in response to questions raised by reporters.

2. 接受…的采访 (to accept an interview with; to be interviewed by)

例: 美国驻中国大使高兴地接受《人民日报》记者的采访。

The U.S. ambassador to China gladly granted an interview to the reporter from the People's Daily.

在接受電視台採訪的時候，美國政府代表團團長對今後的貿易合作表示贊同。

In his televised interview, the head of the U.S. government delegation expressed his approval of the future cooperation in the trade between the two countries.

3. 攀登 (to climb)

例：攀登科學高峰需要有很大的勇氣。

It requires courage to scale the peaks of science.

世界上只有幾個國家的登山運動員攀登過世界第一高峰珠姆朗瑪峰。

In the world, only few country's mountain climbers have climbed Mount Qomolangma which is the highest peak in the world.

4. 像…一樣 (as the same as...)

例：西方人學習東亞語言就像攀登高峰一樣，不是一件輕而易舉的事情。

For Westerners learning East Asian languages is like climbing mountain peaks, it is no easy matter for them.

中英談判就像長跑一樣，要進行很長時間。

The talks between China and Great Britain are like a long distance race, something requiring a lengthy amount of time.

5. 加快…的步伐 (to speed up the pace of...)

例：中國正在加快經濟建設的步伐。

China is right now speeding up the pace of its economic construction.

香港問題的解決可以加快中國經濟和政治發展的步伐。

A resolution to the Hong Kong issue will speed up the pace of China's economic and political development.

在接受电视台采访的时候， 美国政府代表团团长对今后的贸易合作表示赞同。

In his televised interview, the head of the U.S. government delegation expressed his approval of the future cooperation in the trade between the two countries.

3. 攀登 (to climb)

例：攀登科学高峰需要有很大的勇气。

It requires courage to scale the peaks of science.

世界上只有几个国家的登山运动员攀登过世界第一高峰珠姆朗玛峰。

In the world, only few country's mountain climbers have climbed Mount Qomolangma which is the highest peak in the world.

4. 象…一样 (as the same as...)

例：西方人学习东亚语言就象攀登高峰一样，不是一件轻而易举的事情。

For Westerners learning East Asian languages is like climbing mountain peaks, it is no easy matter for them.

中英谈判就象长跑一样， 要进行很长时间。

The talks between China and Great Britain are like a long distance race, something requiring a lengthy amount of time.

5. 加快…的步伐 (to speed up the pace of...)

例：中国正在加快经济建设的步伐。

China is right now speeding up the pace of its economic construction.

香港问题的解决可以加快中国经济和政治发展的步伐。

A resolution to the Hong Kong issue will speed up the pace of China's economic and political development.

6. 達到 (to arrive at)

例：在十年研究中醫的過程中，她刻苦努力，終於達到一個新的高峰。
During ten years of research into Chinese traditional herbal medicine, she worked extremely hard and finally reached a new peak(of her career).

江澤民在會見印尼客人時說，他希望中印兩國根據和平相處的原則，共同努力，以使兩國的關係達到一個新的高度。
When meeting with the Indonesian guests, Jiang Zemin expressed his hopes that China and Indonesia would both observe the principles of peaceful coexistence and make an effort to ensure that relations between the two countries reach a new level.

7. 對⋯表示贊同（反對、支持）(to express agreement with , opposition to, or support of)

例：有一些美國公民對美國政府的新經濟政策表示反對。
Some people in the U.S. oppose the new economic policy of the U.S. government.

昨天我妹妹寫信給《經濟日報》，對他們現在的新聞報道表示贊同。
My sister wrote a letter yesterday to the Economics Daily, expressing her approval of their recent news report.

8. 完成⋯任務 (to complete , to fulfill the task of)

例：昨天我和我的朋友順利地完成了副部長交給的任務。
Yesterday, my friend and I, without any complications, completed the task assigned to us by the deputy minister.

美國駐華大使昨天在大使館會見了美國經濟代表團，祝賀他們完成了訪華任務。
The U.S. ambassador met with the U.S. economic delegation at the embassy yesterday, congratulating them on successfully completing their mission of visiting China.

9. 洩露 (to divulge, to reveal, to leak out)

6. 达到 (to arrive at)

例: 在十年研究中医的过程中，她刻苦努力，终于达到一个新的高峰。
During ten years of research into Chinese traditional herbal medicine, she worked extremely hard and finally reached a new peak(of her career).

江泽民在会见印尼客人时说，他希望中印两国根据和平相处的原则，共同努力，以使两国的关系达到一个新的高度。
When meeting with the Indonesian guests, Jiang Zemin expressed his hopes that China and Indonesia would both observe the principles of peaceful coexistence and make an effort to ensure that relations between the two countries reach a new level.

7. 对…表示赞同（反对、支持）(to express agreement with , opposition to, or support of)

例: 有一些美国公民对美国政府的新经济政策表示反对。
Some people in the U.S. oppose the new economic policy of the U.S. government.

昨天我妹妹写信给《经济日报》，对他们现在的新闻报道表示赞同。
My sister wrote a letter yesterday to the Economics Daily, expressing her approval of their recent news report.

8. 完成…任务 (to complete, to fulfill the task of)

例: 昨天我和我的朋友顺利地完成了副部长交给的任务。
Yesterday, my friend and I, without any complications, completed the task assigned to us by the deputy minister.

美国驻华大使昨天在大使馆会见了美国经济代表团，祝贺他们完成了访华任务。
The U.S. ambassador met with the U.S. economic delegation at the embassy yesterday, congratulating them on successfully completing their mission of visiting China.

例：這些都是很重要的信息，目前不能洩漏。

This is important information. It cannot be allowed to leak out at present.

有消息洩漏出來，美國政府將在本月跟中國政府進行人權會談。

Information to the effect that the U.S. government will hold talks with the Chinese government concerning human rights issues has leaked out.

10. 根據…原則（聲明、協議）(according to the principles [announcement, agreement])

例：根據協議的原則，北京將建立五個經濟技術開發區。

According to the principles of the agreement, five economic and technological development zones will be established in Beijing.

根據七十年代中美聯合聲明，兩國都將致力於維持亞洲乃至世界和平與穩定的工作。

According to the 1972 Sino-American Joint Communique, both countries will strive to maintain peace and stability in Asia as well as in the world.

11. 達成…（協議）(to reach an agreement)

例：昨天在國賓館，中日雙方就出口問題達成協議。

Yesterday, China and Japan arrived at an agreement on the issues of exports at the State Guest House.

中英經過多次會談，一定會在香港問題上達成協議。

After many rounds of talks, China and Great Britain will likely arrive at a formal agreement on the issue of Hong Kong.

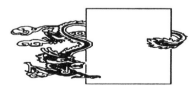

47

9. 泄露 (to divulge, to reveal, to leak out)

例: 这些都是很重要的信息，目前不能泄漏。
This is important information. It cannot be allowed to leak out at present.

有消息泄漏出来，美国政府将在本月跟中国政府进行人权会谈。
Information to the effect that the U.S. government will hold talks with the Chinese
government concerning human rights issues has leaked out.

10. 根据…原则（声明、协议）(according to the principles [announcement, agreement])

例: 根据协议的原则，北京将建立五个经济技术开发区。
According to the principles of the agreement, five economic and technological
development zones will be established in Beijing.

根据七十年代中美联合声明，两国都将致力于维持亚洲乃至世界和平
与稳定的工作。
According to the 1972 Sino-American Joint Communique, both countries will strive to
maintain peace and stability in Asia as well as in the world.

11. 达成…（协议）(to reach an agreement)

例: 昨天在国宾馆，中日双方就出口问题达成协议。
Yesterday, China and Japan arrived at an agreement on the issues of exports at the State
Guest House.

中英经过多次会谈，一定会在香港问题上达成协议。
After many rounds of talks, China and Great Britain will likely arrive at a formal
agreement on the issue of Hong Kong.

小課文

四面楚歌

一、看電視小課文、回答問題 (Answer the following questions)

　　1. 都幾點了，這位老人為甚麼還不能睡覺？

　　2. 那天晚上，老人聽到了一些甚麼聲音？

　　3. 為了睡覺，老人不得不起來做甚麼？

　　4. 為甚麼老人一直在嘆氣？

二、討論 (Discuss the following questions)

　　1. 這個廣告反映了中國當前的甚麼社會問題？

　　2. 比較一下中國的個人空間和美國的個人空間的不同。

　　3. 就廣告談談你對中國住房情況的看法。

　　4. 你有過和這位老人一樣的經歷嗎？請你談一談。

生詞

四面楚歌　　（sì miàn chǔ gē）　　to be besieged on all sides

48

小课文

四面楚歌

一、看电视小课文、回答问题 (Answer the following questions)

   1. 都几点了，这位老人为什么还不能睡觉？

   2. 那天晚上，老人听到了一些什么声音？

   3. 为了睡觉，老人不得不起来做什么？

   4. 为什么老人一直在叹气？

二、讨论 (Discuss the following questions)

   1. 这个广告反映了中国当前的什么社会问题？

   2. 比较一下中国的个人空间和美国的个人空间的不同。

   3. 就广告谈谈你对中国住房情况的看法。

   4. 你有过和这位老人一样的经历吗？请你谈一谈。

生词

四面楚歌	(sì miàn chǔ gē)	to be besieged on all sides

中國歌曲

橄欖樹

不要問我從哪里來，
我的故鄉在遠方。
為甚麼流浪，流浪遠方，
流浪...

為了天空翱翔的小鳥，
為了林中流淌的小溪，
為了寬闊的草原，
流浪遠方，
流浪...

還有，還有，
為了夢中的橄欖樹，橄欖樹。
不要問我從哪里來，
我的故鄉在遠方。

生詞

橄欖樹	(gǎn lǎn shù)	olive tree
故鄉	(gù xiāng)	native place, hometown
遠方	(yuǎn fāng)	far away place
流浪	(líu làng)	to wander around, to roam about
天空	(tiān kōng)	sky
翱翔	(áo xiáng)	to fly, to soar
流淌	(líu tǎng)	running, flowing (water, tears)
小溪	(xiǎo xī)	stream
寬闊	(kuān kuò)	open and wide, spacious
草原	(cǎo yuán)	plains, grassy plains, prairie, grassland

中国歌曲

橄榄树

不要问我从哪里来，
我的故乡在远方。
为什么流浪，流浪远方，
流浪…

为了天空翱翔的小鸟，
为了林中流淌的小溪，
为了宽阔的草原，
流浪远方，
流浪…

还有，还有，
为了梦中的橄榄树，橄榄树。
不要问我从哪里来，
我的故乡在远方。

生词

橄榄树	(gǎn lǎn shù)	olive tree
故乡	(gù xiāng)	native place, hometown
远方	(yuǎn fāng)	far away place
流浪	(líu làng)	to wander around, to roam about
天空	(tiān kōng)	sky
翱翔	(áo xiáng)	to fly, to soar
流淌	(líu tǎng)	running, flowing (water, tears)
小溪	(xiǎo xī)	stream
宽阔	(kuān kuò)	open and wide, spacious
草原	(cǎo yuán)	plains, grassy plains, prairie, grassland

Unit 2: Economic News

第二單元 經濟新聞

第一課

聯合航空公司成立六週年

課文

一、簡介 (Introduction)

中國新聞有一個特點：就是常常只說好話，不說壞話。所以有很多人對中國新聞的真實性表示懷疑。例如，本課的新聞報道說中國聯合航空公司安全飛行六年。可是事實上，中國的航空公司也常有空中和地面事故發生，只是在電視上看不到罷了。

生詞

特點	(tè diǎn)	N.	characteristic(s)
真實性	(zhēn shí xìng)	N.	truthfulness
懷疑	(huái yí)	V.	to suspect, to have doubts about
聯合	(lián hé)	Adj/V.	united , United (Airline), to unite
航空公司	(háng kōng gōng sī)	NP.	airline company
安全	(ān quán)	Adv/N.	safely; safety
飛行	(fēi xíng)	V.	to fly
地面	(dì miàn)	N.	ground
事故	(shì gù)	N.	accident

第二单元 经济新闻

第一课

联合航空公司成立六周年

课文

一、简介 (Introduction)

中国新闻有一个特点：就是常常只说好话，不说坏话。所以有很多人对中国新闻的真实性表示怀疑。例如，本课的新闻报道说中国联合航空公司安全飞行六年。可是事实上，中国的航空公司也常有空中和地面事故发生，只是在电视上看不到罢了。

生词

特点	(tè diǎn)	N.	characteristic(s)
真实性	(zhēn shí xìng)	N.	truthfulness
怀疑	(huái yí)	V.	to suspect, to have doubts about
联合	(lián hé)	Adj/V.	united , United (Airline), to unite
航空公司	(háng kōng gōng sī)	NP.	airline company
安全	(ān quán)	Adv/N.	safely; safety
飞行	(fēi xíng)	V.	to fly
地面	(dì miàn)	N.	ground
事故	(shì gù)	N.	accident

二、對話 (Dialogues)

（一）

白石： 鍾力，我要回中國去。美國有幾家大的航空公司，你看坐哪家的比較
　　　好？

鍾力： 大的航空公司倒有幾家。比方說，聯合、西北、美國航空公司等等。

白石： 我要找一家飛行記錄最好的，很少有空中和地面事故的。

鍾力： 為甚麼？

白石： 我最怕在空中飛行，尤其是飛行20個鐘頭的直航飛機。

鍾力： 那我想，最好的法子就是別飛。

問題： 美國有哪幾家大的航空公司？白石要找一家甚麼樣的航空公司買飛機
　　　票？

生詞

西北	(xī běi)	N.	northwest, Northest Airlines
美國航空公司	(měi guó háng kōng gōng sī)	NP.	American Airlines, AA
記錄	(jì lù)	N.	record
直航	(zhí háng)	NP.	non-stop flight, non-stop routing (air or sea)

（二）

鍾力： 你聽說了嗎？昨天美國(AA)航空公司的空中小姐在全國舉行罷工
　　　了。

白石： 是嗎？

鍾力： 大約有60條航線停止飛行，無法乘坐班機到達他們所要去的地方的人

二、对话 (Dialogues)

（一）

白石： 锤力，我要回中国去。美国有几家大的航空公司，你看坐哪家的比较好？

锤力： 大的航空公司倒有几家。比方说，联合、西北、美国航空公司等等。

白石： 我要找一家飞行记录最好的，很少有空中和地面事故的。

锤力： 为什么？

白石： 我最怕在空中飞行，尤其是飞行20个钟头的直航飞机。

锤力： 那我想，最好的法子就是别飞。

问题： 美国有哪几家大的航空公司？白石要找一家什么样的航空公司买飞机票？

生词

西北	（xī běi）	N.	northwest, Northwest Airlines
美国航空公司	(měi guó háng kōng gōng sī)	NP.	American Airlines, AA
记录	(jì lù)	N.	record
直航	(zhí háng)	NP.	non-stop flight, non-stop routing (air or sea)

（二）

锤力： 你听说了吗？昨天美国(AA)航空公司的空中小姐在全国举行罢工了。

白石： 是吗？

锤力： 大约有60条航线停止飞行，无法乘坐班机到达他们所要去的地方的人有200萬人次。

白石： 那你明天不是要去加州嗎？

鍾力： 對啊，看來我是沒有辦法坐直航去了，也許要在中間甚麼地方停留幾個鐘頭了。

問題： 美國 (AA) 航空公司空中小姐罷工的後果是甚麼？

生詞

空中小姐	(kōng zhōng xiǎo jiě)	N.	stewardess, female flight attendent
罷工	(bà gōng)	VO.	to go on strike
大約	(dà yuē)	Adv.	approximately
航線	(háng xiàn)	N.	air (or shipping) route
人次	(rén cì)	Classifier.	the sum of total people
班機	(bān jī)	N.	flight
停留	(tíng líu)	V.	to stop over at
後果	(hòu guǒ)	N.	result, consequence

三、電視新聞 (The TV news)

聯合航空公司成立六週年

中國聯合航空公司成立6年來，安全飛行3萬5,000多小時，已在國內開闢航線39條，運送中外旅客超過150萬人次，從未發生過任何空中和地面事故，成為我國空中交通的主要力量。

生詞

成立	(chéng lì)	V.	to establish

有200万人次。

白石: 那你明天不是要去加州吗？

锤力: 对啊，看来我是没有办法坐直航去了，也许要在中间什么地方停留几个钟头了。

问题: *美国(AA)航空公司空中小姐罢工的后果是什么？*

生词

空中小姐	(kōng zhōng xiǎo jiě)	*N.*	stewardess, female flight attendent
罢工	(bà gōng)	*VO.*	to go on strike
大约	(dà yuē)	*Adv.*	approximately
航线	(háng xiàn)	*N.*	air (or shipping) route
人次	(rén cì)	*Classifier.*	the sum of total people
班机	(bān jī)	*N.*	flight
停留	(tíng liú)	*V.*	to stop over at
后果	(hòu guǒ)	*N.*	result, consequence

三、电视新闻 (The TV news)

联合航空公司成立六周年

中国联合航空公司成立6年来，安全飞行3万5,000多小时，已在国内开辟航线39条，运送中外旅客超过150万人次，从未发生过任何空中和地面事故，成为我国空中交通的主要力量。

生词

成立	(chéng lì)	*V.*	to establish

週年	(zhōu nián)	N.	anniversary
開闢	(kāi pì)	V.	to open up, to start; to usher in
運送	(yùn sòng)	V.	to transport; to ship
超過	(chāo guò)	V.	to exceed
交通	(jiāo tōng)	N.	transportation
力量	(lì liàng)	N.	force

四、報紙閱讀

莫斯科——香港直航通航
每 周 一 次 来 往 于 两 地

本报香港电　首班由莫斯科直飞香港的班机 8月16日顺利降落启德机场。

据称，今后直航班机将每周一次来往于两地。每周6班自莫斯科起飞，翌日晚从香港飞返莫斯科。

过去，从香港飞往莫斯科通常经曼谷或日本停站，去年6月，有关各方达成协议，在莫斯科和香港两地开设直航班机，协议期到1997年。香港主权移交中国后，另作安排。

莫斯科—香港直航通航
每週一次來往於兩地

　　本報香港電　　　首班由莫斯科直飛香港的班機 8月16日順利降落啟德機場。

　　據稱，今後直航班機將每週一次來往於兩地。每週6班自莫斯科起飛，翌日晚從香港飛返莫斯科。

　　過去，從香港飛往莫斯科通常經曼谷或日本停站，去年6月，有關各方達成協議，在莫斯科和香港兩地開設直航班機，協議期到 1997年。香港主權移交中國後，另作安排。

53

周年	(zhōu nián)	N.	anniversary
开辟	(kāi pì)	V.	to open up, to start; to usher in
运送	(yùn sòng)	V.	to transport; to ship
超过	(chāo guò)	V.	to exceed
交通	(jiāo tōng)	N.	transportation
力量	(lì liàng)	N.	force

四、报纸阅读

莫斯科——香港直航通航
每 周 一 次 来 往 于 两 地

本报香港电 首班由莫斯科直飞香港的班机8月16日顺利降落启德机场。

据称，今后直航班机将每周一次来往于两地。每周6班自莫斯科起飞，翌日晚从香港飞返莫斯科。

过去，从香港飞往莫斯科通常经曼谷或日本停站，去年6月，有关各方达成协议，在莫斯科和香港两地开设直航班机，协议期到1997年。香港主权移交中国后，另作安排。

莫斯科—香港直航通航
每周一次来往于两地

本报香港电 首班由莫斯科直飞香港的班机8月16日顺利降落启德机场。

据称，今后直航班机将每周一次来往于两地。每周6班自莫斯科起飞，翌日晚从香港飞返莫斯科。

过去，从香港飞往莫斯科通常经曼谷或日本停站，去年6月，有关各方达成协议，在莫斯科和香港两地开设直航班机，协议期到 1997年。香港主权移交中国后，另作安排。

生詞

莫斯科	(mò sī kē)	Place N.	Moscow
通航	(tōng háng)	VO.	to be in service
順利	(shùn lì)	Adv/Adj.	smoothly; smooth
啟德機場	(qǐ dé jī chǎng)	NP.	Kaitak Airport in Hong Kong
首班	(shǒu bān)	NP.	the first flight
降落	(jiàng luò)	V.	to land
據稱	(jù chēng)	VP.	it is said＝據說
翌日	(yì rì)	N.	＝第二天
飛返	(fēi fǎn)	V.	to fly back
曼谷	(màn gǔ)	Place N.	Bangkok
有關各方	(yǒu guān gè fāng)	NP.	the parties concerned
開設	(kāi shè)	V.	to provide
主權	(zhǔ quán)	N.	sovereignty
移交	(yí jiāo)	V.	to hand over; to turn over; to transfer

五、幽默小品 (Humor)

遲到原因

老師：“你為甚麼遲到了？”

莉莉：“有人丟了一塊錢。”

老師：“你幫他找著了嗎？”

莉莉：“我踩在那一塊錢上，一直到他走。”

生詞

踩在	(cǎi zài)	V.	to step on

生词

莫斯科	(mò sī kē)	*Place N.*	Moscow
通航	(tōng háng)	*VO.*	to be in service
顺利	(shùn lì)	*Adv/Adj.*	smoothly, smooth
启德机场	(qǐ dé jī chǎng)	*NP.*	Kaitak Airport in Hong Kong
首班	(shǒu bān)	*NP.*	the first flight
降落	(jiàng luò)	*V.*	to land
据称	(jù chēng)	*VP.*	it is said = 据说
翌日	(yì rì)	*N.*	= 第二天
飞返	(fēi fǎn)	*V.*	to fly back
曼谷	(màn gǔ)	*Place N.*	Bangkok
有关各方	(yǒu guān gè fāng)	*NP.*	the parties concerned
开设	(kāi shè)	*V.*	to provide
主权	(zhǔ quán)	*N.*	sovereignty
移交	(yí jiāo)	*V.*	to hand over; to turn over; to transfer

五、幽默小品 (Humor)

迟到原因

老师："你为什么迟到了？"
莉莉："有人丢了一块钱。"
老师："你帮他找着了吗？"
莉莉："我踩在那一块钱上，一直到他走。"

生词

踩在	(cǎi zài)	*V.*	to step on

課文要點 (Key Points)

一、常用文言詞、縮略語與慣用語 (Frequently used classical Chinese phrases, abbreviations, and fixed expressions)

1. 翌日＝第二天 (the next day)

　　例：翌日，中英就貿易問題舉行了會談。
　　　　China and Great Britain held discussions on trade issues the next day.

2. 經＝經過 (via)

　　例：經曼谷到東京的班機早上才有。
　　　　There is only a morning flight to Tokyo via Bangkok.

3. 據稱＝據說 (it is said)

　　例：據稱這家公司六年從未發生過事故。
　　　　It is said that this company has had a perfect record (no accident) for six years.

4. 來往於兩地＝在兩個地方之間來往 (to go back and forth between two places)

　　例：每天有三班飛機來往於兩地。
　　　　There are three flights going back and forth between those two places.

5. 首班＝第一班 (the first flight [bus, car, etc.] of a day)

　　例：從香港到廣州每天有五班汽車，首班在早上八點。
　　　　There is bus service from Hong Kong to Guangzhou, five departures daily, the earliest bus is at 8:00 a.m.

课文要点 (Key Points)

一、常用文言词、缩略语与惯用语 (Frequently used classical Chinese phrases, abbreviations, and fixed expressions)

1. 翌日 = 第二天 (the next day)

例: 翌日，中英就贸易问题举行了会谈。
China and Great Britain held discussions on trade issues the next day.

2. 经 = 经过 (via)

例: 经曼谷到东京的班机早上才有。
There is only a morning flight to Tokyo via Bangkok.

3. 据称 = 据说 (it is said)

例: 据称这家公司六年从未发生过事故。
It is said that this company has had a perfect record (no accident) for six years.

4. 来往于两地 = 在两个地方之间来往 (to go back and forth between two places)

例: 每天有三班飞机来往于两地。
There are three flights going back and forth between those two places.

5. 首班 = 第一班 (the first flight [bus, car, etc.] of a day)

例: 从香港到广州每天有五班汽车，首班在早上八点。
There is bus service from Hong Kong to Guangzhou, five departures daily, the earliest bus is at 8:00 a.m..

6. 直航＝直達航班 (direct flight; a through or direct routing)

例：聯合國負責人坐直航從日內瓦到達伊拉克。

The U.N. representative took a direct flight from Geneva to Iraq.

7. 有關各方＝有關係的各個方面 (parties involved)

例：外交部請來有關各方討論對伊出售武器的問題。

The foreign ministry invited the parties involved to discuss issues pertaining to the selling of weapons to Iraq.

二、常用短語 (Frequently used structures)

1. 成立 + time duration 來 (since the establishment of)

例：這所大學成立二十年來，共收十五萬大學生，現在他們正在全國各地工作。

One hundred fifty thousand students have been enrolled at this university since its establishment twenty years ago. Now these students are working throughout the country.

這家航空公司成立二年以來，共發生了十次空中和地面事故。

Since the establishment of this airline company two years ago, ten accidents both in the air and on the ground have already occurred.

2. 開闢航線（公路 highway）…條 (to inaugurate air routes [to open up highways])

例：最近法國航空公司已經在國內開闢航線幾十條，可供人們四處旅行。

Dozens of new air routes have recently opened up within France, permitting people to travel to every part of the country.

56

6. 直航 = 直达航班 (direct flight; a through or direct routing)

例: 联合国负责人坐直航从日内瓦到达伊拉克。
The U.N. representative took a direct flight from Geneva to Iraq.

7. 有关各方 = 有关系的各个方面 (parties involved)

例: 外交部请来有关各方讨论对伊出售武器的问题。
The foreign ministry invited the parties involved to discuss issues pertaining to the selling of weapons to Iraq.

二、常用短语 (Frequently used structures)

1. 成立 + time duration 来 (since the establishment of)

例: 这所大学成立二十年来，共收十五万大学生，现在他们正在全国各地工作。
One hundred fifty thousand students have been enrolled at this university since its establishment twenty years ago. Now these students are working throughout the country.

这家航空公司成立二年以来，共发生了十次空中和地面事故。
Since the establishment of this airline company two years ago, ten accidents both in the air and on the ground have already occurred.

2. 开辟航线（公路 highway)…条 (to inaugurate air routes [to open up highways])

例: 最近法国航空公司已经在国内开辟航线几十条，可供人们四处旅行。
Dozens of new air routes have recently opened up within France, permitting people to travel to every part of the country.

省政府決定開闢新公路十條，以解決交通問題。

The provincial government decided to open up ten highways in order to resolve the traffic problems.

3. 運送⋯人次 (to transport passengers/people in the number of)

例：這種飛機已經安全飛行兩年，運送旅客100萬人次。

This airplane has been operating for two years, transporting over one million passengers.

在中國，火車是主要的交通工具，每年新年期間運送旅客共5000萬人次。

In China, the railroad is a major means of transportation; it transports 50 million passengers each year at the time of Chinese New Year.

4. ⋯成為⋯的主要力量 (to become the major force in)

例：現在婦女多數要出來工作，她們是美國經濟發展的主要力量之一。

Nowadays, the majority of women want to go out to work. They have become one of the main forces in U.S. economic development.

美國聯合航空公司早就是美國交通的主要力量之一了。

United Airlines has long been a major player in U.S. air travel.

5. 由 place A （直）飛 place B (the [non-stop/direct] flight from place A to place B)

例：我是由紐約坐飛機直飛上海的。

I flew directly from New York to Shanghai.

由伊拉克直飛紐約的飛機現在已經停飛了。

Direct flights from Iraq to New York have been dropped.

省政府决定开辟新公路十条， 以解决交通问题。

The provincial government decided to open up ten highways in order to resolve the traffic problems.

3. 运送…人次 (to transport passengers/people in the number of)

例： 这种飞机已经安全飞行两年， 运送旅客100万人次。

This airplane has been operating for two years, transporting over one million passengers.

在中国， 火车是主要的交通工具， 每年新年期间运送旅客共5000万人次。

In China, the railroad is a major means of transportation; it transports 50 million passengers each year at the time of Chinese New Year.

4. …成为…的主要力量 (to become the major force in)

例： 现在妇女多数要出来工作， 她们是美国经济发展的主要力量之一。

Nowadays, the majority of women want to go out to work. They have become one of the main forces in U.S. economic development.

美国联合航空公司早就是美国交通的主要力量之一了。

United Airlines has long been a major player in U.S. air travel.

5. 由 place A （直）飞 place B (the [non-stop/direct] flight from place A to place B)

例： 我是由纽约坐飞机直飞上海的。

I flew directly from New York to Shanghai.

由伊拉克直飞纽约的飞机现在已经停飞了。

Direct flights from Iraq to New York have been dropped.

6. 開設（班機、學校、工廠、銀行）(to open up flights, schools, factories, banks, etc.)

例：從80年代到現在，在南京和海南已經開設了幾十家私人銀行。
From the 80s up to today, dozens of private banks have opened up in Nanjing and Hainan.

由於中國的經濟開放，很多地區都開設了自己的地方工廠和商店。
Because of China's economic liberalization, many locally owned factories and stores have been launched in all the regions throughout China.

注意："開設"和"開闢"(to open up)

"開設" takes, as its object, nouns of institutions, scheduled flights, buses, etc. For example, "開設直行班機、班車"；"開設銀行、學校"；"開設專欄"，etc.

"開闢" takes nouns referring to routes, roads, etc. as its object. For example, "開闢航線"，"開闢道路"，etc.

7. 經⋯place A 到 place B (to go to place A via place B)

例：美國總統經日本到中國和台灣去訪問。
The U.S. president went via Japan on his visit to China and Taiwan.

我母親昨天經香港到西安去看她二十年沒見的親戚。
My mother went via Hong Kong to Xian to visit relatives whom she hadn't seen for 20 years.

6. 开设（班机、学校、工厂、银行）(to open up flights, schools, factories, banks, etc.)

例： 从80年代到现在，在南京和海南已经开设了几十家私人银行。
From the 80s up to today, dozens of private banks have opened up in Nanjing and Hainan.

由于中国的经济开放，很多地区都开设了自己的地方工厂和商店。
Because of China's economic liberalization, many locally owned factories and stores have been launched in all the regions throughout China.

注意： "开设" 和 "开辟" (to open up)

"开设" takes, as its object, nouns of institutions, scheduled flights, buses, etc. For example, "开设直行班机、班车"； "开设银行、学校"： "开设专栏"，etc.

"开辟" takes nouns referring to routes, roads, etc. as its object. For example, "开辟航线"， "开辟道路"， etc.

7. 经…place A 到 place B (to go to place A via place B)

例： 美国总统经日本到中国和台湾去访问。
The U.S. president went via Japan on his visit to China and Taiwan.

我母亲昨天经香港到西安去看她二十年没见的亲戚。
My mother went via Hong Kong to Xian to visit relatives whom she hadn't seen for 20 years.

第二單元 經濟新聞

第二課

吉諾爾電冰箱／湖南工業生產

課文

一、簡介 (Introduction)

　　由於中國政府的開放政策，最近幾年中國的經濟每年以百分之十到十三的速度增長。這是因為第一，很多大中小型企業都實行中外合資，強化管理系統；第二，不少企業都在努力改變產品形象；第三，很多中國產品打入了其他國家和地區的市場。下面的兩條消息就反映了中國工業的經濟發展。

生詞

開放	(kāi fàng)	*V/Adj.*	to open; to be open (unrestricted)
中外合資	(zhōng wài hé zī)	*Idiom.*	joint venture between China and a foreign count
強化	(qiáng huà)	*V.*	to strengthen
管理	(guǎn lǐ)	*V/N.*	to manage; management of
系統	(xì tǒng)	*N.*	system
形象	(xíng xiàng)	*N.*	appearance; image; form
產品形象	(chǎn pǐn xíng xiàng)	*NP.*	product lines, appearance of products
打入	(dǎ rù)	*V.*	to break into

第二单元 经济新闻

第二课

吉诺尔电冰箱 / 湖南工业生产

课文

一、 简介 (Introduction)

由于中国政府的开放政策，最近几年中国的经济每年以百分之十到十三的速度增长这是因为第一，很多大中小型企业都实行中外合资，强化管理系统；第二，不少企业都在努力改变产品形象；第三，很多中国产品打入了其他国家和地区的市场。下面的两条消息就反映了中国工业的经济发展。

生词

开放	(kāi fàng)	V/Adj.	to open; to be open (unrestricted)
中外合资	(zhōng wài hé zī)	Idiom.	joint venture between China and a foreign count
强化	(qiáng huà)	V.	to strengthen
管理	(guǎn lǐ)	V/N.	to manage; to take care of; management of
系统	(xì tǒng)	N.	system
形象	(xíng xiàng)	N.	appearance; image; form
产品形象	(chǎn pǐn xíng xiàng)	NP.	product lines, appearance of products
打入	(dǎ rù)	V.	to break into

| 地區 | (dì qū) | N. | district; area |
| 市場 | (shì chǎng) | N. | market |

二、對話 (Dialogue)

(一)

趙中祥：問你個問題。甚麼叫"多功能、豪華型"的產品？

劉藍英：讓我一個一個來説。"多功能"就是指一件產品可以有各種不同的作用。比方説：一張桌子既可以做吃飯的桌子，又可以做寫字檯，也可以折起來做床頭櫃等。另外，一件產品的形象很美觀，質量很高，價錢很貴，所以又叫豪華型。

趙中祥：聽你這麼一説，我明白了。其實，這種多功能、豪華型的特徵正説明了中國經濟發展方向的轉變。

問題：甚麼是"多功能、豪華型"的產品？

生詞

多功能	(duō gōng néng)	Adj.	multifunctional
豪華	(háo huá)	Adj.	luxurious; deluxe
型	(xíng)	N.	model, type
豪華型	(háo huá xíng)	N.	deluxe model
產品	(chǎn pǐn)	N.	product
作用	(zuò yòng)	N.	function; role
寫字檯	(xiě zì tái)	N.	desk
折起來	(zhé qǐ lái)	V.	to fold up, to fold together
床頭櫃	(chuáng tóu guì)	N.	night stand, bedside table
美觀	(měi guān)	Adj.	to be attractive; good looking

地区	(dì qū)	*N.*	district; area
市场	(shì chǎng)	*N.*	market

二、对话 (Dialogue)

（一）

赵中祥： 问你个问题。什么叫"多功能、豪华型"的产品？

刘蓝英： 让我一个一个来说。"多功能"就是指一件产品可以有各种不同的作用。比方说：一张桌子既可以做吃饭的桌子，又可以做写字台，也可以折起来做床头柜等。另外，一件产品的形象很美观，质量很高，价钱很贵，所以又叫豪华型。

赵中祥： 听你这么一说，我明白了。其实，这种多功能、豪华型的特征正说明了中国经济发展方向的转变。

问题： 什么是"多功能、豪华型"的产品？

生词

多功能	(duō gōng néng)	*Adj.*	multifunctional
豪华	(háo huá)	*Adj.*	luxurious; deluxe
型	(xíng)	*N.*	model, type
豪华型	(háo huá xíng)	*N.*	deluxe model
产品	(chǎn pǐn)	*N.*	product
作用	(zuò yòng)	*N.*	function; role
写字台	(xiě zì tái)	*N.*	desk
折起来	(zhé qǐ lái)	*V.*	to fold up, to fold together
床头柜	(chuáng tóu guì)	*N.*	night stand, bedside table
美观	(měi guān)	*Adj.*	to be attractive; good looking

質量	(zhì liàng)	N.	quality
特徵	(tè zhēng)	N.	characteristic, trait, distinguishing feature

（二）

趙中祥：中國的工業主要分哪幾種？

劉藍英：主要分兩種，一種是輕工業，比如：紡織品、日用品等；一種是重工業，主要有鋼、鐵等。

趙中祥：可是我還是不懂。為甚麼在這兩個工業中又分全民工業和集體工業？它們的主要特徵是甚麼？

劉藍英：全民工業和集體工業是指兩種不同的管理系統。全民工業是由國家管理的工業，集體工業是由地方自己集中資金，自己管理的工業。這兩種工業都在進行改革。

問題：甚麼是"全民工業"？甚麼是"集體工業"？

生詞

輕工業	(qīng gōng yè)	NP.	light industry
紡織品	(fǎng zhī pǐn)	N.	textile products
日用品	(rì yòng pǐn)	N.	articles of daily use
重工業	(zhòng gōng yè)	NP.	heavy industry
鋼鐵	(gāng tiě)	N.	iron and steel
全民工業	(quán mín gōng yè)	NP.	industries owned and operated by the state, state industry
集體工業	(jí tǐ gōng yè)	NP.	collectively-owned industries
地方	(dì fāng)	N.	locality; local area
集中資金	(jí zhōng zī jīn)	VO.	to pool funds, to amass capital
改革	(gǎi gé)	N/V.	reform; to reform

61

| 质量 | (zhì liàng) | *N.* | quality |
| 特征 | (tè zhēng) | *N.* | characteristic, trait, distinguishing feature |

（二）

赵中祥: 中国的工业主要分哪几种？

刘蓝英: 主要分两种，一种是轻工业，比如：纺织品、日用品等；一种是重工业，主要有钢、铁等。

赵中祥: 可是我还是不懂。为什么在这两个工业中又分全民工业和集体工业？它们的主要特征是什么？

刘蓝英: 全民工业和集体工业是指两种不同的管理系统。全民工业是由国家管理的工业，集体工业是由地方自己集中资金，自己管理的工业。这两种工业都在进行改革。

问题: 什么是"全民工业"？什么是"集体工业"？

生词

轻工业	(qīng gōng yè)	*NP.*	light industry
纺织品	(fǎng zhī pǐn)	*N.*	textile products
日用品	(rì yòng pǐn)	*N.*	articles of daily use
重工业	(zhòng gōng yè)	*NP.*	heavy industry
钢铁	(gāng tiě)	*N.*	iron and steel
全民工业	(quán mín gōng yè)	*NP.*	industries owned and operated by the state, state industry
集体工业	(jí tǐ gōng yè)	*NP.*	collectively-owned industries
地方	(dì fāng)	*N.*	locality; local area
集中资金	(jí zhōng zī jīn)	*VO.*	to pool funds, to amass capital
改革	(gǎi gé)	*N/V.*	reform; to reform

（三）

劉藍英：　趙中祥，現在你這麼努力學習中文，**為甚麼**呢？

趙中祥：　你還不知道嗎？現在中國、香港、台灣、以及新加坡等是世界上**經濟發展**最快的國家和地區之一。自九十年代以來，中國工業和商業都呈現出穩定增長的好勢頭。

劉藍英：　那你是説，東亞地區要是經濟發展起來，會對世界經濟有很大的影**響**。

趙中祥：　**對了**。　這就是為甚麼學中文很要緊，因為它會給我們提供很多工作和打入東亞市場的機會。

問題：趙中祥對中國的經濟發展有甚麼看法？他為甚麼學中文？

生詞

呈現	(chéng xiàn)	*V.*	to present (an appearance); to show forth
增長	(zēng zhǎng)	*V.*	to increase
好勢頭	(hǎo shì tóu)	*Idiom.*	"a good sign", the outlook is very promising; excellent prospects (for)
提供	(tí gòng)	*V.*	to provide; to supply

（三）

刘蓝英：赵中祥，现在你这么努力学习中文，为什么呢？

赵中祥：**你还不知道吗？现在中国、香港、台湾、以及新加坡等是世界上经济发展最快的国家和地区之一。自九十年代以来，中国工业和商业都呈现出稳定增长的好势头。**

刘蓝英：**那你是说，东亚地区要是经济发展起来，会对世界经济有很大的影响。**

赵中祥：**对了。这就是为什么学中文很要紧，因为它会给我们提供很多工作和打入东亚市场的机会。**

问题: 赵中祥对中国的经济发展有什么看法？他为什么学中文？

生词

呈现	(chéng xiàn)	*V.*	to present (an appearance); to show forth
增长	(zēng zhǎng)	*V.*	to increase
好势头	(hǎo shì tóu)	*Idiom.*	"a good sign", the outlook is very promising; excellent prospects (for)
提供	(tí gòng)	*V.*	to provide; to supply

三、電視新聞 (The TV news)

吉諾爾電冰箱出口突破兩萬臺，創匯200萬美元 新聞（一）

　　中國吉林省吉諾爾電冰箱廠電冰箱出口量突破兩萬臺，創匯200萬美元。吉諾爾電冰箱廠強化質量管理系統使產品整體形象向多功能、豪華型轉變。產品打入法國、沙特阿拉伯、巴勒斯坦等十幾個國家和地區。

生詞

吉林省	(jí lín shěng)	*Place N.*	Jilin Province
吉諾爾	(jí nuò ěr)	*Proper.N.*	the name of a company
電冰箱	(diàn bīng xiāng)	*N.*	refrigerator
突破	(tū pò)	*V/N.*	to break through; to surpass, to break (a record); a breakthrough
創匯	(chuàng huì)	*VO.*	to earn foreign currency
沙特阿拉伯	(shā tè ā lā bó)	*Place N.*	Saudi Arabia
巴勒斯坦	(bā lè sī tǎn)	*Place N.*	Palestine

湖南工業生產呈現穩定增長的好勢頭 新聞（二）

　　中國湖南省工業生產呈現穩定增長的好勢頭。1992年湖南省工業企業完成工業銷售額690多億元人民幣。比1991年同期增長15%。1992年湖南省工業生產呈現的主要特徵是輕重工業同步發展，銷售產值增長速度集體工業快於全民工業，大中型企業產銷情況較好。

三、 电视新闻 (The TV news)

吉诺尔电冰箱出口突破两万台，创汇200万美元 新闻（一）

中国吉林省吉诺尔电冰箱厂电冰箱出口量突破两万台，创汇200万美元。吉诺尔电冰箱厂强化质量管理系统使产品整体形象向多功能、豪华型转变。产品打入法国、沙特阿拉伯、巴勒斯坦等十几个国家和地区。

生词

吉林省	(jí lín shěng)	*Place N.*	Jilin Province
吉诺尔	(jí nuò ěr)	*Proper.N.*	the name of a company
电冰箱	(diàn bīng xiāng)	*N.*	refrigerator
突破	(tū pò)	*V/N.*	to break through; to surpass, to break (a record); a breakthrough
创汇	(chuàng huì)	*VO.*	to earn foreign currency
沙特阿拉伯	(shā tè ā lā bó)	*Place N.*	Saudi Arabia
巴勒斯坦	(bā lè sī tǎn)	*Place N.*	Palestine

湖南工业生产呈现稳定增长的好势头 新闻（二）

中国湖南省工业生产呈现稳定增长的好势头。1992年湖南省工业企业完成工业销售额690多亿元人民币。比1991年同期增长15%。1992年湖南省工业生产呈现的主要特征是轻重工业同步发展，销售产值增长速度集体工业快于全民工业，大中型企业产销情况较好。

生詞

銷售	(xiāo shòu)	*V/N.*	to sell, to market; sale
銷售額	(xiāo shòu é)	*N.*	total sales of ...; volume of sales or sales quota
同期	(tóng qī)	*N.*	(in) the same period, (at) the same time, during the corresponding period
輕重工業	(qīng zhòng gōng yè)	*NP.*	light and heavy industry
同步	(tóng bù)	*Adj.*	synchronous, simultaneous, synchronic
產值	(chǎn zhí)	*N.*	value of output, total value of what was produced
企業	(qǐ yè)	*N.*	enterprise, business
產銷	(chǎn xiāo)	*V/N.*	to produce and sell; production and sales
大中型	(dà zhōng xíng)	*NP.*	large-size and middle-size

四、報紙閱讀

上海籌建大型鑽石加工基地

　　上海將籌建東南亞規模最大的鑽石加工基地—"鑽石城"。

　　位於浦東新區金橋出口加工區的"鑽石城"1995年建成後，計劃每年出口總產量達2億美元。日前"鑽石城"內舉辦了浦東新區首屆鑽石對外貿易洽談會，兩天成交700萬美元。

上海籌建大型
钻石加工基地
　　上海将筹建东南亚规模最大的钻石加工基地——"钻石城"。
　　位于浦东新区金桥出口加工区的"钻石城"1995年建成后，计划每年出口总产量达2亿美元。日前"钻石城"内举办了浦东新区首届钻石对外贸易洽谈会，两天成交700万美元。　　（钱承飞　刘士安）

生词

销售	(xiāo shòu)	*V/N.*	to sell, to market; sale
销售额	(xiāo shòu é)	*N.*	total sales of ...; volume of sales or sales quota
同期	(tóng qī)	*N.*	(in) the same period, (at) the same time, during the corresponding period
轻重工业	(qīng zhòng gōng yè)	*NP.*	light and heavy industry
同步	(tóng bù)	*Adj.*	synchronous, simultaneous, synchronic
产值	(chǎn zhí)	*N.*	value of output, total value of what was produced
企业	(qǐ yè)	*N.*	enterprise, business
产销	(chǎn xiāo)	*V/N.*	to produce and sell; production and sales
大中型	(dà zhōng xíng)	*NP.*	large-size and middle-size

四、报纸阅读

上海筹建大型钻石加工基地

上海将筹建东南亚规模最大的钻石加工基地—"钻石城"。

位于浦东新区金桥出口加工区的"钻石城"1995年建成后，计划每年出口总产量达2亿美元。日前"钻石城"内举办了浦东新区首届钻石对外贸易洽谈会，两天成交700万美元。

上海筹建大型钻石加工基地

上海将筹建东南亚规模最大的钻石加工基地——"钻石城"。

位于浦东新区金桥出口加工区的"钻石城"1995年建成后，计划每年出口总产量达2亿美元。日前"钻石城"内举办了浦东新区首届钻石对外贸易洽谈会，两天成交700万美元。　（钱承飞　刘士安）

<h1 style="text-align:center">生詞</h1>

籌建	(chóu jiàn)	V.	to plan to establish
大型	(dà xíng)	N/Adj.	large scale, large, large-sized; on a large scale
鑽石	(zuàn shí)	N.	diamond
加工	(jiā gōng)	V/N.	to process; processing
基地	(jī dì)	N.	base; source
東南亞	(dōng nán yà)	Place N.	Southeast Asia
位於	(wèi yú)	V.	to be located at/in
浦東	(pǔ dōng)	Place N.	district east of Huang Pu River in Shanghai (an important special enterprise zone)
加工區	(jiā gōng qū)	N.	zone specializing in manufacturing
出口	(chū kǒu)	V/N.	to export; exports
總產量	(zǒng chǎn liàng)	NP.	total output
達	(dá)	V.	to reach; to be as high as
日前	(rì qián)	N.	at present; now
首屆	(shǒu jiè)	N.	the first session of;
洽談會	(qià tán huì)	N.	talks (often business talks or informal negotiations)
成交	(chéng jiāo)	VO.	to clinch a deal

生词

筹建	(chóu jiàn)	*V.*	to plan to establish
大型	(dà xíng)	*N/Adj.*	large scale, large; large sized; on a large scale
钻石	(zuàn shí)	*N.*	diamond
加工	(jiā gōng)	*V/N.*	to process; processing
基地	(jī dì)	*N.*	base; source
东南亚	(dōng nán yà)	*Place N.*	Southeast Asia
位于	(wèi yú)	*V.*	to be located at/in
浦东	(pǔ dōng)	*Place N.*	district east of Huang Pu River in Shanghai (an important special enterprise zone)
加工区	(jiā gōng qū)	*N.*	zone specializing in manufacturing
出口	(chū kǒu)	*V/N.*	to export; exports
总产量	(zǒng chǎn liàng)	*NP.*	total output
达	(dá)	*V.*	to reach; to be as high as
日前	(rì qián)	*N.*	at present; now
首届	(shǒu jiè)	*N.*	the first session of
洽谈会	(qià tán huì)	*N.*	talks (often business talks or informal negotiations)
成交	(chéng jiāo)	*VO.*	to clinch a deal

五、幽默小品 (Humor)

縮寫

　　老師要求學生把一篇一百五十字的文章縮寫成五十字，下課時，小華把作業交了。

　　老師看了以後，生氣地問："為甚麼你要把文章內四十五米高的建築物寫成十五米，六輛汽車寫成兩輛，三個人寫成一個人？"

　　小華答："老師，我這篇文章是嚴格按比例縮寫的。"

生詞

縮寫	(suō xiě)	*V.*	to reduce, to shrink
嚴格	(yán gé)	*Adj.*	strict
按比例	(àn bǐ lì)	*Prep P.*	proportionally

五、幽默小品 (Humor)

缩写

老师要求学生把一篇一百五十字的文章缩写成五十字，下课时，小华把作业交了。

老师看了以后，生气地问："为什么你要把文章内四十五米高的建筑物写成十五米，六辆汽车写成两辆，三个人写成一个人？"

小华答："老师，我这篇文章是严格按比例缩写的。"

生词

缩写	(suō xiě)	*V.*	to reduce, to shrink
严格	(yán gé)	*Adj.*	strict
按比例	(àn bǐ lì)	*Prep P.*	proportionally

課文要點 (Key Points)

一、常用縮略語與慣用語 (Frequently used abbreviations and fixed expressions)

1. 創匯＝創造外匯 (to earn foreign currency)

　　例：這家電冰箱廠上個月創匯五千萬。

　　This refrigerator factory earned 50 million in foreign currency last month.

2. 日前＝幾天以前 (a few days ago)

　　例：聯航日前又開闢了三條新航線。

　　United Airlines opened up another three air routes a few days ago.

3. 首屆＝第一屆 (the first session)

　　例：首屆工業企業洽談會在湖南進行。

　　The First Indutrial Enterprise Convention is being held in Hunan.

4. 成交＝辦成交易 (to clinch a deal; to conclude a business transaction)

　　例：昨天這家國際電話公司和中國一家集體企業成交一筆一百萬元人民幣的生意。

　　This international telephone company yesterday clinched a deal of one million Yuan in RMB with a collective enterprise in China.

5. 產銷＝生產和銷售 (to produce and sell; to combine production and marketing)

　　例：要想創匯，必須改變產品形象，**產銷**結合。

　　If you want to earn foreign currency, the image of your products must be changed and your production must be coordinated with the marketing of the products.

课文要点(Key Points)

一、 常用缩略语与惯用语 (Frequently used abbreviations and fixed expressions)

1. 创汇 = 创造外汇 (to earn foreign currency)

例: 这家电冰箱厂上个月创汇五千万。
This refrigerator factory earned 50 million in foreign currency last month.

2. 日前 = 几天以前 (a few days ago)

例: 联航日前又开辟了三条新航线。
United Airlines opened up another three air routes a few days ago.

3. 首届 = 第一届 (the first session)

例: 首届工业企业洽谈会在湖南进行。
The First Indutrial Enterprise Convention is being held in Hunan.

4. 成交 = 办成交易 (to clinch a deal; to conclude a business transaction)

例: 昨天这家国际电话公司和中国一家集体企业成交一笔一百万元人民币
的生意。
This international telephone company yesterday clinched a deal of one million Yuan in
RMB with a collective enterprise in China.

5. 产销 = 生产和销售 (to produce and sell; to combine production and marketing)

例: 要想创汇，必须改变产品形象，产销结合。
If you want to earn foreign currency, the image of your products must be changed and
your production must be coordinated with the marketing of the products.

6. (快、高) 於＝比…(快) (than)

例：今年浙江省的工業產品銷售額高於去年。

This year the sales volume of industrial products in Zhejiang Province is greater than last year.

7. 集體工業 (collective industries)

例：集體工業是由地方(local) 政府和地方人民集資建立的工業。

Collective Industries refer to those industrial or commercial enterprises established with funds raised by the local government and the local people.

8. 全民工業 (State-owned industry)

例：全民工業是由中國政府出資(to invest) 和管理的工業。

State-owned industries refer to those enterprises which are capitalized and managed by the Chinese government.

9. 大中型 (large and middle-sized)

例：德國的經濟主要來自大中型企業。

The mainstay of the German economy comes from large and medium-sized enterprises.

二、常用短語 (Frequently used structures)

1. …突破… (to break through, to have a breakthrough in)

例：吉林省江海電冰箱廠創匯已突破200萬美元。

The foreign currency earned by the Jianghai Refrigerator factory in JiLin Province has broken the (previous high) record of 2 million dollars.

6. (快、高）于 = 比…（快）(than)

例：今年浙江省的工业产品销售额高于去年。
This year the sales volume of industrial products in Zhejiang Province is greater than last year.

7. 集体工业 (collective industries)

例：集体工业是由地方(local)政府和地方人民集资建立的工业。
Collective Industries refer to those industrial or commercial enterprises established with funds raised by the local government and the local people.

8. 全民工业 (State-owned industry)

例：全民工业是由中国政府出资(to invest)和管理的工业。
State-owned industries refer to those enterprises which are capitalized and managed by the Chinese government.

9. 大中型 (large and middle-sized)

例：德国的经济主要来自大中型企业。
The mainstay of the German economy comes from large and medium-sized enterprises.

二、常用短语 (Frequently used structures)

1. …突破… (to break through, to have a breakthrough in)

例：吉林省江海电冰箱厂创汇已突破200万美元。
The foreign currency earned by the Jianghai Refrigerator factory in JiLin Province has broken the (previous high) record of 2 million dollars.

中英就香港問題的談判已有新的突破，雙方已經在很多重要問題上達成了**協議**。

The negotiations between China and Great Britain on the Hong Kong issue has achieved new breakthroughs. Both sides have now reached agreement on many important questions.

2. …**強化**… (to strengthen; to be intensive)

例：美國的醫療保險常常貴得可怕，很多人都買不起。克林頓（Clinton）政府提出要強化對保險公司的管理，不許他們隨意提價。

Because medical insurance in the U.S. is often extremely expensive, many people cannot affort it. The Clinton administration has emphasized strengthening the supervision on insurance companies, restraining them from arbitrarily raising prices

對中文的聽力和閱讀理解一定要進行強化訓練，不然，學生是學不好的。

The listening and reading comprehension in Chinese require intensive training. Otherwise, the students will not be able to learn Chinese well.

3. …**使**…**向**…**轉變** (to cause to shift toward)

例：中國的經濟開放使中國的生產方式向高效率、快速度轉變。

The economic open door policy has caused China to shift toward a high efficiency and high speed production mode.

聯合國對伊拉克政府採取的行動并沒有使伊拉克向民主、自由的方向**轉變**。

The action taken by the U.N. did not cause Iraq to shift toward democracy and liberty.

4. …**打入**（＋place） (to break in)

例：現在，中國的很多產品已經打入北美和南美市場。

Nowadays, many Chinese-made products have broken into markets in North and South America.

69

中英就香港问题的谈判已有新的突破， 双方已经在很多重要问题上达成了协议。

The negotiations between China and Great Britain on the Hong Kong issue has achieved new breakthroughs. Both sides have now reached agreement on many important questions.

2. …强化… (to strengthen; to be intensive)

例： 美国的医疗保险常常贵得可怕， 很多人都买不起。克林顿（Clinton）政府提出要强化对保险公司的管理， 不许他们随意提价。

Because medical insurance in the U.S. is often extremely expensive, many people cannot affort it. The Clinton administration has emphasized strengthening the supervision on insurance companies, restraining them from arbitrarily raising prices

对中文的听力和阅读理解一定要进行强化训练， 不然， 学生是学不好的。

The listening and reading comprehension in Chinese require intensive training. Otherwise, the students will not be able to learn Chinese well.

3. …使…向…转变… (to cause to shift toward)

例： 中国的经济开放使中国的生产方式向高效率、快速度转变。

The economic open door policy has caused China to shift toward a high efficiency and high speed production mode.

联合国对伊拉克政府采取的行动并没有使伊拉克向民主、自由的方向转变。

The action taken by the U.N. did not cause Iraq to shift toward democracy and liberty.

4. …打入（＋place） (to break in)

例： 现在， 中国的很多产品已经打入北美和南美市场。

Nowadays, many Chinese-made products have broken into markets in North and South America.

美國政府、三大汽車公司以及許多公民都對日本汽車產品大規模打入美國市場表示擔心。

The American government, the big three car companies, and many U.S. citizens all expressed their concern over Japanese cars large-scale penatration of the U.S. market.

5. ⋯位於（＋place）(to be located)

例：休斯敦位於美國的南部，是德州人口最多、商業最集中的城市之一。

Houston is located in the southern United States. It is one of the most populated and commercialized cities in Texas.

吉林省位於中國的東北部，是中國東北三省之一。

Jilin Province is located in the northeast of China. It is one of the three northernmost provinces of China.

6. ⋯呈現⋯勢頭 (to show the tendency of)

例：美國經濟今年呈現較好的勢頭。

The economy in the U.S. is looking relatively strong for this year.

明後年世界經濟將呈現穩定增長的好勢頭。

The world economy gives every sign of strong prospects for steady improvement over the next year or two.

7. ⋯比⋯同期增長（減少）⋯ (to increase more...than... at the same time last year)

例：巴勒斯坦貿易出口總量比去年同期增長百分之二十。

The amount of trade and export of Palestine has increased 20% compared to the same time last year.

今年我校學生比去年同期減少百分之十。

The number of students in our school has decreased 10% as compared with the number at this same period last year.

美国政府、三大汽车公司以及许多公民都对日本汽车产品大规模打入美国市场表示担心。

The American government, the big three car companies, and many U.S. citizens all expressed their concern over Japanese cars large-scale penatration of the U.S. market.

5. …位于（+ place）(to be located)

例: 休斯敦位于美国的南部，是德州人口最多、商业最集中的城市之一。

Houston is located in the southern United States. It is one of the most populated and commercialized cities in Texas.

吉林省位于中国的东北部，是中国东北三省之一。

Jilin Province is located in the northeast of China. It is one of the three northernmost provinces of China.

6. …呈现…势头 (to show the tendency of)

例: 美国经济今年呈现较好的势头。

The economy in the U.S. is looking relatively strong for this year.

明后年世界经济将呈现稳定增长的好势头。

The world economy gives every sign of strong prospects for steady improvement over the next year or two.

7. …比…同期增长（减少）… (to increase more...than... at the same time last year)

例: 巴勒斯坦贸易出口总量比去年同期增长百分之二十。

The amount of trade and export of Palestine has increased 20% compared to the same time last year.

今年我校学生比去年同期减少百分之十。

The number of students in our school has decreased 10% as compared with the number at this same period last year.

8. …快於… (...faster than...)

例：中國的經濟改革似乎快於政治改革。

The economic reform of China appears to be faster than political reform.

聯合航空公司的航線開關似乎快於西北航空公司。

The opening up of new routes by United Airlines seems even faster than that of Northwest Airlines.

8. ⋯快于⋯ (...faster than...)

例: 中国的经济改革似乎快于政治改革。

The economic reform of China appears to be faster than political reform.

联合航空公司的航线开辟似乎快于西北航空公司。

The opening up of new routes by United Airlines seems even faster than that of Northwest Airlines.

小課文

請愛護人民幣

一、看電視小課文、回答問題 (Answer the following questions)

    1. 在廣告中人民幣被當成了甚麼？

    2. 為甚麼要保護人民幣？

    3. 在美國有沒有廣告中所提到的各種現象？

二、討論 (Discuss the following questions)

    1. 為甚麼中國有這種不愛護人民幣的現象？這跟經濟發展和文化習慣有**沒有關係？**

    2. 這樣的廣告對老百姓有沒有意義？

    3. 政府應該採取甚麼好的措施？

小课文

请爱护人民币

一、看电视小课文、回答问题 (Answer the following questions)

1. 在广告中人民币被当成了什么？

2. 为什么要保护人民币？

3. 在美国有没有广告中所提到的各种现象？

二、讨论 (Discuss the following questions)

1. 为什么中国有这种不爱护人民币的现象？这跟经济发展和文化习惯有没有关系？

2. 这样的广告对老百姓有没有意义？

3. 政府应该采取什么好的措施？

第二單元 經濟新聞

第三課

中國在哈薩克斯坦建立合資酒廠
中國唯一對外國人出售絹花的商店

課文

一、簡介 (Introduction)

目前在中國，中外合資企業以及對外服務公司越來越多。這兩種經濟形式為中國的經濟繁榮作了不少貢獻。中外合資企業是指中方和外方合資經營的企業。對外服務公司是指專門買給外國人商品、或者為外國人提供服務的機構與商店。下面的兩條新聞就是報道這兩種經濟形式的。

生詞

合資	(hé zī)	NP.	joint venture(s)
對外	(duìwài)	Adj.	open to foreigners
服務公司	(fú wù gōng sī)	NP.	service agency
貢獻	(gòng xiàn)	N.	contribution
指	(zhǐ)	V.	to refer to
中方	(zhōng fāng)	N.	the China side
外方	(wài fāng)	N.	the foreign side
經營	(jīng yíng)	V.	to manage
專門	(zhuān mén)	V.	to specialize in
商品	(shāng pǐn)	N.	commodity; goods

第二单元 经济新闻

第三课

中国在哈萨克斯坦建立合资酒厂
中国唯一对外国人出售绢花的商店

课文

一、简介 (Introduction)

目前在中国，中外合资企业以及对外服务公司越来越多。这两种经济形式为中国的经济繁荣作了不少贡献。中外合资企业是指中方和外方合资经营的企业。对外服务公司是指专门买给外国人商品、或者为外国人提供服务的机构与商店。下面的两条新闻就是报道这两种经济形式的。

生词

合资	(hé zī)	*NP.*	joint venture(s)
对外	(duìwài)	*Adj.*	open to foreigners
服务公司	(fú wù gōng sī)	*NP.*	service agency
贡献	(gòng xiàn)	*N.*	contribution
指	(zhǐ)	*V.*	to refer to
中方	(zhōng fāng)	*N.*	the China side
外方	(wài fāng)	*N.*	the foreign side
经营	(jīng yíng)	*V.*	to manage
专门	(zhuān mén)	*V.*	to specialize in
商品	(shāng pǐn)	*N.*	commodity; goods

| 服務 | (fú wù) | N/V. | service; to serve |
| 機構 | (jī gòu) | N. | institution; organization; administrative organization |

二、對話 (Dialogues)

（一）

周錦：李蘭，在北京你最喜歡上哪兒買東西？

李蘭：我想是銀河商社。因為這是一家跨國經營的合資公司。產品質量好，服務熱情周到，特別受到老百姓的讚賞。

周錦：這種商社的商品會不會很貴呢？

李蘭：我倒不覺得，有些東西比在美國還便宜。

問題：為甚麼李蘭喜歡去銀河買東西？

生詞

銀河	(yín hé)	N.	the Milky Way
商社	(shāng shè)	NP.	trading firm or company, shop, store
跨國經營	(kuà guó jīng yíng)	VP.	to manage transnationally
周到	(zhōu dào)	Adj.	attentive, considerate, paying attention to every detail, carefully worked out
熱情	(rè qíng)	Adj.	warm, enthusiastic
讚賞	(zàn shǎng)	V/N.	to praise and appreciate; praise and appreciation, appreciation

| 服务 | (fú wù) | N/V. | service; to serve |
| 机构 | (jī gòu) | N. | institution; organization; administrative organization |

二、对话 (Dialogues)

（一）

周锦：李兰，在北京你最喜欢上哪儿买东西？

李兰：我想是银河商社。因为这是一家跨国经营的合资公司。产品质量好，服务热情周到，特别受到老百姓的赞赏。

周锦：这种商社的商品会不会很贵呢？

李兰：我倒不觉得，有些东西比在美国还便宜。

问题： 为什么李兰喜欢去银河买东西？

生词

银河	(yín hé)	N.	the Milky Way
商社	(shāng shè)	NP.	trading firm or company, shop, store
跨国经营	(kuà guó jīng yíng)	VP.	to manage transnationally
周到	(zhōu dào)	Adj.	attentive, considerate, paying attention to every detail, carefully worked out
热情	(rè qíng)	Adj.	warm, enthusiastic
赞赏	(zàn shǎng)	V/N.	to praise and appreciate; praise and appreciation, appreciation

（二）

李蘭：現在在中國辦一個合資企業，需要做些甚麼事情？

周錦：首先要獲得雙方國家的批准，然後在中國商業部門註冊。一般的合資
企業都是外方以技術專用設備入股，中方以廠房、人力、和通用設備
入股。

李蘭：現在這種中外合資的有限公司在中國很多嗎？

周錦：多極了。尤其是在中國的東部及東南部，這種公司到處都是。它們對
中國的經濟穩步發展起了很大的作用。

問題：辦合資企業的手續是甚麼？

生詞

首先	(shǒu xiān)	*Adv.*	first of all; firstly
批准	(pī zhǔn)	*N/V.*	approval; to approve
商業部門	(shāng yè bù mén)	*NP.*	the commerce department
註冊	(zhù cè)	*V.*	to register
專用設備	(zhuān yòng shè bèi)	*NP.*	specialized equipment
入股	(rù gǔ)	*VO.*	to buy a share; to become a share holder
廠房	(chǎng fáng)	*N.*	factory shop, workshop, factory bldg., factory floor
通用設備	(tōng yòng shè bèi)	*NP.*	general equipment
有限公司	(yǒu xiàn gōng sī)	*NP.*	limited company-co., ltd.
手續	(shǒu xù)	*N.*	procedure

（二）

李兰： 现在在中国办一个合资企业，需要做些什么事情？

周锦： 首先要获得双方国家的批准，然后在中国商业部门注册。一般的合资企业都是外方以技术专用设备入股，中方以厂房、人力、和通用设备入股。

李兰： 现在这种中外合资的有限公司在中国很多吗？

周锦： 多极了。尤其是在中国的东部及东南部，这种公司到处都是。它们对中国的经济稳步发展起了很大的作用。

问题: 办合资企业的手续是什么？

生词

首先	(shǒu xiān)	*Adv.*	first of all; firstly
批准	(pī zhǔn)	*N/V.*	approval; to approve
商业部门	(shāng yè bù mén)	*NP.*	the commerce department
注册	(zhù cè)	*V.*	to register
专用设备	(zhuān yòng shè bèi)	*NP.*	specialized equipment
入股	(rù gǔ)	*VO.*	to buy a share; to become a share holder
厂房	(chǎng fáng)	*N.*	factory shop, workshop, factory bldg., factory floor
通用设备	(tōng yòng shè bèi)	*NP.*	general equipment
有限公司	(yǒu xiàn gōng sī)	*NP.*	limited company-co., ltd.
手续	(shǒu xù)	*N.*	procedure

（三）

李蘭：周錦，甚麼是"產、供、銷"一條龍？

周錦：這是經濟管理上用的術語。"產"就是生產，"供"就是供應，
"銷"就是銷售，也就是賣出的意思。"一條龍"就是說把生產、供
應、銷售結合起來，一個公司既要負責製作產品，保證質量，又要負
責把產品送到代辦處那里，還要負責產品的銷售。

李蘭：這倒是一種很好的管理方法。

問題：甚麼是"產、供、銷一條龍"？

生詞

術語	(shù yǔ)	N.	term, jargon
供應	(gòng yìng)	V/N.	to supply, to provide; supply
結合	(jié hé)	V.	to combine
負責	(fù zé)	V.	to be responsible
製作	(zhì zuò)	V.	to manufacture, to turn out (products), to make
代辦處	(dài bàn chù)	N.	agency

76

（三）

李兰: 周锦，什么是"产、供、销"一条龙？

周锦: 这是经济管理上用的术语。"产"就是生产，"供"就是供应，"销"就是销售，也就是卖出的意思。"一条龙"就是说把生产、供应、销售结合起来，一个公司既要负责制作产品，保证质量，又要负责把产品送到代办处那里，还要负责产品的销售。

李兰: 这倒是一种很好的管理方法。

问题: 什么是"产、供、销一条龙"？

生词

术语	(shù yǔ)	*N.*	term, jargon
供应	(gòng yìng)	*V/N.*	to supply, to provide; supply
结合	(jié hé)	*V.*	to combine
负责	(fù zé)	*V.*	to be responsible
制作	(zhì zuò)	*V.*	to manufacture, to turn out (products), to make
代办处	(dài bàn chù)	*N.*	agency

三、電視新聞 (The TV news)

中國在哈薩克斯坦建立合資酒廠　新聞（一）

中國貴州省鴨溪酵酒廠與哈薩克斯坦共和國合資在哈薩克建立銀河酒業有限公司。近日獲得雙方國家的批准，並在哈薩克斯坦註冊。

這是中國在獨聯體國家建立的第一家合資酒廠。這個項目是中國政府批准的第一家對哈薩克斯坦小麥、白酒技術出口，並跨國經營的產、供、銷一條龍的酒類合資企業。中方以技術專用設備入股，哈方以廠房、通用設備等入股。

生詞

哈薩克斯坦	(hā sā kè sī tǎn)	*Place N.*	Kazakhstan
貴州	(guì zhōu)	*Place N.*	a province in South China
鴨溪	(yā xī)	*Place N.*	Duck Creek
酵酒	(jiào jiǔ)	*NP.*	naturally fermented alcoholic beverages
獨聯體	(dú lián tǐ)	*Place N.*	The Commonwealth of Independent States
項目	(xiàng mù)	*N.*	item(s)
小麥	(xiǎo mài)	*N.*	wheat
白酒	(bái jiǔ)	*N.*	colorless spirits, usually 40-50% alcohol, distilled from sorghum, corn, wheat or other grains
一條龍	(yī tiáo lóng)	*N.*	a series of (a continuous process), an uninterrupted run of a series

77

三、电视新闻 (The TV news)

中国在哈萨克斯坦建立合资酒厂 新闻（一）

　　中国贵州省鸭溪酵酒厂与哈萨克斯坦共和国合资在哈萨克建立银河酒业有限公司。近日获得双方国家的批准，并在哈萨克斯坦注册。

　　这是中国在独联体国家建立的第一家合资酒厂。这个项目是中国政府批准的第一家对哈萨克斯坦小麦、白酒技术出口，并跨国经营的产、供、销一条龙的酒类合资企业。中方以技术专用设备入股，哈方以厂房、通用设备等入股。

生词

哈萨克斯坦	(hā sā kè sī tǎn)	*Placce N.*	Kazakhstan
贵州	(guì zhōu)	*Placce N.*	a province in South China
鸭溪	(yā xī)	*Place N.*	Duck Creek
酵酒	(jiào jiǔ)	*NP.*	naturally fermented alcoholic beverages
独联体	(dú lián tǐ)	*Placce N.*	The Commonwealth of Independent States
项目	(xiàng mù)	*N.*	item(s)
小麦	(xiǎo mài)	*N.*	wheat
白酒	(bái jiǔ)	*N.*	colorless spirits, usually 40-50% alcohol, distilled from sorghum, corn, wheat or other grains
一条龙	(yī tiáo lóng)	*N.*	a series of (a continuous process), an uninterrupted run of a series

中國唯一對外國人出售絹花的商店 新聞 (二)

在中國北京的各國駐華使館、駐北京公司商社、外國銀行代辦處的外國人，都愛到新建的北京永龍絹花工藝品商場購買色彩繽紛的絹花。

這家商場是中國唯一一家專門定點為外國人生產出售絹花的商店，各國駐華機構、涉外飯店工作生活所需絹花的百分之九十五來自這家商店。他們製作的絹花和周到熱情的服務受到各國用戶的歡迎和讚賞。

生詞

唯一	(wéi yī)	*Adv.*	only
絹花	(juàn huā)	*N.*	silk flowers
新建的	(xīn jiàn de)	*Adj.*	newly established
工藝品	(gōng yì pǐn)	*N.*	handicrafts
購買	(gòu mǎi)	*V.*	to purchase
色彩繽紛	(sè cǎi bīn fēn)	*Idiom.*	extremely colorful, all the colors of the rainbow
定點	(dìng diǎn)	*N.*	fixed place
涉外	(shè wài)	*Abbrev.*	involving foreign affairs or foreign nationals
所需	(suǒ xū)	*Abbrev.*	what is needed
用戶	(yòng hù)	*N.*	customers, consumers, users

中国唯一对外国人出售绢花的商店 新闻（二）

在中国北京的各国驻华使馆、驻北京公司商社、外国银行代办处的外国人，都爱到新建的北京永龙绢花工艺品商场购买色彩缤纷的绢花。

这家商场是中国唯一一家专门定点为外国人生产出售绢花的商店，各国驻华机构、涉外饭店工作生活所需绢花的百分之九十五来自这家商店。他们制做的绢花和周到热情的服务受到各国用户的欢迎和赞赏。

生词

唯一	(wéi yī)	*Adv.*	only
绢花	(juàn huā)	*N.*	silk flowers
新建的	(xīn jiàn de)	*Adj.*	newly established
工艺品	(gōng yì pǐn)	*N.*	handicrafts
购买	(gòu mǎi)	*V.*	to purchase
色彩缤纷	(sè cǎi bīn fēn)	*Idiom.*	extremely colorful, all the colors of the rainbow
定点	(dìng diǎn)	*N.*	fixed place
涉外	(shè wài)	*Abbrev.*	involving foreign affairs or foreign nationals
所需	(suǒ xū)	*Abbrev.*	what is needed
用户	(yòng hù)	*N.*	customers, consumers, users

四、幽默小品 (Humor)

留級理由

　　父親看到兒子的成績表，發現有好幾門不及格。

　　父：“你的外國地理不行啊？”

　　子：“因為我沒有去過外國。”

　　父：“歷史也不行！”

　　子：“我出生得太晚，以前的事大部分都不知道。”

生詞

理由	(lǐ yóu)	N.	reason
留級	(líu jí)	VO.	to be held back a year, to fail to advance to the next grade
不及格	(bù jí gé)	V.	fail to pass

四、幽默小品 (Humor)

留级理由

父亲看到儿子的成绩表，发现有好几门不及格。

父："你的外国地理不行啊？"

子："因为我没有去过外国。"

父："历史也不行！"

子："我出生得太晚，以前的事大部分都不知道。"

生词

理由	(lǐ yóu)	N.	reason
留级	(líu jí)	VO.	to be held back a year, to fail to advance to the next grade
不及格	(bù jí gé)	V.	fail to pass

課文要點 (Key Points)

一、常用文言詞、縮略語與慣用語 (Frequently used classical Chinese phrases, abbreviations, and fixed expressions)

1. 以＝用 (by)

   例：中方以技術專用設備入股。

   China will invest its technology.

2. 為＝給 (for)

   例：多功能產品為用戶提供了很多方便。

   The multifunctional products provide tremendous convenience for customers.

3. 自＝自從、從 (from)

   例：自去年以來，美國的工業管理系統有了很大的轉變。

   Since last year, the industrial management system in the U.S. has undergone many changes.

4. 並＝並且 (furthermore, moreover)

   例：合資酒廠是國家批准，並在國外註冊的工廠。

   The joint venture winery is approved by the state, and is also registered in other countries.

5. 該＝這、此 (this, these)

   例：該公司專門定點為外國人服務。

   This company sets up special places to provide services to foreigners.

课文要点 (Key Points)

一、常用文言词、缩略语与惯用语 (Frequently used classical Chinese phrases, abbreviations, and fixed expressions)

1. 以 = 用 (by)

　　例: 中方以技术专用设备入股。
　　China will invest its technology.

2. 为 = 给 (for)

　　例: 多功能产品为用户提供了很多方便。
　　The multifunctional products provide tremendous convenience for customers.

3. 自 = 自从、从 (from)

　　例: 自去年以来，美国的工业管理系统有了很大的转变。
　　Since last year, the industrial management system in the U.S. has undergone many changes.

4. 并 = 并且 (furthermore, moreover)

　　例: 合资酒厂是国家批准，并在国外注册的工厂。
　　The joint venture winery is approved by the state, and is also registered in other countries.

5. 该 = 这、此 (this, these)

　　例: 该公司专门定点为外国人服务。
　　This company sets up special places to provide services to foreigners.

6. 產＝生產 (to produce)

　　例：產、供、銷一條龍是一種新的管理系統。
　　　　A coherent system of production, supply, and sales is a new way of management.

7. 供＝供應 (to supply)

8. 銷＝銷售 (to sell)

9. 近日＝最近、這些天 (recently)

　　例：中國和沙特阿拉伯今日舉行貿易會談。
　　　　China and Saudi Arabia will hold trade talks today.

10. 合資＝聯合投資 (joint investment)

　　例：合資就是兩個政府或公司聯合投資。
　　　　Joint investment refers to two governments or companies that jointly invest money into a project.

11. 涉外＝涉及外國事物 (concerning foreign affairs or foreigners)

　　例：涉外飯店是專門為外國人開的飯店。
　　　　She wai hotels refers to hotels which provide services specifically for foreigners.

二、常用短語 (Frequently used structures)

1. 與…合資… (to have a joint venture with)

　　例：這幾年，北京啤酒廠與德國啤酒廠合資建立了中國最大的啤酒公司。
　　　　In recent years, the Beijing Beer Company and the German Beer Company jointly established the largest beer company in China.

6. 产 = 生产 (to produce)

例: 产、供、销一条龙是一种新的管理系统。
A coherent system of production, supply, and sales is a new way of management.

7. 供 = 供应 (to supply)

8. 销 = 销售 (to sell)

9. 近日 = 最近、这些天 (recently)

例: 中国和沙特阿拉伯今日举行贸易会谈。
China and Saudi Arabia will hold trade talks today.

10. 合资 = 联合投资 (joint investment)

例: 合资就是两个政府或公司联合投资。
Joint investment refers to two governments or companies that jointly invest money into a project.

11. 涉外 = 涉及外国事物 (concerning foreign affairs or foreigners)

例: 涉外饭店是专门为外国人开的饭店。
She wai hotels refers to hotels which provide services specifically for foreigners.

二、常用短语 (Frequently used structures)

1. 与…合资… (to have a joint venture with)

例: 这几年，北京啤酒厂与德国啤酒厂合资建立了中国最大的啤酒公司。
In recent years, the Beijing Beer Company and the German Beer Company jointly established the largest beer company in China.

中國與美國合資的酵酒有限公司已經在北京註冊。
The Winery Limited, a joint venture by China and the U.S., has already been registered in Beijing.

2. 由…發展到… (to have developed from)

例：中國的絹花由以前的手工生產發展到現在的機器生產，速度加快了很多。
The production of silk flowers has progressed from man made to machine made. The speed of making flowers has increased a great deal.

中國葡萄酒業已經由自己管理發展到跨國經營。
The grape winery enterprise in China has progressed from self-management to multi-national management.

3. 因…而… (because)

例：那家公司因投資和入股的人太少而關閉了。
That company is closed due to limited investment and very few share holders.

他的學習成績因經常不上課而受到影響。
His grades have been influenced by his frequent absence from classes.

4. 遠銷 (to sell [something] to a distant market)

例：黑龍江生產的電冰箱現在遠銷歐洲很多國家。
The refrigerators produced in Hei Long Jiang Province are now sold to countries as far as Europe.

中國工藝品遠銷世界各地。
China's handicrafts are sold all over the world.

5. 同…建立 (to establish...with)

例：中國目前已經跟獨聯體的多數國家建立了外交關系。
China has established diplomatic relations with most of the nations in the Commonwealth of Independent States.

中国与美国合资的酵酒有限公司已经在北京注册。
The Winery Limited, a joint venture by China and the U.S., has already been registered in Beijing.

2. 由 ··· 发展到 ··· (to have developed from)

例: 中国的绢花由以前的手工生产发展到现在的机器生产，速度加快了很多。
The production of silk flowers has progressed from man made to machine made. The speed of making flowers has increased a great deal.

中国葡萄酒业已经由自己管理发展到跨国经营。
The grape winery enterprise in China has progressed from self-management to multi-national management.

3. 因 ··· 而 ··· (because)

例: 那家公司因投资和入股的人太少而关闭了。
That company is closed due to limited investment and very few share holders.

他的学习成绩因经常不上课而受到影响。
His grades have been influenced by his frequent absence from classes.

4. 远销 (to sell [something] to a distant market)

例: 黑龙江生产的电冰箱现在远销欧洲很多国家。
The refrigerators produced in Hei Long Jiang Province are now sold to countries as far as Europe.

中国工艺品远销世界各地。
China's handicrafts are sold all over the world.

5. 同 ··· 建立 (to establish...with)

例: 中国目前已经跟独联体的多数国家建立了外交关系。
China has established diplomatic relations with most of the nations in the Commonwealth of Independent States.

現在中國已經同許多國家建立了合資企業。
Many joint ventures with other countries have been established in China.

6. 集…於一體 (to combine something into one unit)

例：這個新廠的管理方法是集產、供、銷於一體。
The way of management in this new factory is to combine production, supply, and sales into one system.

中國的社會體制是集政治、經濟、個人、國家於一體。
The (characteristics) of the social system in China is to combine politics, economy, individual, and the country into one entity.

7. …來自… (place) (to come from)

例：在昨天的記者招待會上，有來自五十幾個國家的記者參加。
At yesterday's press conference, journalists from more than 50 countries participated in it.

來自獨聯體哈薩克斯坦的白酒很受中國用戶的歡迎。
The liquor from Kazakhstan of the Commonwealth of Independent States is very popular among Chinese customers.

8. 受到…歡迎和讚賞 (to receive welcome and praise from)

例：中國的茅台酒總是受到各國客人的歡迎和讚賞。
The Chinese Mao Tai (liquor) has always been popular and well received by foreign guests.

多功能、豪華型的產品現在開始受到中國用戶的歡迎和讚賞。
Now the multifunctional and deluxe products are gaining popularity among Chinese.

现在中国已经同许多国家建立了合资企业。
Many joint ventures with other countries have been established in China.

6. 集…于一体 (to combine something into one unit)

例: 这个新厂的管理方法是集产、供、销于一体。
The way of management in this new factory is to combine production, supply, and sales into one system.

中国的社会体制是集政治、经济、个人、国家于一体。
The (characteristics) of the social system in China is to combine politics, economy, individual, and the country into one entity.

7. …来自… (place) (to come from)

例: 在昨天的记者招待会上，有来自五十几个国家的记者参加。
At yesterday's press conference, journalists from more than 50 countries participated in it.

来自独联体哈萨克斯坦的白酒很受中国用户的欢迎。
The liquor from Kazakhstan of the Commonwealth of Independent States is very popular among Chinese customers.

8. 受到…欢迎和赞赏 (to receive welcome and praise from)

例: 中国的茅台酒总是受到各国客人的欢迎和赞赏。
The Chinese Mao Tai (liquor) has always been popular and well received by foreign guests.

多功能、豪华型的产品现在开始受到中国用户的欢迎和赞赏。
Now the multifunctional and deluxe products are gaining popularity among Chinese.

第二單元　經濟新聞

第四課

中國大學生百縣千鄉服務工程拉開帷幕

課文

一、簡介 (Introduction)

　　現在，中國大學生不再有"鐵飯碗"了，因為政府不再給大學生分配工作了。這樣，一方面，大學生需要把自己作為商品向市場推銷；另一方面，高校也要改革課程，使學生學的知識與經濟建設和社會發展的實際需要結合起來。

生詞

鐵飯碗	(tiě fàn wǎn)	*N.*	"the iron rice bowl" (refers to a job which one can not lose)
分配	(fēn pèi)	*V.*	to assign (a job, a part, etc.)
推銷	(tuī xiāo)	*V.*	to promote (a product)
高校	(gāo xiào)	*Abbrev.*	universities and colleges, technical institutions; institutions of higher education＝高等學校
實際需要	(shí jì xū yào)	*NP.*	actual needs, practical needs

84

第二单元　经济新闻

第四课

中国大学生百县千乡服务工程拉开帷幕

课文

一、简介 (Introduction)

　　现在，中国大学生不再有"铁饭碗"了，因为政府不再给大学生分配工作了。这样，一方面，大学生需要把自己作为商品向市场推销；另一方面，高校也要改革课程，使学生学的知识与经济建设和社会发展的实际需要结合起来。

生词

铁饭碗	(tiě fàn wǎn)	*N.*	"the iron rice bowl" (refers to a job which one can not lose)
分配	(fēn pèi)	*V.*	to assign (a job, a part, etc.)
推销	(tuī xiāo)	*V.*	to promote (a product)
高校	(gāo xiào)	*Abbrev.*	universities and colleges, technical institutions; institutions of higher education = 高等学校
实际需要	(shí jì xū yào)	*NP.*	actual needs, practical needs

二、對話 (Dialogues)

(一)

大平： 中國高校學生有沒有他們自己的組織？

小敏： 可以說有， 也可以說沒有。 因為像中國共產主義青年團， 全國學生
聯合會都是一些大學生的組織。 但是， 這些組織都受中國共產黨的
控制， 並沒有自己的活動自由和獨立權利。 所以很難說學生有自己
的組織。

問題：為甚麼說中國高校學生組織是 "可以說有， 也可以說沒有"？

生詞

共產主義	(gòng chǎn zhǔ yì)	N.	communism, communist
青年團	(qīng nián tuán)	N.	Youth League
聯合會	(lián hé huì)	N.	federation
學生聯合會	(xué shēng lián hé huì)	NP.	student federation
控制	(kòng zhì)	V/N.	to control; control

(二)

大平： 小敏， "百縣千鄉服務工程" 到底是一個甚麼工程？ 怎麼我看了半
天也看不懂這條新聞？

小敏： 大平， 雖然這條新聞中用的詞好像都很複雜， 但其實內容很簡單。
它的主要意思就是讓高校學生把他們所學的科學技術以及文化知識用
到社會實踐中去。也就是說讓大學生利用暑假去跟地方政府和企業界
人士見面洽談，讓他們了解社會需要，同時也把學到的知識用到社
會實踐中去。

問題： "百縣千鄉服務工程" 到底是個甚麼工程？

二、对话 (Dialogues)

（一）

大平： 中国高校学生有没有他们自己的组织？

小敏： 可以说有，也可以说没有。因为像中国共产主义青年团，全国学生联合会都是一些大学生的组织。但是，这些组织都受中国共产党的控制，并没有自己的活动自由和独立权利。所以很难说学生有自己的组织。

问题： *为什么说中国高校学生组织是"可以说有，也可以说没有"？*

生词

共产主义	(gòng chǎn zhǔ yì)	N.	communism, communist
青年团	(qīng nián tuán)	N.	Youth League
联合会	(lián hé huì)	N.	federation
学生联合会	(xué shēng lián hé huì)	NP.	student federation
控制	(kòng zhì)	V/N.	to control; control

（二）

大平： 小敏，"百县千乡服务工程"到底是一个什么工程？怎么我看了半天也看不懂这条新闻？

小敏： 大平，虽然这条新闻中用的词好像都很复杂，但其实内容很简单。它的主要意思就是让高校学生把他们所学的科学技术以及文化知识用到社会实践中去。也就是说让大学生利用暑假去跟地方政府和企业界人士见面洽谈，让他们了解社会需要，同时也把学到的知识用到社会实践中去。

问题： *"百县千乡服务工程"到底是个什么工程？*

85

生詞

百縣千鄉	(bǎi xiàn qiān xiāng)	*Idiom.*	hundreds of counties, thousands of small towns and villages
工程	(gōng chéng)	*N.*	an undertaking, a project; engineering or construction project(s)
複雜	(fù zá)	*Adj.*	complicated; complex
實踐	(shí jiàn)	*N/V.*	practice; to put into practice
企業界	(qǐ yè jiè)	*N.*	business circles, entrepreneurial circles
洽談	(qià tán)	*V.*	to hold talks, to have consultation, to talk about (business, trade, commerce)
運用	(yùn yòng)	*V.*	to utilize; to make use of

（三）

大平： 明天晚上在城里有一個街市，你要不要去？

小敏： 甚麼是街市？

大平： 是一種市場。就是由很多商人在街上擺攤設點，一方面為市民提供各種服務，一方面促進城市的貿易交流。

小敏： 聽起來還不錯，那我一定去。

問題： 甚麼是街市？

生詞

街市	(jiē shì)	*V.*	street fair
商人	(shāng rén)	*N.*	businessman
擺攤	(bǎi tān)	*VO.*	to set up a booth
設點	(shè diǎn)	*VO.*	to select a spot, set something up
市民	(shì mín)	*N.*	residents (of a city), townspeople
貿易	(mào yì)	*N.*	trade; commerce

生词

百县千乡	(bǎi xiàn qiān xiāng)	*Idiom.*	hundreds of counties, thousands of small towns and villages
工程	(gōng chéng)	*N.*	an undertaking, a project; engineering or construction project(s)
复杂	(fù zá)	*Adj.*	complicated; complex
实践	(shí jiàn)	*N/V.*	practice; to put into practice
企业界	(qǐ yè jiè)	*N.*	business circles, entrepreneurial circles
洽谈	(qià tán)	*V.*	to hold talks, to have consultation, to talk about (business, trade, commerce)
运用	(yùn yòng)	*V.*	to utilize; to make use of

（三）

大平：明天晚上在城里有一个街市，你要不要去？

小敏：什么是街市？

大平：是一种市场。就是由很多商人在街上摆摊设点，一方面为市民提供各种服务，一方面促进城市的贸易交流。

小敏：听起来还不错，那我一定去。

问题: 什么是街市？

生词

街市	(jiē shì)	*V.*	street fair
商人	(shāng rén)	*N.*	businessman
摆摊	(bǎi tān)	*VO.*	to set up a booth
设点	(shè diǎn)	*VO.*	to select a spot, set something up
市民	(shì mín)	*N.*	residents (of a city), townspeople
贸易	(mào yì)	*N.*	trade; commerce

三、電視新聞 (The TV news)

中國大學生百縣千鄉服務工程拉開帷幕

　　由中國共產主義青年團中央、中國全國學生聯合會等單位主辦的中國大學生百縣千鄉科技文化服務工程6月17號在北京圖書館拉開序幕。

　　這次活動選擇了中國一百二十多個縣市，根據當地經濟建設和社會發展的實際需要來這里擺攤設點，與全國高校開展科技文化服務洽談。各高校採取大學生社會實踐的方式，利用暑假組織他們有針對性地進行科技文化服務。一方面把高校的科技成果推向市場，一方面引導大學生在經濟建設方面鍛煉成材。這一新的嘗試吸引了眾多高校師生、地方政府和企業界人士參加。

生詞

拉開	(lā kāi)	V.	to pull open (curtain, drawer, etc.), to raise (curtain)
帷幕	(wéi mù)	N.	curtain(s)
中央	(zhōng yāng)	Adj/N.	central; the center, central committee or "Party Central"
單位	(dān wèi)	N.	unit (as in "work unit", administrative unit, organization)
主辦	(zhǔ bàn)	V.	to sponsor
序幕	(xù mù)	N.	prelude, "inaugural curtain", opening
縣	(xiàn)	N.	county
市	(shì)	N.	city
當地	(dāng dì)	N.	local
有針對性地	(yǒu zhēn duì xìng de)	Adv.	purposefully, with a focused goal
科技文化	(kē jì wén huà)	NP.	science and technology, "scientific and

三、电视新闻 (The TV news)

中国大学生百县千乡服务工程拉开帷幕

由中国共产主义青年团中央、中国全国学生联合会等单位主办的中国大学生百县千乡科技文化服务工程6月17号在北京图书馆拉开序幕。

这次活动选择了中国一百二十多个县市，根据当地经济建设和社会发展的实际需要来这里摆摊设点，与全国高校开展科技文化服务洽谈。各高校采取大学生社会实践的方式，利用暑假组织他们有针对性地进行科技文化服务。一方面把高校的科技成果推向市场，一方面引导大学生在经济建设方面锻炼成材。这一新的尝试吸引了众多高校师生、地方政府和企业界人士参加。

生词

拉开	(lā kāi)	V.	to pull open (curtain, drawer, etc.), to raise (curtain)
帷幕	(wéi mù)	N.	curtain(s)
中央	(zhōng yāng)	Adj/N.	central; the center, central committee or "Party Central"
单位	(dān wèi)	N.	unit (as in "work unit", administrative unit, organization)
主办	(zhǔ bàn)	V.	to sponsor
序幕	(xù mù)	N.	prelude, "inaugural curtain", opening
县	(xiàn)	N.	county
市	(shì)	N.	city
当地	(dāng dì)	N.	local
有针对性地	(yǒu zhēn duì xìng de)	Adv.	purposefully, with a focused goal
科技文化	(kē jì wén huà)	NP.	science and technology, "scientific and

technological literacy"

科技成果	(kē jì chéng guǒ)	*NP.*	the fruits (achievements) of science and technology
推向	(tuī xiàng)	*V.*	to promote, to introduce into, to propel into
引導	(yǐn dǎo)	*V.*	to guide, to draw into
鍛煉	(duàn liàn)	*V.*	to build up strength and will power; to temper (steel); to exercise, to train
成材	(chéng cái)	*VO.*	to become useful (people, materials)
鍛煉成材	(duàn liàn chéng cái)	*Idiom.*	to be tempered and molded into a useful person
嘗試	(cháng shì)	*N.*	attempt, trial run
吸引	(xī yǐn)	*V.*	to attract
眾多	(zhòng duō)	*Adj.*	many, a large number of
師生	(shī shēng)	*Abbrev.*	teachers and students＝老師和學生

			technological literacy"
科技成果	(kē jì chéng guǒ)	*NP.*	the fruits (achievements) of science and technology
推向	(tuī xiàng)	*V.*	to promote, to introduce into, to propel into
引导	(yǐn dǎo)	*V.*	to guide, to draw into
锻炼	(duàn liàn)	*V.*	to build up strength and will power; to temper (steel); to exercise, to train
成材	(chéng cái)	*VO.*	to become useful (people, materials)
锻炼成材	(duàn liàn chéng cái)	*Idiom.*	to be tempered and molded into a useful person
尝试	(cháng shì)	*N.*	attempt, trial run
吸引	(xī yǐn)	*V.*	to attract
众多	(zhòng duō)	*Adj.*	many, a large number of
师生	(shī shēng)	*Abbrev.*	teachers and students=老师和学生

四、報紙閱讀 (Newspaper reading)

中英将培训合作企业经理

　　北京商学院与英国兰开夏大学联合举办的中英合作企业经理培训第一期培训班日前在结业典礼上透露，中英将继续实施合作企业经理培训项目。来自全国各主要城市大型零售商场的总经理或副总经理参加了中英合作企业经理培训第一期培训班。学员们先后在国内和英国听取了中英双方专家教授的讲课，并到英国的有关企业进行了实地考察，具体了解了西方市场的状况以及对我国商品的需求情况。通过培训，学员们对英国的管理理论、方法与技巧，对英国经济和企业的运作情况和贸易习惯，有了第一手的了解。　　　　　　　　　（严　冰）

中英將培訓合作企業經理

　　北京商學院與英國蘭開夏大學聯合舉辦的中英合作企業經理培訓第一期培訓班日前在結業典禮上透露，中英將繼續實施合作企業經理培訓項目。來自全國各主要城市大型零售商場的總經理或副總經理參加了中英合作企業經理培訓第一期培訓班。學員們先後在國內和英國聽取了中英雙方專家教授的講課，並到英國的有關企業進行了實地考察，具體了解了西方市場的狀況以及對我國商品的需求情況。通過培訓，學員們對英國的管理理論、方法與技巧，對英國經濟和企業的運作情況和貿易習慣，有了第一手了解。

四、报纸阅读 (Newspaper reading)

中英将培训合作企业经理

北京商学院与英国兰开夏大学联合举办的中英合作企业经理培训第一期培训班日前在结业典礼上透露，中英将继续实施合作企业经理培训项目。来自全国各主要城市大型零售商场的总经理或副总经理参加了中英合作企业经理培训第一期培训班。学员们先后在国内和英国听取了中英双方专家教授的讲课，并到英国的有关企业进行了实地考察，具体了解了西方市场的状况以及对我国商品的需求情况。通过培训，学员们对英国的管理理论、方法与技巧，对英国经济和企业的运作情况和贸易习惯，有了第一手的了解。　　　　　　（严　冰）

中英将培训合作企业经理

北京商学院与英国兰开夏大学联合举办的中英合作企业经理培训第一期培训班日前在结业典礼上透露，中英将继续实施合作企业经理培训项目。来自全国各主要城市大型零售商场的总经理或副总经理参加了中英合作企业经理培训第一期培训班。学员们先后在国内和英国听取了中英双方专家教授的讲课，并到英国的有关企业进行了实地考察，具体了解了西方市场的状况以及对我国商品的需求情况。通过培训，学员们对英国的管理理论、方法与技巧，对英国经济和企业的运作情况和贸易习惯，有了第一手了解。

生詞

培訓	（péi xùn）	V.	to train
經理	（jīng lǐ）	N.	manager
商學院	（shāng xué yuàn）	N.	business school
蘭開夏	（lán kāi xià）	Place N.	Lancashire (nothern England shire)
舉辦	（jǔ bàn）	V.	to conduct, to put on or to hold (an exhibition), to give (a concert), to sponsor＝主辦
結業	（jié yè）	N.	graduation
典禮	（diǎn lǐ）	N.	ceremony
實施	（shí shī）	V.	to implement, to carry out, to put into effect
零售	（líng shòu）	N.	retail
聽取	（tīng qǔ）	V.	listen carefully
專家	（zhuān jiā）	N.	expert(s)
實地	（shí dì）	N.	on the spot, on site
考察	（kǎo chá）	N.	investigation, inspection
狀況	（zhuàng kuàng）	N.	state, condition, state of affairs
理論	（lǐ lùn）	N.	theory, theories
技巧	（jì qiǎo）	N.	technique(s), skill(s)
運作	（yùn zuò）	N.	operation(s), procedures (business, manufacturing)
第一手	（dì yī shǒu）	N.	first-hand

生词

培训	(péi xùn)	*V.*	to train
经理	(jīng lǐ)	*N.*	manager
商学院	(shāng xué yuàn)	*N.*	business school
兰开夏	(lán kāi xià)	*Place N.*	Lancashire (nothern England shire)
举办	(jǔ bàn)	*V.*	to conduct, to put on or to hold (an exhibition), to give (a concert), to sponsor = 主办
结业	(jié yè)	*N.*	graduation
典礼	(diǎn lǐ)	*N.*	ceremony
实施	(shí shī)	*V.*	to implement, to carry out, to put into effect
零售	(líng shòu)	*N.*	retail
听取	(tīng qǔ)	*V.*	listen carefully
专家	(zhuān jiā)	*N.*	expert(s)
实地	(shí dì)	*N.*	on the spot, on site
考察	(kǎo chá)	*N.*	investigation, inspection
状况	(zhuàng kuàng)	*N.*	state, condition, state of affairs
理论	(lǐ lùn)	*N.*	theory, theories
技巧	(jì qiǎo)	*N.*	technique(s), skill(s)
运作	(yùn zuò)	*N.*	operation(s), procedures (business, manufacturing)
第一手	(dì yī shǒu)	*N.*	first-hand

五、幽默小品 (Humor)

電報快

　　媽媽手里拿著電報，高興地説："小強，你爸爸來電報説明天乘飛機回家啦。"

　　小強問："媽媽，電報快還是飛機快？"

　　"當然是電報快。"

　　"爸爸真傻，如果他乘電報，現在不是已經到家了嗎？"

生詞

電報	（diàn bào）	N.	telegram
乘	（chéng）	V.	to take (a vehicle), to ride on
傻	（shǎ）	Adj.	stupid

五、幽默小品 (Humor)

电报快

妈妈手里拿著电报，高兴地说："小强，你爸爸来电报说明天乘飞机回家啦。"

小强问："妈妈，电报快还是飞机快？"

"当然是电报快。"

"爸爸真傻，如果他乘电报，现在不是已经到家了吗？"

生词

电报	(diàn bào)	N.	telegram
乘	(chéng)	V.	to take (a vehicle), to ride on
傻	(shǎ)	Adj.	stupid

課文要點 (Key Points)

一、常用文言詞、縮略語與慣用語 (Frequently used classical Chinese phrases, abbreviations, and fixed expressions)

1. 眾多＝很多、非常多 (many)

　例：現在中國已經出現了眾多中外合資企業。
　　　In China many joint venture enterprises are emerging.

2. 培訓＝培養訓練 (to nurture/cultivate and train)

　例：培訓管理人員很要緊。
　　　It is crucial to train the managerial personnel.

3. 高校＝高等學校 (higher educational institutions)

　例：很多高校大學生利用暑假到社會上去實踐。
　　　Many university students take advantage of their summer vacation to get practical experience in society.

4. 百縣千鄉＝很多縣、鄉、跟地方單位 (hundreds of counties, thousands of villages)

5. 擺攤設點 (to set up booths for)

　例：經濟開放以來，很多人離開自己的工作，根據社會需要去街上擺攤設點賣東西。
　　　Since the economic open door policy, many people have left their own jobs to set up a small stand selling things according to the needs of the society.

课文要点 (Key Points)

一、常用文言词、缩略语与惯用语 (Frequently used classical Chinese phrases, abbreviations, and fixed expressions)

1. 众多 = 很多、非常多 (many)

   例: 现在中国已经出现了众多中外合资企业。
      In China many joint venture enterprises are emerging.

2. 培训 = 培养训练 (to nurture/cultivate and train)

   例: 培训管理人员很要紧。
      It is crucial to train the managerial personnel.

3. 高校 = 高等学校 (higher educational institutions)

   例: 很多高校大学生利用暑假到社会上去实践。
      Many university students take advantage of their summer vacation to get practical
      experience in society.

4. 百县千乡 = 很多县、乡、跟地方单位 (hundreds of counties, thousands of villages)

5. 摆摊设点 (to set up booths for)

   例: 经济开放以来, 很多人离开自己的工作, 根据社会需要去街上摆摊
      设点卖东西。
      Since the economic open door policy, many people have left their own jobs to set up a
      small stand selling things according to the needs of the society.

6. 拉開帷幕（序幕）(to raise the curtain on, to have a grand opening)

　　例：首屆大學生文化討論會在天津拉開帷幕。
　　　　The first University Students' Cultural Conference held its grand opening in Tianjin.

二、常用短語 (Frequently used structures)

1. 由…主辦 (to be sponsored by, conducted under the auspices of)

　　例：這次晚會是由當地的學校主辦的。
　　　　This party is sponsored by the local schools.

　　　　由市政府主辦的科技大會今天中午拉開帷幕。
　　　　The Science and Technology Conference sponsored by the city government had its grand opening today at noon.

2. …拉開帷幕（序幕）(to raise the curtain on)

　　例：由小學生聯合會主辦的詩歌比賽昨天拉開帷幕。
　　　　The poetry reading contest sponsored by the elementary student union began yesterday.

　　　　奧林匹克運動會將在亞特蘭大 (Atlanta) 拉開序幕。
　　　　The next Olympic Games will be held in Atlanta.

3. 與…洽談 (to hold talks with)

　　例：從上月起，中國開始跟歐洲國家洽談進出口貿易。
　　　　From last month, China began to hold talks with European countries on import and export trade.

　　　　自從北美自由貿易協定通過以來，很多進出口有限公司開始與加拿大、墨西哥洽談合資貿易。
　　　　Ever since the North America Free Trade Agreement was ratified, many import/export companies began to hold trade talks with Canada and Mexico concerning setting up joint venture trade.

6. 拉开帷幕（序幕）(to raise the curtain on, to have a grand opening)

例: 首届大学生文化讨论会在天津拉开帷幕。
The first University Students' Cultural Conference held its grand opening in Tianjin.

二、常用短语 (Useful structures)

1. 由⋯主办 (to be sponsored by, conducted under the auspices of)

例: 这次晚会是由当地的学校主办的。
This party is sponsored by the local schools.

由市政府主办的科技大会今天中午拉开帷幕。
The Science and Technology Conference sponsored by the city government had its grand opening today at noon.

2. ⋯拉开帷幕（序幕）(to raise the curtain on)

例: 由小学生联合会主办的诗歌比赛昨天拉开帷幕。
The poetry reading contest sponsored by the elementary student union began yesterday.

奥林匹克运动会将在亚特兰大 (Atlanta) 拉开序幕。
The next Olympic Games will be held in Atlanta.

3. 与⋯洽谈 (to hold talks with)

例: 从上月起，中国开始跟欧洲国家洽谈进出口贸易。
From last month, China began to hold talks with European countries on import and export trade.

自从北美自由贸易协定通过以来，很多进出口有限公司开始与加拿大、墨西哥洽谈合资贸易。
Ever since the North America Free Trade Agreement was ratified, many import/export companies began to hold trade talks with Canada and Mexico concerning setting up joint venture trade.

4. 採取⋯的方式 (via; by means of; by taking the path of)

例：採取產、供、銷一條龍的方式使這家酒廠一年創匯100萬美元。
The adoption of the coherent system of production, supply, and sales has enabled this winery to earn 1 milliom U.S. dollars in a single year.

這家電冰箱廠採取科學的管理方式，生產出各種多功能產品，受到用戶的讚賞。
This refrigerator factory adopted a scientific way of management and produced many multifunctional products which are popular with their customers.

5. 進行⋯服務 (to serve as, to provide a service for)

例：這家公司是專門進行涉外服務的。
This company provides special services for foreigners.

各國駐華大使館的任務之一就是對本國公民進行各種涉外服務。
One of the tasks of the various foreign embassies in China is to provide assistance to their own citizens involved in foreign affairs.

6. 一方面⋯一方面 (on one hand... on the other hand...)

例：中國大學生在這次活動中一方面實踐了自己的書本知識，一方面也了解了實際市場對他們所學的科學技術的需要。
The university students of China on one hand have put their knowledge into practice with this activity, and on the other hand, they have also gained an understanding of actual market demand for the science and technology they are studying.

中國學生聯合會一方面受中共中央的控制，一方面又控制全國高校的大學生政治活動。
The Chinese Students Union, on one hand, is controlled by the central committee of CCP; on the other hand, it also controls the political activities of students at all universities in the country.

4. 采取…的方式 (via; by means of; by taking the path of)

例: 采取产、供、销一条龙的方式使这家酒厂一年创汇100万美元。
The adoption of the coherent system of production, supply, and sales in one year has enabled this winery to earn 1 milliom U.S. dollars in a single year.

这家电冰箱厂采取科学的管理方式，生产出各种多功能产品，受到用户的赞赏。
This refrigerator factory adopted a scientific way of management and produced many multifunctional products which are popular with their customers.

5. 进行…服务 (to serve as, to provide a service for)

例: 这家公司是专门进行涉外服务的。
This company provides special services for foreigners.

各国驻华大使馆的任务之一就是对本国公民进行各种涉外服务。
One of the tasks of the various foreign embassies in China is to provide assistance to their own citizens involved in foreign affairs.

6. 一方面…一方面 (on one hand... on the other hand...)

例: 中国大学生在这次活动中一方面实践了自己的书本知识，一方面也了解了实际市场对他们所学的科学技术的需要。
The university students of China on one hand have put their knowledge into practice with this activity, and on the other hand, they have also gained an understanding of actual market demand for the science and technology they are studying.

中国学生联合会一方面受中共中央的控制，一方面又控制全国高校的大学生政治活动。
The Chinese Students Union, on one hand, is controlled by the central committee of CCP; on the other hand, it also controls the political activities of students at all universities in the country.

7. 吸引…參加 (to attract someone to join in, to succeed in eliciting the participation of)

例：這個洽談會吸引了三十二個國家的企業界人士參加。
This meeting attracted enterprise representatives from 32 countries to participate.

中英第十次會談吸引了很多中外記者來採訪。
The tenth talk between China and Great Britain attracted many foreign and domestic reporters to come and cover this story.

8. 進行…考察 (to inspect; to pay an inspection to)

例：美國政府派出了專家對南非的經濟進行考察。
The U.S. government sent experts to study the economy of South Africa.

進行了一年多的考察，美國政府決定跟北美幾個國家達成自由貿易的協定。
After more than one year of study, the U.S. government decided to reach a free trade agreement with several North American countries.

9. 了解…的情況 (to understand the situation of)

例：我們校長這次去德國了解了很多德國的社會和經濟情況。
Our university president's visit to Germany this time helped him understand many social and economic problems of Germany

舉行大學生科技洽談會是為了讓大學生對社會和市場有進一步的了解。
The purpose of sponsoring a university students' trade talk is to enable students to gain further understanding of society and the market.

7. 吸引…参加 (to attract someone to join in, to succeed in eliciting the participation of)

例: 这个洽谈会吸引了三十二个国家的企业界人士参加。
This meeting attracted enterprise representatives from 32 countries to participate.

中英第十次会谈吸引了很多中外记者来采访。
The tenth talk between China and Great Britain attracted many foreign and domestic reporters to come and cover this story.

8. 进行…考察 (to inspect; to pay an inspection to)

例: 美国政府派出了专家对南非的经济进行考察。
The U.S. government sent experts to study the economy of South Africa.

进行了一年多的考察，美国政府决定跟北美几个国家达成自由贸易的协定。
After more than one year of study, the U.S. government decided to reach a free trade agreement with several North American countries.

9. 了解…的情况 (to understand the situation of)

例: 我们校长这次去德国了解了很多德国的社会和经济情况。
Our university president's visit to Germany this time helped him understand many social and economic problems of Germany

举行大学生科技洽谈会是为了让大学生对社会和市场有进一步的了解。
The purpose of sponsoring a university students' trade talk is to enable students to gain further understanding of society and the market.

小課文

如此八小時。。。

一、看電視小課文、回答問題 (Answer the following questions)

　　1. 從廣告中你知道那些人在上班的時候做甚麼？
　　　1) 兩個女的：
　　　2) 坐在桌子旁邊的那兩個男的：
　　2. 打電話的人説了些甚麼？
　　3. 為甚麼桌子上的報紙上寫著"無聊"？它説明了中國企業管理上的一個甚麼問題？

二、討論 (Discuss the following questions)

　　1. 廣告中的現像反映了中國的一個甚麼社會問題？
　　2. 你認為應該用甚麼辦法解決這個問題？
　　3. 美國有沒有這種問題？
　　4. 政府應該採取甚麼好的措施？

小课文

如此八小时...

一、看电视小课文、回答问题 (Answer the following questions)

1. 从广告中你知道那些人在上班的时候做什么?

   1) 两个女的:

   2) 坐在桌子旁边的那两个男的:

2. 打电话的人说了些什么?

3. 为什么桌子上的报纸上写著"无聊"?它说明了中国企业管理上的一个什么问题?

二、讨论 (Discuss the following questions)

1. 广告中的现象反映了中国的一个什么社会问题?

2. 你认为应该用什么办法解决这个问题?

3. 美国有没有这种问题?

4. 政府应该采取什么好的措施?

中國歌曲

彎彎的月亮

遙遠的夜空有一個彎彎的月亮，
彎彎的月亮下是那彎彎的小橋，
小橋的旁邊有一條彎彎的小船，
彎彎的小船悠悠是那童年的阿嬌
嘟…

阿嬌搖著船唱著那古老的歌謠，
歌聲隨風飄呀飄飄到我的臉上，
臉上淌著淚像那彎彎的河水，
彎彎的河水流呀流進我的心上。
嘟…

我的心中充滿惆悵，
不為那彎彎的月亮，
只為那今天的村莊，
還唱著那古老的歌謠。

啊，故鄉的月亮，
你那彎彎的憂傷，
穿透了我的胸膛。

啦…

生詞

彎彎	(wān wān)	curving, bent
遙遠	(yáo yuǎn)	far away
悠悠	(yōu yōu)	leisurely
搖船	(yáo chuán)	row a boat
歌謠	(gē yáo)	ballad
隨風	(suí fēng)	with the wind (following the wind)
淌著	(tǎng zhe)	shedding (tears)
充滿	(chōng mǎn)	full of; to be filled with
惆悵	(chóu chàng)	sad, depressed; sadness, depression
村莊	(cūn zhuāng)	village
憂傷	(yōu shāng)	sorrow
胸膛	(xiōng táng)	chest

中国歌曲

弯弯的月亮

遥远的夜空有一个弯弯的月亮，
弯弯的月亮下是那弯弯的小桥，
小桥的旁边有一条弯弯的小船，
弯弯的小船悠悠是那童年的阿娇
嘟…

阿娇摇著船唱著那古老的歌谣，
歌声随风飘呀飘飘到我的脸上，
脸上淌著泪象那弯弯的河水，
弯弯的河水流呀流进我的心上。
嘟…

我的心中充满惆怅，
不为那弯弯的月亮，
只为那今天的村庄，
还唱著那古老的歌谣。

啊，故乡的月亮，
你那弯弯的忧伤，
穿透了我的胸膛。

啦…

生词

弯弯	(wān wān)	curving, bent
遥远	(yáo yuǎn)	far away
悠悠	(yōu yōu)	leisurely
摇船	(yáo chuán)	row a boat
歌谣	(gē yáo)	ballad
随风	(suí fēng)	with the wind (following the wind)
淌著	(tǎng zhe)	shedding (tears)
充满	(chōng mǎn)	full of; to be filled with
惆怅	(chóu chàng)	sad, depressed; sadness, depression
村庄	(cūn zhuāng)	village
忧伤	(yōu shāng)	sorrow
胸膛	(xiōng táng)	chest

Unit 3: Culture News

第三單元　文化新聞

第一課

九二年長春電影節
《秋菊打官司》獲金獅獎

課文

一、簡介

　　中國文化新聞常常報道一些與社會文化發展和交流有關的消息。例如：全國性的文化藝術活動和節日、或國際性的節日和獎勵等。本課的兩篇新聞都是有關電影界的報道。

生詞

藝術	(yì shù)	*N.*	art, the arts
國際性	(guó jì xìng)	*N.*	internationality
節日	(jié rì)	*N.*	holidays, festival
獎勵	(jiǎng lì)	*N./V.*	award(s), reward(s); to encourage and reward
有關	(yǒu guān)	*Prep.*	related; concerning; about

第三单元　文化新闻

第一课

九二年长春电影节
《秋菊打官司》获金狮奖

课文

一、简介

　　中国文化新闻常常报道一些与社会文化发展和交流有关的消息。例如:
全国性的文化艺术活动和节日、或国际性的节日和奖励等。本课的两篇新闻
都是有关电影界的报道。

生词

艺术	(yì shù)	*N.*	art, the arts
国际性	(guó jì xìng)	*N.*	internationality
节日	(jié rì)	*N.*	holidays, festival
奖励	(jiǎng lì)	*N/V.*	award(s), reward(s); to encourage and reward
有关	(yǒu guān)	*Prep.*	related; concerning; about

二、 對話

（一）

林東：小芳，我正在準備去中國的旅行計劃，據說長春是一個好地方，我不知道該去不該去。你能不能給我一些有關長春的信息？

小芳：你知道，長春在中國的東北部，是吉林省的省會，也是中國著名的電影城。

林東：是嗎？那長春可能跟美國的好萊塢一樣是一個電影文化中心。

小芳：對，對。長春有全國最大的電影製片廠，攝製過很多大型故事片，那里也有展映電影的電影宮。此外，長春還開始舉辦國際性的電影節，邀請各種中外電影角逐長春杯。

林東：看來，長春這個城市還是值得去看看。

問題：請你說說長春市的特點。

生詞

長春	(cháng chūn)	*Place N.*	Changchun, capital city of Jilin Province
信息	(xìn xī)	N.	information
省會	(shěng huì)	N.	capital city of a province
電影城	(diàn yǐng chéng)	N.	movie city
好萊塢	(Hǎo lái wū)	*Place N.*	Hollywood
製片廠	(zhì piān chǎng)	N.	film studio
攝製	(shè zhì)	V.	to film, to produce (a film), to make (a movie)
故事片	(gù shì piān)	N.	feature film
展映	(zhǎn yìng)	V.	to exhibit, to show (a film)

二、 对话

（一）

林东： 小芳，我正在准备去中国的旅行计划，据说长春是一个好地方，我不知道该去不该去。你能不能给我一些有关长春的信息？

小芳： 你知道，长春在中国的东北部，是吉林省的省会，也是中国著名的电影城。

林东： 是吗？那长春可能跟美国的好莱坞一样是一个电影文化中心。

小芳： 对，对。长春有全国最大的电影制片厂，摄制过很多大型故事片，那里也有展映电影的电影宫。此外，长春还开始举办国际性的电影节，邀请各种中外电影角逐长春杯。

林东： 看来，长春这个城市还是值得去看看。

问题: 请你说说长春市的特点。

生词

长春	(cháng chūn)	*Place N.*	Changchun, capital city of Jilin Province
信息	(xìn xī)	*N.*	information
省会	(shěng huì)	*N.*	capital city of a province
电影城	(diàn yǐng chéng)	*N.*	movie city
好莱坞	(Hǎo lái wū)	*Place N.*	Hollywood
制片厂	(zhì piān chǎng)	*N.*	film studio
摄制	(shè zhì)	*V.*	to film, to produce (a film), to make (a movie)
故事片	(gù shì piān)	*N.*	feature film
展映	(zhǎn yìng)	*V.*	to exhibit, to show (a film)

| 電影宮 | (diàn yǐng gōng) | N. | movie theater, film palace |
| 角逐 | (jué zhú) | V. | to compete for, to vie for |

(二)

小芳：昨天晚上的大型表演晚會你去了嗎？

林東：沒有。因為有朋友來，我沒有去成，怎麼樣？

小芳：好極了，每個年級的學生都登台獻藝，並且角逐最佳表演獎。

林東：那誰獲得了這個表演獎？

小芳：當然是四年級的學生，因為他們差不多排練了一個月，而且他們的表演也最成功，最圓滿。

問題：為甚麼四年級的學生獲得了表演獎？

生詞

畢業晚會	(bì yè wǎn huì)	NP.	graduation party
登台獻藝	(dēng tái xiàn yì)	VP.	to perform on stage
最佳	(zuì jiā)	Adj.	the best
表演	(biǎo yǎn)	V/N.	to perform, performance
排練	(pái liàn)	V.	to rehearse (play, performance, etc.)
圓滿	(yuán mǎn)	Adv.	successfully, satisfactorily

(三)

小芳：你看過幾部由張藝謀執導、鞏俐主演的電影？

林東：差不多四部，每一部我都非常喜歡。

小芳：是啊，差不多每一部都獲得了世界電影節的最高獎勵。他真是一個好導演。

| 电影宫 | (diàn yǐng gōng) | N. | movie theater, film palace |
| 角逐 | (jué zhú) | V. | to compete for, to vie for |

（二）

小芳：昨天晚上的大型表演晚会你去了吗？

林东：没有。因为有朋友来，我没有去成，怎么样？

小芳：好极了，每个年级的学生都登台献艺，并且角逐最佳表演奖。

林东：那谁获得了这个表演奖？

小芳：当然是四年级的学生，因为他们差不多排练了一个月，而且他们的表演也最成功，最圆满。

问题：为什么四年级的学生获得了表演奖？

生词

毕业晚会	(bì yè wǎn huì)	NP.	graduation party
登台献艺	(dēng tái xiàn yì)	VP.	to perform on stage
最佳	(zuì jiā)	Adj.	the best
表演	(biǎo yǎn)	V/N.	to perform, performance
排练	(pái liàn)	V.	to rehearse (play, performance, etc.)
圆满	(yuán mǎn)	Adv.	successfully, satisfactorily

（三）

小芳：你看过几部由张艺谋执导、巩俐主演的电影？

林东：差不多四部，每一部我都非常喜欢。

小芳：是啊，差不多每一部都获得了世界电影节的最高奖励。他真是一个好导演。

林東：我覺得鞏俐也是一個十分好的演員，在《秋菊打官司》里，鞏俐把農村婦女秋菊演得真實極了。遺憾的是，這麼好的影片過去在中國是不許放映的，所以很多中國的老百姓都沒有看過她的電影。

問題：林東和小芳對張藝謀、鞏俐的看法是甚麼？

生詞

張藝謀	(zhāng yì móu)	*Personal N.*	personal name: a famous Chinese film director, directed "Red Sorghum", "Judou", "Raise the Red Lantern", etc.
執導	(zhí dǎo)	*V.*	to direct
鞏俐	(gǒng lì)	*Personal N.*	personal name: a famous Chinese female star, plays the lead role in "Red Sorghum", "Raise the Red Lantern", "Judou", "Qiuju", etc.
主演	(zhǔ yǎn)	*V.*	to have the leading role (in a film, drama, etc.)
電影節	(diàn yǐng jié)	*N.*	film festival
導演	(dǎo yǎn)	*N.*	director
演員	(yǎn yuán)	*N.*	actor or actress
秋菊	(qīu jú)	*Personal N.*	personal name, "Autumn Chrysanthemum(s)"
打官司	(dǎ guān sī)	*VO.*	to sue someone, to bring a suit against, to take legal action against
遺憾	(yí hàn)	*V/N.*	to regret; regret

101

林东： 我觉得巩俐也是一个十分好的演员，在《秋菊打官司》里，巩俐把农村妇女秋菊演得真实极了。遗憾的是，这么好的影片过去在中国是不许放映的，所以很多中国的老百姓都没有看过她的电影。

问题： 林东和小芳对张艺谋、巩俐的看法是什么？

生词

张艺谋	(zhāng yì móu)	*Personal N.*	personal name: a famous Chinese film director, directed "Red Sorghum", "Judou", "Raise the Red Lantern", etc.
执导	(zhí dǎo)	*V.*	to direct
巩俐	(gǒng lì)	*Personal N.*	personal name: a famous Chinese female star, plays the lead role in "Red Sorghum", "Raise the Red Lantern", "Judou", "Qiuju", etc.
主演	(zhǔ yǎn)	*V.*	to have the leading role (in a film, drama, etc.)
电影节	(diàn yǐng jié)	*N.*	film festival
导演	(dǎo yǎn)	*N.*	director
演员	(yǎn yuán)	*N.*	actor or actress
秋菊	(qīu jú)	*Personal N.*	personal name, "Autumn Chrysanthemum(s)"
打官司	(dǎ guān sī)	*VO.*	to sue someone, to bring a suit against, to take legal action against
遗憾	(yí hàn)	*V/N.*	to regret; regret

三、電視新聞

九二年長春電影節 新聞（一）

　　九二中國長春電影節是我國舉辦的第一個電影節。這次電影盛會邀請了七十多位國內外及港台地區著名影星登台獻藝，將由五十多部中外影片角逐長春杯。目前總建築面積為七千多平方米的電影宮總體工程已全部完成。開幕式大型晚會"走向輝煌"正在加緊排練。電影節期間，長春市還將組成二十五個交易團，提供十五大類，四千多個品種的新產品，開展經貿活動。這是吉林台和長春台報道的。

生詞

盛會	(shèng huì)	N.	a grand meeting; distinguished conclave
港台地區	(gǎng tái dì qū)	Abbrev.	Hong Kong and Taiwan areas＝香港跟台灣地區
部	(bù)	Classifier.	a classifier for movies
長春杯	(cháng chūn bēi)	Title.	the Changchun Cup (top award in a film festival)
建築	(jiàn zhù)	N.	building, structure, edifice, architecture
面積	(miàn jī)	N.	area, floor space; surface area
平方米	(píng fāng mǐ)	N.	square meter
總體工程	(zǒng tǐ gōng chéng)	NP.	the overall project
開幕式	(kāi mù shì)	N.	the opening ceremony
走向輝煌	(zǒu xiàng huī huáng)	VO.	"Bound for Glory", "advancing towards brilliant splendor"
加緊	(jiā jǐn)	V.	to speed up, to intensify
交易團	(jiāo yì tuán)	N.	the trade delegation
大類	(dà lèi)	N.	major kind, major type

三、电视新闻

九二年长春电影节 新闻（一）

九二中国长春电影节是我国举办的第一个电影节。这次电影盛会邀请了七十多位国内外及港台地区著名影星登台献艺，将由五十多部中外影片角逐长春杯。目前总建筑面积为七千多平方米的电影宫总体工程已全部完成。开幕式大型晚会"走向辉煌"正在加紧排练。电影节期间，长春市还将组成二十五个交易团，提供十五大类，四千多个品种的新产品，开展经贸活动。这是吉林台和长春台报道的。

生词

盛会	(shèng huì)	N.	a grand meeting; distinguished conclave
港台地区	(gǎng tái dì qū)	Abbrev.	Hong Kong and Taiwan areas = 香港跟台湾地区
部	(bù)	Classifier.	a classifier for movies
长春杯	(cháng chūn bēi)	Title.	the Changchun Cup (top award in a film festival)
建筑	(jiàn zhù)	N.	building, structure, edifice, architecture
面积	(miàn jī)	N.	area, floor space; surface area
平方米	(píng fāng mǐ)	N.	square meter
总体工程	(zǒng tǐ gōng chéng)	NP.	the overall project
开幕式	(kāi mù shì)	N.	the opening ceremony
走向辉煌	(zǒu xiàng huī huáng)	VO.	"Bound for Glory", "advancing towards brilliant splendor"
加紧	(jiā jǐn)	V.	to speed up, to intensify
交易团	(jiāo yì tuán)	N.	the trade delegation
大类	(dà lèi)	N.	major kind, major type

| 品種 | (pǐn zhǒng) | N. | type, design, variety, breed(s), strain(s) |

電影《秋菊打官司》獲四十九屆
威尼斯電影節金獅獎　新聞（二）

　　張藝謀執導，著名女演員鞏俐主演的《秋菊打官司》9月13號在第四十九屆威尼斯電影節上獲得該項活動的最高獎勵—金獅獎。鞏俐榮獲威尼斯電影節最佳女演員獎，並榮獲了烏爾提杯。

　　電影《秋菊打官司》主要描寫了當代中國農村的一名婦女打官司的經過。

生詞

威尼斯	(wēi ní sī)	Place N.	Venice
金獅獎	(jīn shī jiǎng)	N.	Golden Lion Award
榮獲	(róng huò)	V.	to have the honor of winning, to be awarded (the prize, the distinction of)
烏爾提杯	(wū ěr tí bēi)	N.	the Ugarti Cup
描寫	(miáo xiě)	V.	to describe; to depict
經過	(jīng guò)	N.	process; experiences from beginning to end, whole course of events

品种	(pǐn zhǒng)	N.	type, design, variety, breed(s), strain(s)

电影《秋菊打官司》获四十九届威尼斯电影节金狮奖　新闻（二）

　　张艺谋执导，著名女演员巩俐主演的《秋菊打官司》9月13号在第四十九届威尼斯电影节上获得该项活动的最高奖励—金狮奖。巩俐荣获威尼斯电影节最佳女演员奖，并荣获了乌尔提杯。

　　电影《秋菊打官司》主要描写了当代中国农村的一名妇女打官司的经过。

生词

威尼斯	(wēi ní sī)	Place N.	Venice
金狮奖	(jīn shī jiǎng)	N.	Golden Lion Award
荣获	(róng huò)	V.	to have the honor of winning, to be awarded (the prize, the distinction of)
乌尔提杯	(wū ěr tí bēi)	N.	the Ugarti Cup
描写	(miáo xiě)	V.	to describe; to depict
经过	(jīng guò)	N.	process; experiences from beginning to end, whole course of events

四、報紙閱讀

长春电影节圆满闭幕

影片《秋菊打官司》获本届电影节最高奖

新华社长春8月28日电（记者周长庆、陈美凤）为期6天的'92中国长春电影节今天圆满结束。由中国著名导演张艺谋执导、影星巩俐主演的新作《秋菊打官司》，获得本届电影节唯一的最高奖——"长春金杯"及20000元人民币奖金。

同时获得"长春银杯"奖的有长春电影制片厂摄制的《葛老爷子》、上海电影制片厂的《蝴里人家》和儿童电影制片厂的《人之初》。峨眉厂的《毛泽东的故事》和上影的《烛光里的微笑》获得电影节的"特别奖"。获"长春银杯"和"特别奖"的影片剧组各获本届电影节组委会颁发的10000元人民币奖金。

长春电影节是一次国际性的大型中外文化交流活动。电影节期间共展映中国以及美、日、法、意、印等12个国家及港台地区的影片55部。自8月初至今在长春共上映3000场，观众达100多万人次。

被广播电影电视部电影局局长、评委会评委滕进贤誉为"艺术性和观赏性完美结合"的影片《秋菊打官司》，是由香港银都机构和中国青年电影制片厂联合摄制的。它描写了九十年代中国北方农村一群普通农民的故事。该片导演张艺谋打破传统的拍摄手段，影片一半镜头采用偷拍，从而以纪实性手段真实地记录了影片女主人公秋菊（巩俐饰）围绕一场从村、乡、县、市的几经周折的"官司"所表现出的朴实心态。

'92中国长春电影节集电影、文化、经贸、旅游活动于一体，共有30000多名国内外客人参加。

長春電影節圓滿閉幕
影片《秋菊打官司》獲本屆電影節最高獎　（節選）

新華社長春8月28日電（記者周長慶、陳美鳳）為期 6天的92中國長春電影節今天圓滿結束。由中國著名導演張藝謀執導、影星鞏俐主演的新作《秋菊打官司》，獲得本屆電影節唯一的最高獎—"長春金杯"及20,000元人民幣獎金。…

長春電影節是一次國際性的大型中外文化交流活動。電影節期間共展映中國以及美、日、法、意、印等12個國家及港台地區的影片55部。自8月初至今在長春共上映3,000場，觀眾達100多萬人次。

四、报纸阅读

长春电影节圆满闭幕

影片《秋菊打官司》获本届电影节最高奖

新华社长春8月28日电（记者周长庆、陈美凤）为期6天的'92中国长春电影节今天圆满结束。由中国著名导演张艺谋执导、影星巩俐主演的新作《秋菊打官司》，获得本届电影节唯一的最高奖——"长春金杯"及20000元人民币奖金。

同时获得"长春银杯"奖的有长春电影制片厂摄制的《葛老爷子》、上海电影制片厂的《阙里人家》和儿童电影制片厂的《人之初》。峨眉厂的《毛泽东的故事》和上影的《烛光里的微笑》获得电影节的"特别奖"。获"长春银杯"和"特别奖"的影片剧组各获本届电影节组委会颁发的10000元人民币奖金。

长春电影节是一次国际性的大型中外文化交流活动。电影节期间共展映中国以及美、日、法、意、印等12个国家及港台地区的影片55部。自8月初至今在长春共上映3000场，观众达100多万人次。

被广播电影电视部电影局局长、评委会评委滕进贤誉为"艺术性和观赏性完美结合"的影片《秋菊打官司》，是由香港银都机构和中国青年电影制片厂联合摄制的。它描写了九十年代中国北方农村一群普通农民的故事。该片导演张艺谋打破传统的拍摄手段，影片一半镜头采用偷拍，从而以纪实性手段真实地记录了影片女主人公秋菊（巩俐饰）围绕一场从村、乡、县、市的几经周折的"官司"所表现出的朴实心态。

'92中国长春电影节集电影、文化、经贸、旅游活动于一体，共有30000多名国内外客人参加。

长春电影节圆满闭幕
影片《秋菊打官司》获本届电影节最高奖（节选）

新华社长春8月28日电（记者周长庆、陈美凤）为期 6天的92中国长春电影节今天圆满结束。由中国著名导演张艺谋执导、影星巩俐主演的新作《秋菊打官司》，获得本届电影节唯一的最高奖一"长春金杯"及20,000元人民币奖金。…

长春电影节是一次国际性的大型中外文化交流活动。电影节期间共展映中国以及美、日、法、意、印等12个国家及港台地区的影片55部。自8月初至今在长春共上映3,000场，观众达100多万人次。

生詞

節選	(jié xuǎn)	*N.*	excerpt
新作	(xīn zuò)	*Abbrev.*	new works＝新的作品
閉幕	(bì mù)	*VO.*	to close, to conclude
獲	(huò)	*V.*	to obtain
屆	(jiè)	*Classifier.*	session
金杯	(jīn bēi)	*N.*	gold cup
銀杯	(yín bēi)	*N.*	silver cup
上映	(shàng yìng)	*V.*	to screen (a film), to be shown (in a cinema)
場	(chǎng)	*Classifier.*	showing (of films), screening(s)

五、幽默小品

行人問路

　　行人問路，看到了一個小孩子，他拍拍孩子的肩膀説：“小弟弟，這兒是廣東路嗎？”孩子看了他一眼説：“這兒是我的肩膀。”

生詞

行人	(xíng rén)	*N.*	pedestrian
肩膀	(jiān bǎng)	*N.*	shoulder
廣東路	(guǎng dōng lù)	*Place N.*	Canton road

生词

节选	(jié xuǎn)	*N.*	excerpt
新作	(xīn zuò)	*Abbrev.*	new works = 新的作品
闭幕	(bì mù)	*VO.*	to close, to conclude
获	(huò)	*V.*	to obtain
届	(jiè)	*Classifier.*	session
金杯	(jīn bēi)	*N.*	gold cup
银杯	(yín bēi)	*N.*	silver cup
上映	(shàng yìng)	*V.*	to screen (a film), to be shown (in a cinema)
场	(chǎng)	*Classifier.*	showing (of films), screening(s)

五、幽默小品

行人问路

行人问路，看到了一个小孩子，他拍拍孩子的肩膀说："小弟弟，这儿是广东路吗？"孩子看了他一眼说："这儿是我的肩膀。"

生词

行人	(xíng rén)	*N.*	pedestrian
肩膀	(jiān bǎng)	*N.*	shoulder
广东路	(guǎng dōng lù)	*Place N.*	Canton road

課文要點

一、常用文言詞、縮略語與慣用語

1. 港台地區＝香港跟台灣地區 (Taiwan and Hong Kong areas)

> 例：這個大型建築工程吸引了很多港台地區的企業界人士來投資合作。
> This large scale architectural project has attracted the investment and involvement (co-operation) of many entrepreneurs from Hong Kong and Taiwan.

2. 影星＝電影明星 (film stars)

> 例：加拿大影星代表團昨天到北京電影製片廠訪問。
> The delegation of Canada's famous film stars paid a visit to Beijing Film Studio yesterday.

3. 交易團＝貿易團 (trade delegation)

> 例：東北三省組成了十個交易團與海南省洽談貿易。
> The three provinces from northeast China formed ten delegations in order to hold trade talks with Hainan.

4. 經貿＝經濟和貿易 (economy and trade)

> 例：中國與港台地區經貿往來很多。
> There are many economical and trade activities btween China, Taiwan, and Hong Kong.

5. 為期＝所用的時間是 (the fixed time is)

> 例：為期三天的經貿活動現已結束。
> The trade activities which were allotted 3 days have now been concluded.

课文要点

一、常用文言词、缩略语与惯用语

1. 港台地区 = 香港跟台湾地区 (Taiwan and Hong Kong areas)

例： 这个大型建筑工程吸引了很多港台地区的企业界人士来投资合作。
This large scale architectural project has attracted the investment and involvement (co-operation) of many entrepreneurs from Hong Kong and Taiwan.

2. 影星 = 电影明星 (film stars)

例： 加拿大影星代表团昨天到北京电影制片厂访问。
The delegation of Canada's famous film stars paid a visit to Beijing Film Studio yesterday.

3. 交易团 = 贸易团 (trade delegation)

例： 东北三省组成了十个交易团与海南省洽谈贸易。
The three provinces from northeast China formed ten delegations in order to hold trade talks with Hainan.

4. 经贸 = 经济和贸易 (economy and trade)

例： 中国与港台地区经贸往来很多。
There are many economical and trade activities btween China, Taiwan, and Hong Kong.

5. 为期 = 所用的时间是 (the fixed time is)

例： 为期三天的经贸活动现已结束。
The trade activities which were allotted 3 days have now been concluded.

6. 獲＝獲得 (to gain)

例：哈薩克斯坦的葡萄酒獲最佳酒獎。
The wine made in Kazakhstan has garnered the best wine award.

7. 最佳＝最好的 (the best)

例：今年電影節的最佳男演員是誰？
Who is/was the best male actor for this year's film festival ?

8. 新作＝新作品 (new works)

例：《秋菊》是著名導演張藝謀的新作。
"Qiuju" is the new work by the famous director Zhang Yimou.

9. 上影＝上海電影製片廠 (Shanghai Film Studio)

例：上影是上海電影製片廠的簡稱。
Shang Ying is the abbreviation of Shanghai Film Studio.

10. 中外＝中國和外國 (China and foreign countries)

例：中外合資是現在中國的一種新的重要經濟形式。
The joint venture between China and a foreign country has become an important new economic form for modern China.

11. 共＝一共 (total, totally)

例：西北航空公司共開設了十五條新航線。
Northwest Airlines has inaugurated 15 new routes.

6. 获 = 获得 (to gain)

例: 哈萨克斯坦的葡萄酒获最佳酒奖。

The wine made in Kazakhstan has garnered the best wine award.

7. 最佳 = 最好的 (the best)

例: 今年电影节的最佳男演员是谁？

Who is/was the best male actor for this year's film festival ?

8. 新作 = 新作品 (new works)

例 《秋菊》是著名导演张艺谋的新作。

"Qiuju" is the new work by the famous director Zhang Yimou.

9. 上影 = 上海电影制片厂 (Shanghai Film Studio)

例: 上影是上海电影制片厂的简称。

Shang Ying is the abbreviation of Shanghai Film Studio.

10. 中外 = 中国和外国 (China and foreign countries)

例: 中外合资是现在中国的一种新的重要经济形式。

The joint venture between China and a foreign country has become an important new economic form for modern China.

11. 共 = 一共 (total, totally)

例: 西北航空公司共开设了十五条新航线。

Northwest Airlines has inaugurated 15 new routes.

12. 展映＝展覽放映 (to exhibit, to show)

例：昨天在長春電影宮展映了中國著名影星鞏俐的新作《秋菊打官司》。
Yesterday the renowned movie star Gong Li's new film was shown in the Changchun Film Palace.

二、常用短語

1. 在⋯(place) 舉辦⋯　(to be held at)

例：據CBS報道,洛衫磯將舉辦全國美式足球賽。
According to a CBS report, Los Angeles will play host to a national football tournament.

由新加坡政府舉辦的大型新年晚會昨天閉幕。
The big New Year Party put on by the Singapore government came to an end last night.

2. 由⋯角逐　(to be contested by, competed for by)

例：今年世界杯足球冠軍將由意大利隊與巴西隊角逐。
This year's World Cup soccer championship will be contested by the teams from Italy and Brazil.

今年有一百多部電影角逐奧斯卡 (Oscar) 獎。
More than one hundred films will vie for this year's Oscars (Academy Awards).

3. ⋯的面積為⋯ (to cover an area of)

例：中國土地的總面積為九百六十多萬平方公里。
The total area of China exceeds nine million six hundred thousand square kilometers.

美國白宮的建築總面積是多少平英尺？
What is the total square footage of the White House as an edifice?

12. 展映 = 展览放映 (to exhibit, to show)

例：昨天在长春电影宫展映了中国著名影星巩俐的新作《秋菊打官司》。

Yesterday the renowned movie star Gong Li's new film was shown in the Changchun Film Palace.

二、常用短语

1. 在…(place) 举办…　(to be held at)

例：据CBS报道, 洛衫矶将举办全国美式足球赛。

According to a CBS report, Los Angeles will play host to a national football tournament.

由新加坡政府举办的大型新年晚会昨天闭幕。

The big New Year Party put on by the Singapore government came to an end last night.

2. 由…角逐　(to be contested by, competed for by)

例：今年世界杯足球冠军将由意大利队与巴西队角逐。

This year's World Cup soccer championship will be contested by the teams from Italy and Brazil.

今年有一百多部电影角逐奥斯卡 (Oscar) 奖。

More than one hundred films will vie for this year's Oscars (Academy Awards).

3. …的面积为…　(to cover an area of)

例：中国土地的总面积为九百六十多万平方公里。

The total area of China exceeds nine million six hundred thousand square kilometers.

美国白宫的建筑总面积是多少平英尺？

What is the total square footage of the White House as an edifice?

4. 提供…產品、材料、幫助 (to provide ... products, materials, help, etc.)

例：廣州一年兩次的交易會為外商提供了很多中國製造的新產品。

The semi-annual Guangzhou Trade Fair provides foreign business people with a variety of new products made in China

全國大學生科技交流會為大學生找工作提供了很多機會。

The all-China university students science and technology fair provided many chances for university students to find jobs.

5. 開展…活動 (to launch a campaign against)

例：由於中學生吸毒問題越來越嚴重，很多學校組織學生開展反對吸毒活動。

Due to the worsening problem of drug abuse at high schools, many schools have organized the students to launch a campaign against drug abuse.

現在有很多動物的生命都面臨危險，所以很多地方的老百姓都開展愛護野外動物的活動。

Due to the fact that there are many endangered species nowadays, people in many places have launched a campaign to protect the animals in the wild.

4. 提供…产品、材料、帮助 (to provide ... products, materials, help, etc.)

例: 广州一年两次的交易会为外商提供了很多中国制造的新产品。
The semi-annual Guangzhou Trade Fair provides foreign business people with a variety of new products made in China

全国大学生科技交流会为大学生找工作提供了很多机会。
The all-China university students science and technology fair provided many chances for university students to find jobs.

5. 开展…活动 (to launch a campaign against)

例: 由于中学生吸毒问题越来越严重，很多学校组织学生开展反对吸毒活动。
Due to the worsening problem of drug abuse at high schools, many schools have organized the students to launch a campaign against drug abuse.

现在有很多动物的生命都面临危险，所以很多地方的老百姓都开展爱护野外动物的活动。
Due to the fact that there are many endangered species nowadays, people in many places have launched a campaign to protect the animals in the wild.

第三單元 文化新聞

第二課

華南虎繁殖成功/非洲黑猩猩在北京產仔

課文

一、簡介

中國的文化新聞中也常常有一些關於稀有動物的報道。 這種報道一方面比較新奇可以引起觀眾的注意，另一方面也讓人們了解政府如何重視保護面臨滅絕的動物。

生詞

稀有	(xī yǒu)	*Adj.*	rare; scarce
新奇	(xīn qí)	*Adj.*	novel; strange
引起	(yǐn qǐ)	*V.*	to arouse
保護	(bǎo hù)	*V.*	to protect
面臨	(miàn lín)	*V.*	to be faced with (a crisis, extinction), to be up against
滅絕	(miè jué)	*N/V.*	extinction; to become extinct

110

第三单元　文化新闻

第二课

华南虎繁殖成功/非洲黑猩猩在北京产仔

课文

一、简介

中国的文化新闻中也常常有一些关于稀有动物的报道。这种报道一方面比较新奇可以引起观众的注意，另一方面也让人们了解政府如何重视保护面临灭绝的动物。

生词

稀有	(xī yǒu)	Adj.	rare; scarce
新奇	(xīn qí)	Adj.	novel; strange
引起	(yǐn qǐ)	V.	to arouse
保护	(bǎo hù)	V.	to protect
面临	(miàn lín)	V.	to be faced with (a crisis, extinction), to be up against
灭绝	(miè jué)	N/V.	extinction; to become extinct

二、對話

（一）

小麗：白蘭，你喜歡飼養小動物嗎？

白蘭：我很喜歡，我尤其喜歡小貓，因為牠們非常活潑可愛。不過飼養起來也很麻煩。有一次，我的花貓產仔，可是遇到難產，我晝夜沒睡，對牠精心管理，才使一胎三仔都成活了。

小麗：現在你的花貓呢，還跟著你嗎？

白蘭：早就送給當地的動物園去飼養了。現在花貓的女兒都已產下幼仔了。

問題：白蘭說養貓也很麻煩的原因是甚麼？

生詞

飼養	(sì yǎng)	*V.*	to feed; to raise
貓	(māo)	*N.*	cat
活潑	(huó pō)	*Adj.*	active; lively
可愛	(kě ài)	*Adj.*	cute
產仔	(chǎn zǐ)	*VO.*	to give birth to a baby animal ＝產下幼仔
難產	(nán chǎn)	*N.*	difficult labor
晝夜	(zhòu yè)	*N.*	day and night; 24 hour, round the clock
精心	(jīng xīn)	*Adv.*	with the best care, painstakingly, meticulously
一胎	(yī tāi)	*N.*	one litter of
仔	(zǐ)	*N.*	offspring; baby
成活	(chéng huó)	*V.*	to survive, to be born successfully, to be born alive and to survive
動物園	(dòng wù yuán)	*N.*	zoo

二、对话

（一）

小丽：白兰，你喜欢饲养小动物吗？

白兰：我很喜欢，我尤其喜欢小猫，因为它们非常活泼可爱。不过饲养起来也很麻烦。有一次，我的花猫产仔，可是遇到难产，我昼夜没睡，对它精心管理，才使一胎三仔都成活了。

小丽：现在你的花猫呢，还跟著你吗？

白兰：早就送给当地的动物园去饲养了。现在花猫的女儿都已产下幼仔了。

问题: 白兰说养猫也很麻烦的原因是什么？

生词

饲养	(sì yǎng)	*V.*	to feed; to raise
猫	(māo)	*N.*	cat
活泼	(huó pō)	*Adj.*	active; lively
可爱	(kě ài)	*Adj.*	cute
产仔	(chǎn zǐ)	*VO.*	to give birth to a baby animal = 产下幼仔
难产	(nán chǎn)	*N.*	difficult labor
昼夜	(zhòu yè)	*N.*	day and night; 24 hour, round the clock
精心	(jīng xīn)	*Adv.*	with the best care, painstakingly, meticulously
一胎	(yī tāi)	*N.*	one litter of
仔	(zǐ)	*N.*	offspring; baby
成活	(chéng huó)	*V.*	to survive, to be born successfully, to be born alive and to survive
动物园	(dòng wù yuán)	*N.*	zoo

（二）

白蘭： 世界上有多少面臨滅絕、需要一級保護的動物？

小麗： 多極了。據調查，中國的大熊貓、華南虎、非洲的黑猩猩、美國的北
斑鷹等等都已經面臨滅絕的境地了。

白蘭： 那麼這些國家採取了甚麼措施保護這些動物呢？

小麗： 有的國家列出國家級保護動物，讓人們特別注意；有的國家把稀少動
物送到動物園進行科學飼養，讓動物很快繁殖；還有的國家規定一些
政策，保護這些野外動物的生活環境。

白蘭： 看來，保護稀少動物現在很要緊。

問題： 世界上有些甚麼面臨滅絕的動物？ 有關國家採取了甚麼措施？

生詞

一級	（yī jí）	*N.*	of the first rank; grade one (or of top priority)
動物	（dòng wù）	*N.*	animal
大熊貓	（dà xióng māo）	*N.*	giant panda
華南虎	（huá nán hǔ）	*N.*	Indo-Chinese tiger
黑猩猩	（hēi xīng xing）	*N.*	chimpanzee
北斑鷹	（běi bān yīng）	*N.*	northern spotted owl
境地	（jìng dì）	*N.*	situation; predicament; plight
措施	（cuò shī）	*N.*	measures; method
列出	（liè chū）	*V.*	to specify, to name, to list as
國家級	（guó jiā jí）	*N.*	at the national level
稀少	（xī shǎo）	*Adj.*	rare; scarce
繁殖	（fán zhí）	*V.*	to breed; to reproduce
規定	（guī dìng）	*V.*	to regulate; to set the rule

（二）

白兰： 世界上有多少面临灭绝、需要一级保护的动物？

小丽： 多极了。据调查，中国的大熊猫、华南虎、非洲的黑猩猩、美国的北
斑鹰等等都已经面临灭绝的境地了。

白兰： 那么这些国家采取了什么措施保护这些动物呢？

小丽： 有的国家列出国家级保护动物，让人们特别注意；有的国家把稀少动
物送到动物园进行科学饲养，让动物很快繁殖；还有的国家规定一些
政策，保护这些野外动物的生活环境。

白兰： 看来，保护稀少动物现在很要紧。

问题: 世界上有些什么面临灭绝的动物？有关国家采取了什么措施？

生词

一级	(yī jí)	*N.*	of the first rank; grade one (or of top priority)
动物	(dòng wù)	*N.*	animal
大熊猫	(dà xióng māo)	*N.*	giant panda
华南虎	(huá nán hǔ)	*N.*	Indo-Chinese tiger
黑猩猩	(hēi xīng xing)	*N.*	chimpanzee
北斑鹰	(běi bān yīng)	*N.*	northern spotted owl
境地	(jìng dì)	*N.*	situation; predicament; plight
措施	(cuò shī)	*N.*	measures; method
列出	(liè chū)	*V.*	to specify, to name, to list as
国家级	(guó jiā jí)	*N.*	at the national level
稀少	(xī shǎo)	*Adj.*	rare; scarce
繁殖	(fán zhí)	*V.*	to breed; to reproduce
规定	(guī dìng)	*V.*	to regulate; to set the rule

| 野外 | (yě wài) | N. | in the wild |
| 環境 | (huán jìng) | N. | environment |

（三）

白蘭： 為甚麼每一次奧運會都有一個吉祥物？牠的作用是甚麼？

小麗： 我想吉祥物是人們美好祝願的象徵。一方面用牠來象徵奧運會召開的
喜慶，一方面用牠來祝願運動會的順利進行。

白蘭： 那下一次奧運會的吉祥物是甚麼呢？

小麗： 我還不知道。

問題： 吉祥物的作用是甚麼？

生詞

吉祥物	(jí xiáng wù)	N.	mascot
祝願	(zhù yuàn)	V.	to wish
象徵	(xiàng zhēng)	N/V.	symbol; to symbolize
喜慶	(xǐ qìng)	N/Adj.	happy event; joyous; jubilant

三、電視新聞

華南虎繁殖成功 新聞（一）

福州動物園繁殖成功的四隻華南虎現已經兩個多月了，長得活潑可愛。
華南虎是國家一級保護動物。據調查，全世界華南虎在野外不足五十
頭，比大熊貓還要稀少，面臨滅絕的境地。福州動物園在華南虎繁殖期間組
織攻關小組，對華南虎進行了科學飼養、精心管理，並堅持二十四小時晝夜
值班，終於創造出一胎四仔全部成活的好成績。

野外	(yě wài)	*N.*	in the wild
环境	(huán jìng)	*N.*	environment

（三）

白兰： 为什么每一次奥运会都有一个吉祥物？它的作用是什么？

小丽： 我想吉祥物是人们美好祝愿的象征。一方面用它来象征奥运会召开的喜庆，一方面用它来祝愿运动会的顺利进行。

白兰： 那下一次奥运会的吉祥物是什么呢？

小丽： 我还不知道。

问题: 吉祥物的作用是什么？

生词

吉祥物	(jí xiáng wù)	*N.*	mascot
祝愿	(zhù yuàn)	*V.*	to wish
象征	(xiàng zhēng)	*N/V.*	symbol; to symbolize
喜庆	(xǐ qìng)	*N/Adj.*	happy event; joyous; jubilant

三、电视新闻

华南虎繁殖成功 新闻（一）

福州动物园繁殖成功的四只华南虎现已经两个多月了，长得活泼可爱。

华南虎是国家一级保护动物。据调查，全世界华南虎在野外不足五十头，比大熊猫还要稀少，面临灭绝的境地。福州动物园在华南虎繁殖期间组织攻关小组，对华南虎进行了科学饲养、精心管理，并坚持二十四小时昼夜值班，终于创造出一胎四仔全部成活的好成绩。

生詞

非洲	(fēi zhōu)	*Place N.*	Africa
福州	(fú zhōu)	*Place N.*	provincial capital of Fujian
調查	(diào chá)	*N/V.*	survey (s), investigation; to investigate, to take a survey
不足	(bù zú)	*Adj/Adv.*	less than; insufficient to/for
頭	(tóu)	*Classifier.*	head, classifier for animals
攻關	(gōng guān)	*VO.*	to tackle key problems
值班	(zhí bān)	*VO.*	to be on duty
創造	(chuàng zào)	*V/N.*	to create; creation; to make a record of

非洲黑猩猩在北京產仔　新聞（二）

　　生活繁殖在非洲的黑猩猩第一次在寒冷的中國北京產下幼仔。

　　這隻名叫璐璐的雄性黑猩猩，是 1992年10月12號在北京動物園出生的。生下時，體重兩公斤多。由於牠的母親沒有哺育經驗，小璐璐一直由飼養員精心喂養，目前體重已有三公斤多。

生詞

寒冷	(hán lěng)	*Adj.*	bitter cold
璐璐	(lù lu)	*Personal N.*	personal name or pet name
雄性	(xióng xìng)	*N/A.*	male gender; male
體重	(tǐ zhòng)	*N.*	weight
公斤	(gōng jīn)	*Classifier.*	kilogram
哺育	(bǔ yù)	*V.*	to nurse; to feed; to nurture
經驗	(jīng yàn)	*N.*	experience
飼養員	(sì yǎng yuán)	*N.*	animal keeper
喂養	(wèi yǎng)	*V.*	to raise; to feed＝飼養

生词

非洲	(fēi zhōu)	*Place N.*	Africa
福州	(fú zhōu)	*Place N.*	provincial capital of Fujian
调查	(diào chá)	*N/V.*	survey (s), investigation; to investigate, to take a survey
不足	(bù zú)	*Adj/Adv.*	less than; insufficient to/for
头	(tóu)	*Classifier.*	head, classifier for animals
攻关	(gōng guān)	*VO.*	to tackle key problems
值班	(zhí bān)	*VO.*	to be on duty
创造	(chuàng zào)	*V/N.*	to create; creation; to make a record of

非洲黑猩猩在北京产仔 新闻（二）

生活繁殖在非洲的黑猩猩第一次在寒冷的中国北京产下幼仔。

这只名叫璐璐的雄性黑猩猩，是1992年10月12号在北京动物园出生的。生下时，体重两公斤多。由于它的母亲没有哺育经验，小璐璐一由饲养员精心喂养，目前体重已有三公斤多。

生词

寒冷	(hán lěng)	*Adj.*	bitter cold
璐璐	(lù lu)	*Personal N.*	personal name or pet name
雄性	(xióng xìng)	*N/A.*	male gender; male
体重	(tǐ zhòng)	*N.*	weight
公斤	(gōng jīn)	*Classifier.*	kilogram
哺育	(bǔ yù)	*V.*	to nurse; to feed; to nurture
经验	(jīng yàn)	*N.*	experience
饲养员	(sì yǎng yuán)	*N.*	animal keeper
喂养	(wèi yǎng)	*V.*	to raise; to feed = 饲养

四、 報紙閱讀

成都熊貓"苏苏"喜得贵子
萨翁欣然为其取名"科比"

新华社成都8月18日电（记者王文俊）国际奥林匹克运动委员会主席萨马兰奇，为在第25届奥运会开幕时出生的大熊猫"苏苏"的幼仔取名为"科比"（COBI）。

小狗科比，是25届奥林匹克运动会的吉祥物。

1992年7月26日北京时间凌晨2时，正是巴塞罗那时间7月25日20时，第25届奥林匹克运动会宣告开幕，成都动物园的大熊猫"苏苏"恰在此时顺利产下一仔。守护在一旁的成都动物园何园长和其他职工高兴地说，今天是个喜庆日子，如果让萨马兰奇主席为"苏苏"的贵子取个名字就好了。这个建议很快传到巴塞罗那。中国奥运代表团团长伍绍祖请萨马兰奇主席为刚出生的大熊猫取个名字。

8月9日上午，国家体委转来伍绍祖从巴塞罗那发回电报。

电报称：萨马兰奇欣然为刚诞生的大熊猫取名"科比"（COBI）。

成都动物园是一个保护大熊猫的有功单位。从八十年代以来，这个动物园已成功地人工繁殖大熊猫18只。

成都熊貓 "蘇蘇" 喜得貴子
薩翁欣然為其取名 "科比"

新華社成都8月18日電 （記者王文俊） 國際奧林匹克運動委員會主席薩馬蘭奇，為在第25屆奧運會開幕時出生的大熊貓"蘇蘇"的幼仔取名為"科比"(Cobi)。

小狗科比，是25屆奧林匹克運動會的吉祥物。

四、 报纸阅读

成都熊猫"苏苏"喜得贵子
萨翁欣然为其取名"科比"

新华社成都8月18日电（记者**王文俊**）国际奥林匹克运动委员会主席萨马兰奇，为在第25届奥运会开幕时出生的大熊猫"苏苏"的幼仔取名为"科比"（COBI）。

小狗科比，是25届奥林匹克运动会的吉祥物。

1992年7月26日北京时间凌晨2时，正是巴塞罗那时间7月25日20时，第25届奥林匹克运动会宣告开幕，成都动物园的大熊猫"苏苏"恰在此时顺利产下一仔。守护在一旁的成都动物园何园长和其他职工高兴地说，今天是个喜庆日子，如果让萨马兰奇主席为"苏苏"的贵子取个名字就好了。这个建议很快传到巴塞罗那。中国奥运代表团团长伍绍祖请萨马兰奇主席为刚出生的大熊猫取个名字。

8月9日上午，国家体委转来伍绍祖从巴塞罗那发回电报。

电报称：萨马兰奇欣然为刚诞生的大熊猫取名"科比"（COBI）。

成都动物园是一个保护大熊猫的有功单位。从八十年代以来，这个动物园已成功地人工繁殖大熊猫18只。

成都熊猫 "苏苏" 喜得贵子
萨翁欣然为其取名 "科比"

新华社成都8月18日电　　（记者王文俊）国际奥林匹克运动委员会主席萨马兰奇，为在第25届奥运会开幕时出生的大熊猫"苏苏"的幼仔取名为"科比"（Cobi）。

小狗科比，是25届奥林匹克运动会的吉祥物。

115

　　1992年7月26日北京時間凌晨2時，正是巴塞羅那時間7月25日20時，第25屆奧林匹克運動會宣告開幕，成都動物園的大熊貓"蘇蘇"恰在此時順利產下一仔。守護在一旁的成都動物園何園長和其他職工高興地說，今天是個喜慶日子，如果讓薩馬蘭奇主席為"蘇蘇"的貴子取個名字就好了。這個建議很快傳到巴塞羅那。中國奧運會代表團團長伍紹祖請薩馬蘭奇主席為剛出生的大熊貓取個名字。

　　8月9日上午，國家體委轉來伍紹祖從巴塞羅那發回電報。

　　電報稱：薩馬蘭奇欣然為剛誕生的大熊貓取名"科比"(Cobi)。

　　成都動物園是一個保護大熊貓的有功單位。從八十年代以來，這個動物園已成功地人工繁殖大熊貓18隻。

生詞

成都	(chéng dū)	*Place N.*	provincial capital of Sichuan
蘇蘇	(sū su)	*Personal N.*	personal name or pet name
薩翁	(sà wēng)	*N.*	personal name: Saimlech, head of International Olympic Committee＝薩馬蘭奇
貴子	(guì zǐ)	*N.*	"honorable son"
欣然	(xīn rán)	*Adv.*	gladly; happily
取名	(qǔ míng)	*VO.*	to name, to choose a name for
凌晨	(líng chén)	*N.*	early morning, before dawn
巴塞羅那	(bā sài luó nà)	*Place N.*	Barcelona
宣告	(xuān gào)	*V/N.*	to announce; announcement
恰	(qià)	*Adv.*	just; right
守護	(shǒu hù)	*V.*	to be keeping watch over, to be on (sentry) duty
職工	(zhí gōng)	*N.*	staff member
建議	(jiàn yì)	*N/V.*	suggestions; to suggest, to make a proposal

1992年7月26日北京时间凌晨2时，正是巴塞罗那时间7月25日20时，第25届奥林匹克运动会宣告开幕，成都动物园的大熊猫"苏苏"恰在此时顺利产下一仔。守护在一旁的成都动物园何园长和其他职工高兴地说，今天是个喜庆日子，如果让萨马兰奇主席为"苏苏"的贵子取个名字就好了。这个建议很快传到巴塞罗那。中国奥运会代表团团长伍绍祖请萨马兰奇主席为刚出生的大熊猫取个名字。

8月9日上午，国家体委转来伍绍祖从巴塞罗那发回电报。

电报称：萨马兰奇欣然为刚诞生的大熊猫取名"科比"(Cobi)。

成都动物园是一个保护大熊猫的有功单位。从八十年代以来，这个动物园已成功地人工繁殖大熊猫18只。

生词

成都	(chéng dū)	Place N.	provincial capital of Sichuan
苏苏	(sū su)	Personal N.	personal name or pet name
萨翁	(sà wēng)	N.	personal name: Saimlech, head of International Olympic Committee = 萨马兰奇
贵子	(guì zǐ)	N.	"honorable son"
欣然	(xīn rán)	Adv.	gladly; happily
取名	(qǔ míng)	VO.	to name, to choose a name for
凌晨	(líng chén)	N.	early morning, before dawn
巴塞罗那	(bā sài luó nà)	Place N.	Barcelona
宣告	(xuān gào)	V/N.	to announce; announcement
恰	(qià)	Adv.	just; right
守护	(shǒu hù)	V.	to be keeping watch over, to be on (sentry) duty
职工	(zhí gōng)	N.	staff member
建议	(jiàn yì)	N/V.	suggestions; to suggest, to make a proposal

傳到	(chuán dào)	*V.*	to pass on to, to convey to
伍紹祖	(wǔ shào zǔ)	*Personal N.*	the name of a person
體委	(tǐ wěi)	*Abbrev.*	sports committee＝中國體育委員會
誕生	(dàn shēng)	*V.*	to be born
有功	(yǒu gōng)	*VO.*	to have made contributions to, to have rendered service to, commendable, noteworthy
人工	(rén gōng)	*Adj/Adv.*	artificial; artificially

五、幽默小品

猩猩難看

　　小明："爸爸！姐姐上星期罵我是猩猩。"

　　爸爸："姐姐不對，為甚麼你今天才告訴我？"

　　小明："昨天我到動物園去才知道猩猩真難看！"

传到	（chuán dào）	*V.*	to pass on to, to convey to
伍绍祖	（wǔ shào zǔ）	*Personal N.*	the name of a person
体委	（tǐ wěi）	*Abbrev.*	sports committee = 中国体育委员会
诞生	（dàn shēng）	*V.*	to be born
有功	（yǒu gōng）	*VO.*	to have made contributions to, to have rendered service to, commendable, noteworthy
人工	（rén gōng）	*Adj/Adv.*	artificial; artificially

五、 幽默小品

猩猩难看

小明： "爸爸！姐姐上星期骂我是猩猩。"

爸爸： "姐姐不对，为什么你今天才告诉我？"

小明： "昨天我到动物园去才知道猩猩真难看！"

課文要點

一、常用文言詞、縮略語與慣用語

1. 據＝根據 (according to)

　　例：據調查, 中國男性吸煙者占吸煙者數的百分之八十。
　　　　According to the investigation, male smokers make up 80% of the total smokers in China.

　　　　據了解，在中國農村，一家一個孩子的人口政策很難實行。
　　　　According to what was said, the one-child policy is hard to carry out in China's rural areas.

2. 不足＝不夠 (less than)

　　例：這個建築面積不足五十平方米的小企業現在可以創匯幾千萬。
　　　　This small enterprise with its building occupying less than 50 square meters can at present generate several millions in foreign exchange earnings.

3. 產下＝生下 (give birth to)

　　例：上個月華南虎東東產下一隻幼仔。
　　　　Last month the Indo-Chinese tiger Dongdong gave birth to a baby tiger.

4. 由＝被、歸 (by)

　　例：這隻幼虎由動物園的飼養員喂養。
　　　　This baby tiger is being raised by the animal keeper of the zoo.

课文要点

一、常用文言词、缩略语与惯用语

1. 据 = 根据 (according to)

例: 据调查,中国男性吸烟者占吸烟者总数的百分之八十。
According to the investigation, male smokers make up 80% of the total smokers in China.

据了解, 在中国农村, 一家一个孩子的人口政策很难实行。
According to what was said, the one-child policy is hard to carry out in China's rural areas.

2. 不足 = 不够 (less than)

例: 这个建筑面积不足五十平方米的小企业现在可以创汇几千万。
This small enterprise with its building occupying less than 50 square meters can at present generate several millions in foreign exchange earnings.

3. 产下 = 生下 (give birth to)

例: 上个月华南虎东东产下一只幼仔。
Last month the Indo-Chinese tiger Dongdong gave birth to a baby tiger.

4. 由 = 被、归 (by)

例: 这只幼虎由动物园的饲养员喂养。
This baby tiger is being raised by the animal keeper of the zoo.

5. 欣然＝很高興地 (gladly, happily , to be delighted to)

例：該影星欣然為小黑猩猩取名"小藝"。

Said film star was delighted to name the baby chimpanzee "Xiao Yi".

6. 喜得＝高興地獲得 (to be thrilled to obtain)

例：我朋友昨天喜得貴子， 我們都向他祝賀。

My friend had a baby son yesterday. We all congratulated him.

7. 為其＝為牠（他、她） (for it, for him or her)

例：今天第一家中法合資公司成立，法國駐華大使欣然為其取名"法華第一家"。

The first Sino-Franco joint venture was founded today, the French ambassador to China happily came and gave it a name "the first joint venture of Sino-Franco".

8. 幼仔＝剛生下不久的小動物（這里指小熊貓） (the baby animal)

例：大猩猩產下幼仔不久就病了。

The gorilla got sick soon after giving birth to a baby gorilla.

9. 二時＝兩點 (two o'clock)

例：昨晚二時，聯合航空公司九五三號發生了一起空中事故。

At 2 o'clock last night, United Airlines Flight 953 had an accident in the air.

10. 恰在此時＝正好在這個時候 (right at this moment)

例：恰在此時，上海動物園的猩猩一胎產下三仔。

Just at this moment, the chimpanzee at Shanghai Zoo gave birth to triplets.

5. 欣然 = 很高兴地 (gladly, happily, to be delighted to)

例: 该影星欣然为小黑猩猩取名"小艺"。
Said film star was delighted to name the baby chimpanzee "Xiao Yi".

6. 喜得 = 高兴地获得 (to be thrilled to obtain)

例: 我朋友昨天喜得贵子，我们都向他祝贺。
My friend had a baby son yesterday. We all congratulated him.

7. 为其 = 为它（他、她）(for it, for him or her)

例: 今天第一家中法合资公司成立，法国驻华大使欣然为其取名"法华第一家"。
The first Sino-Franco joint venture was founded today, the French ambassador to China happily came and gave it a name "the first joint venture of Sino-Franco".

8. 幼仔 = 刚生下不久的小动物（这里指小熊猫）(the baby animal)

例: 大猩猩产下幼仔不久就病了。
The gorilla got sick soon after giving birth to a baby gorilla.

9. 二时 = 两点 (two o'clock)

例: 昨晚二时，联合航空公司九五三号发生了一起空中事故。
At 2 o'clock last night, United Airlines Flight 953 had an accident in the air.

10. 恰在此时 = 正好在这个时候 (right at this moment)

例: 恰在此时，上海动物园的猩猩一胎产下三仔。
Just at this moment, the chimpanzee at Shanghai Zoo gave birth to triplets.

二、常用短語

1. 據調查 (according to the investigation; according to a survey)

例： 據調查，中國政府在近期電影節期間禁演了三部電影。
According to the investigation, during a recent film festival the Chinese government banned three films.

據官方調查，中國人口到1993年11月已為13.1億。
According to an official survey, by November 1993 the population of China had reached 1.31 billion.

2. 比⋯稀少 (to be rarer as compared to)

例：據說中國的白熊比熊貓還稀少。
It is said that in China albino bears are even rarer than pandas.

世界上大熊貓比非洲黑猩猩稀少得多。
In the world, pandas are much rarer than African gorillas.

3. 面臨⋯的境地 (to be confronted with/up against the predicament or plight of)

例：現在很多動物都面臨滅絕的境地。
Many species of animals are now on the verge of extinction .

在中國，許多全民所有制的企業面臨破產的境地。
In China, many state-owned enterprises are facing the predicament of impending bankruptcy.

4. 對⋯進行了⋯（飼養、訪問等） (to carry out)

例：因為熊貓很稀少，所以動物園對現有的熊貓進行精心的飼養。
Because pandas are very rare animals, the zoos usually take extra pains in caring for the pandas they have.

二、常用短语

1. 据调查 (according to the investigation; according to a survey)

例: 据调查，中国政府在近期电影节期间禁演了三部电影。
According to the investigation, during a recent film festival the Chinese government banned three films.

据官方调查，中国人口到 1993 年 11 月已为 13.1 亿。
According to an official survey, by November 1993 the population of China had reached 1.31 billion.

2. 比…稀少 (to be rarer as compared to)

例: 据说中国的白熊比熊猫还稀少。
It is said that in China albino bears are even rarer than pandas.

世界上大熊猫比非洲黑猩猩稀少得多。
In the world, pandas are much rarer than African gorillas.

3. 面临…的境地 (to be confronted with/up against the predicament or plight of)

例: 现在很多动物都面临灭绝的境地。
Many species of animals are now on the verge of extinction .

在中国，许多全民所有制的企业面临破产的境地。
In China, many state-owned enterprises are facing the predicament of impending bankruptcy.

4. 对…进行了…（饲养、访问等） (to carry out)

例: 因为熊猫很稀少，所以动物园对现有的熊猫进行精心的饲养。
Because pandas are very rare animals, the zoos usually take extra pains in caring for the pandas they have.

美國總統克林頓6月對歐洲進行了正式訪問。

The U.S. President Clinton paid an official visit to Europe in June.

5. 創造出…的（好）成績(to make great progress in; make the best record of)

例：上個月，上海的工業生產創造了今年以來最好的成績。

Last month, industrial production in Shanghai attained its best record since the begining of the year.

這家電冰箱廠由於採取了科學管理，今年創造出了出口量達百分之四十的好成績。

Because of the adoption of scientific management, this refrigerator factory has made the best record in exporting 40% more of its products.

美国总统克林顿6月对欧洲进行了正式访问。

The U.S. President Clinton paid an official visit to Europe in June.

5. 创造出…的（好）成绩(to make great progress in; make the best record of)

例: 上个月，上海的工业生产创造了今年以来最好的成绩。

Last month, industrial production in Shanghai attained its best record since the begining of the year.

这家电冰箱厂由于采取了科学管理，今年创造出了出口量达百分之四十的好成绩。

Because of the adoption of scientific management, this refrigerator factory has made the best record in exporting 40% more of its products.

小課文

"少兒不宜" 只是招徠觀眾的招牌嗎？

一、看電視小課文、回答問題

1. 為甚麼有很多人擠在那兒買票？
2. 廣告中的 "少兒不宜" 是甚麼意思？真正的 "少兒不宜" 是甚麼意思？
3. 這個廣告說明了一個甚麼社會問題？美國有沒有這樣的問題？

二、討論

1. 你認為甚麼電影應該讓少兒看？甚麼電影應該禁止 (prohibit) 少兒看？區分成人片和少兒片有沒有必要？
2. 政府應該怎樣解決這種問題？

生詞

少兒不宜	(shào ér bù yí)	"not suitable (films) for children", parental discretion
招徠	(zhāo lái)	to drum up (business), to solicit or entice (customers into buying)
招牌	(zhāo pái)	signboard, shop sign, store front sign

小课文

"少儿不宜" 只是招徕观众的招牌吗？

一、看电视小课文、回答问题

1. 为什么有很多人挤在那儿买票？
2. 广告中的 "少儿不宜" 是什么意思？真正的 "少儿不宜" 是什么意思？
3. 这个广告说明了一个什么社会问题？美国有没有这样的问题？

二、讨论

1. 你认为什么电影应该让少儿看？什么电影应该禁止 (prohibit) 少儿看？区分成人片和少儿片有没有必要？
2. 政府应该怎样解决这种问题？

生词

少儿不宜	(shào ér bù yí)	"not suitable (films) for children", parental discretion
招徕	(zhāo lái)	to drum up (business), to solicit or entice (customers into buying)
招牌	(zhāo pái)	signboard, shop sign, store front sign

第三單元　文化新聞

第三課

中國美術館建館三十周年
中國古代蒙漢合璧書法大展

課文

一、簡介

　　中國有關藝術的新聞常常包括一些全國性的和國際性的藝術活動。這類新聞往往有自己的獨特詞彙，文學語言很多，專業性也較強。要想看懂這類新聞必須多聽、多看才行。

生詞

包括	(bāo kuò)	*V.*	to include
獨特	(dú tè)	*Adj.*	special; unique
專業性	(zhuān yè xìng)	*Adj.*	specialized; technical

第三单元　文化新闻

第三课

中国美术馆建馆三十周年
中国古代蒙汉合璧书法大展

课文

一、简介

　　中国有关艺术的新闻常常包括一些全国性的和国际性的艺术活动。这类新闻往往有自己的独特词汇，文学语言很多，专业性也较强。要想看懂这类新闻必须多听、多看才行。

生词

包括	(bāo kuò)	*V.*	to include
独特	(dú tè)	*Adj.*	special; unique
专业性	(zhuān yè xìng)	*Adj.*	specialized; technical

二、對話

（一）

于一： 你在北京的時候，去過中國美術館嗎？

齊天： 去過。那里可真是中國最具代表性的藝術殿堂。他們收藏的藝術珍品種類多，質量好。既有中國傳統的和民間的，又有西方的。

于一： 你最喜歡那里誰的畫兒？

齊天： 齊白石的傑作《牡丹》。可惜太貴了，我買不起。

問題： 齊天對中國美術館的描述是甚麼？

生詞

美術	(měi shù)	N.	fine arts (as fields of study)
美術館	(měi shù guǎn)	N.	Art Center, Museum of Fine Arts
最具	(zuì jù)	V.	to possess the greatest..., the most...
代表性	(dài biǎo xìng)	N.	characteristics
最具代表性	(zuì jù dài biǎo xìng)	VO.	to be the leading example of
殿堂	(diàn táng)	N.	palace; hall
收藏	(shōu cáng)	V.	to collect (works of art)
珍品	(zhēn pǐn)	N.	treasures, master works
傳統	(chuán tǒng)	N/Adj.	tradition; traditional
民間	(mín jiān)	N.	folk
傑作	(jié zuò)	N.	the outstanding work
齊白石	(qí bái shí)	Personal N.	Qi Baishi, great ink painter, 1863-1957
《牡丹》	(mǔ dān)	N.	peony, the name of a painting
可惜	(kě xī)	Adj.	it is a pity that

二、对话

（一）

于一： 你在北京的时候，去过中国美术馆吗？

齐天： 去过。那里可真是中国最具代表性的艺术殿堂。他们收藏的艺术珍品种类多，质量好。既有中国传统的和民间的，又有西方的。

于一： 你最喜欢那里谁的画儿？

齐天： 齐白石的杰作《牡丹》。可惜太贵了，我买不起。

问题: 齐天对中国美术馆的描述是什么？

生词

美术	(měi shù)	*N.*	fine arts (as fields of study)
美术馆	(měi shù guǎn)	*N.*	Art Center, Museum of Fine Arts
最具	(zuì jù)	*V.*	to possess the greatest..., the most...
代表性	(dài biǎo xìng)	*N.*	characteristics
最具代表性	(zuì jù dài biǎo xìng)	*VO.*	to be the leading example of
殿堂	(diàn táng)	*N.*	palace; hall
收藏	(shōu cáng)	*V.*	to collect (works of art)
珍品	(zhēn pǐn)	*N.*	treasures, master works
传统	(chuán tǒng)	*N/Adj.*	tradition; traditional
民间	(mín jiān)	*N.*	folk
杰作	(jié zuò)	*N.*	the outstanding work
齐白石	(qí bái shí)	*Personal N.*	Qi Baishi, great ink painter, 1863-1957
《牡丹》	(mǔ dān)	*N.*	peony, the name of a painting
可惜	(kě xī)	*Adj.*	it is a pity that

（二）

于一：　你喜歡中國的書法嗎？

齊天：　當然。中國的書法真是一種藝術。每次看書法家寫字都是在看他們創
　　　　作。他們寫一個字就是畫一張畫，字字有力，渾為一體。我真希望我
　　　　也甚麼時候能寫出那樣的字來。

問題：　齊天對中國書法的看法是甚麼？

生詞

書法	(shū fǎ)	N.	calligraphy (usually brush writing with Chinese brush pen and ink)
創作	(chuàng zuò)	N/V.	creation; to create
渾為一體	(hún wéi yī tǐ)	VP.	to merge into a single whole/entity（＝渾然一體）

（三）

齊天：　紐約大都會博物館是美國最大的博物館嗎？

于一：　我想是的。它已經建館一百多年了，是美國最大的國家級藝術博物
　　　　館，早就躋身於世界著名美術館之列。這個博物館是收藏世界名畫、
　　　　藝術精品最多的博物館之一。那里還有中國著名的蘇州園林。

齊天：　是嗎，那我甚麼時候一定去看看。

問題：　于一是怎麼描述紐約大都會博物館的？

（二）

于一：　你喜欢中国的书法吗？

齐天：　当然。中国的书法真是一种艺术。每次看书法家写字都是在看他们创作。他们写一个字就是画一张画，字字有力，浑为一体。我真希望我也什么时候能写出那样的字来。

问题：*齐天对中国书法的看法是什么？*

生词

书法	(shū fǎ)	*N.*	calligraphy (usually brush writing with Chinese brush pen and ink)
创作	(chuàng zuò)	*N/V.*	creation; to create
浑为一体	(hún wéi yī tǐ)	*VP.*	to merge into a single whole/entity（＝浑然一体）

（三）

齐天：　纽约大都会博物馆是美国最大的博物馆吗？

于一：　我想是的。它已经建馆一百多年了，是美国最大的国家级艺术博物馆，早就跻身于世界著名美术馆之列。这个博物馆是收藏世界名画、艺术精品最多的博物馆之一。那里还有中国著名的苏州园林。

齐天：　是吗，那我什么时候一定去看看。

问题：*于一是怎么描述纽约大都会博物馆的？*

生詞

大都會	(dà dū huì)	N.	metropolitan
博物館	(bó wù guǎn)	N.	museum
大都會博物館	(dà dū huì bó wù guǎn)	N.	the Metropolitan Museum of Art
躋身	(jī shēn)	VO.	to be ranked among, to be placed in
列	(liè)	N.	rank (s)
精品	(jīng pǐn)	N.	choice works (of artistic creation), "representative" works of highest quality
蘇州	(sū zhōu)	Place N.	Suzhou, an old, scenic city located in Jiangsu
園林	(yuán lín)	N.	garden

三、電視新聞

中國美術館建館三十周年 新聞（一）

　　被喻為藝術殿堂、國之瑰寶的中國美術館　6月17號迎來了她的三十歲生日，中國黨和國家領導人題辭祝賀。同時中國美術館藏精品特展隆重開幕。

　　中國美術館在建館三十年的歷程中受到中國黨和國家的高度重視。現在已成為中國最具代表性的國家級美術博物館，躋身於世界著名美術館之列。美術館設有收藏、保管、研究、展覽、陳列和民間美術、博物館籌備組等美術學術機構，擁有中國近代和現代美術傑作珍藏和民間美術藏品約五萬餘件。這次展出的有吳昌碩的《綠梅》、齊白石的《牡丹》、董希文的《哈薩克牧羊女》和羅東立的《父親》、楊東海的《飲水的熊》等著名老畫家和近年獲得中國美展金獎的中青年畫家的百餘幅作品。

生词

大都会	(dà dū huì)	N.	metropolitan
博物馆	(bó wù guǎn)	N.	museum
大都会博物馆	(dà dū huì bó wù guǎn)	N.	the Metropolitan Museum of Art
跻身	(jī shēn)	VO.	to be ranked among, to be placed in
列	(liè)	N.	rank (s)
精品	(jīng pǐn)	N.	choice works (of artistic creation), "representative" works of highest quality
苏州	(sū zhōu)	Place N.	Suzhou, an old, scenic city located in Jiangsu
园林	(yuán lín)	N.	garden

三、电视新闻

中国美术馆建馆三十周年 新闻（一）

　　被喻为艺术殿堂、国之瑰宝的中国美术馆 6月17号迎来了她的三十岁生日，中国党和国家领导人题辞祝贺。同时中国美术馆藏精品特展隆重开幕。

　　中国美术馆在建馆三十年的历程中受到中国党和国家的高度重视。现在已成为中国最具代表性的国家级美术博物馆，跻身于世界著名美术馆之列。美术馆设有收藏、保管、研究、展览、陈列和民间美术、博物馆筹备组等美术学术机构，拥有中国近代和现代美术杰作珍藏和民间美术藏品约五万余件。这次展出的有吴昌硕的《绿梅》、齐白石的《牡丹》、董希文的《哈萨克牧羊女》和罗东立的《父亲》、杨东海的《饮水的熊》等著名老画家和近年获得中国美展金奖的中青年画家的百余幅作品。

生詞

建館	(jiàn guǎn)	VO.	to establish or to open a hall/a gallery/a public building
喻為	(yù wéi)	VP.	to be referred to as, to be likened to
國之瑰寶	(guó zhī guī bǎo)	NP.	national treasures (art works, antiquities, masterpices,etc.)
迎來	(yíng lái)	V.	to welcome; to meet
領導人	(lǐng dǎo rén)	N.	leaders
題辭	(tí cí)	VO.	to inscribe, to write a few words of commemoration
藏	(cáng)	V.	to collect, to hold (of a museum's collection)
特展	(tè zhǎn)	N.	a special exhibition
隆重	(lóng zhòng)	Adj/Adv.	impressive, impressive and solemn, ceremonious; ceremoniously, solemnly
歷程	(lì chéng)	N.	the course of, the process of
高度	(gāo dù)	N.	high degree of
重視	(zhòng shì)	V.	to place emphasis on, to take seriously, to devote much attention to, to value, to attach importance to
設有	(shè yǒu)	V.	to include within it, incorporate, to have established within it...
保管	(bǎo guǎn)	V/N.	to store, to preserve; storage, preservation
展覽	(zhǎn lǎn)	N/V.	exhibition; to exhbit
陳列	(chén liè)	V.	to display; to show
民間美術	(mín jiān měi shù)	NP.	folk art
籌備組	(chóu bèi zǔ)	N.	preparatory committee
學術	(xué shù)	Adj.	academic
擁有	(yōng yǒu)	V.	to possess

生词

建馆	(jiàn guǎn)	*VO.*	to establish or to open a hall/a gallery/a public building
喻为	(yù wéi)	*VP.*	to be referred to as, to be likened to
国之瑰宝	(guó zhī guī bǎo)	*NP.*	national treasures (art works, antiquities, masterpices,etc.)
迎来	(yíng lái)	*V.*	to welcome; to meet
领导人	(lǐng dǎo rén)	*N.*	leaders
题辞	(tí cí)	*VO.*	to inscribe, to write a few words of commemoration
藏	(cáng)	*V.*	to collect, to hold (of a museum's collection)
特展	(tè zhǎn)	*N.*	a special exhibition
隆重	(lóng zhòng)	*Adj/Adv.*	impressive, impressive and solemn, ceremonious; ceremoniously, solemnly
历程	(lì chéng)	*N.*	the course of, the process of
高度	(gāo dù)	*N.*	high degree of
重视	(zhòng shì)	*V.*	to place emphasis on, to take seriously, to devote much attention to, to value, to attach importance to
设有	(shè yǒu)	*V.*	to include within it, incorporate, to have established within it...
保管	(bǎo guǎn)	*V/N.*	to store, to preserve; storage, preservation
展览	(zhǎn lǎn)	*N/V.*	exhibition; to exhbit
陈列	(chén liè)	*V.*	to display; to show
民间美术	(mín jiān měi shù)	*NP.*	folk art
筹备组	(chóu bèi zǔ)	*N.*	preparatory committee
学术	(xué shù)	*Adj.*	academic
拥有	(yōng yǒu)	*V.*	to possess

珍藏	(zhēn cáng)	*V.*	to collect (valuable, rare object d'art)
吳昌碩	(wú chāng shuò)	*Personal N.*	Wu Changshuo, great ink painter, 1844-1927
《綠梅》	(lù méi)	*N.*	Green Plum blossom, the name of the art work
董希文	(dǒng xī wén)	*Personal N.*	Dong Xiwen, a well known professor of oil painting and artist, Central Academy of Fine Arts
哈薩克	(hā sā kè)	*N.*	Kazak
牧羊女	(mù yáng nǚ)	*N.*	herd woman
羅中立	(luó zhōng lì)	*Personal N.*	Luo Zhongli, a well known Sichuanese oil painter, 1950-
楊東海	(yáng dōng hǎi)	*Personal N.*	Yang Donghai, a well known artist
飲水	(yǐn shuǐ)	*VO.*	to drink water＝喝水
熊	(xióng)	*N.*	bear

中國古代蒙漢合璧書法大展 新聞（二）

　　中國古代蒙古族領袖成吉思汗箴言蒙漢合璧書法大展6月16號在北京民族文化宮正式展出。

　　這次大展由中國新安蒙大展組委會主辦。參展的作品在書法整體結構上突破了書法藝術歷來單一文字的傳統模式，兩種文字的書法各顯技藝，同時又渾為一體，相得益彰。展出薈萃了中國二十九個省區書法名家的精品。

生詞

古代	(gǔ dài)	*N.*	ancient time
蒙漢	(měng hàn)	*NP.*	Mongolian and Han

珍藏	(zhēn cáng)	*V.*	to collect (valuable, rare object d'art)
吴昌硕	(wú chāng shuò)	*Personal N.*	Wu Changshuo, great ink painter, 1844-1927
《绿梅》	(lǜ méi)	*N.*	Green Plum blossom, the name of the art work
董希文	(dǒng xī wén)	*Personal N.*	Dong Xiwen, a well known professor of oil painting and artist, Central Academy of Fine Arts
哈萨克	(hā sā kè)	*N.*	Kazak
牧羊女	(mù yáng nǚ)	*N.*	herd woman
罗中立	(luó zhōng lì)	*Personal N.*	Luo Zhongli, a well known Sichuanese oil painter, 1950-
杨东海	(yáng dōng hǎi)	*Personal N.*	Yang Donghai, a well known artist
饮水	(yǐn shuǐ)	*VO.*	to drink water = 喝水
熊	(xióng)	*N.*	bear

中国古代蒙汉合璧书法大展 新闻（二）

中国古代蒙古族领袖成吉思汗箴言蒙汉合璧书法大展6月16号在北京民族文化宫正式展出。

这次大展由中国新安蒙大展组委会主办。参展的作品在书法整体结构上突破了书法艺术历来单一文字的传统模式，两种文字的书法各显技艺，同时又浑为一体，相得益彰。展出荟萃了中国二十九个省区书法名家的精品。

生词

古代	(gǔ dài)	*N.*	ancient time
蒙汉	(měng hàn)	*NP.*	Mongolian and Han

合璧	(hé bì)	*VO.*	to blend together harmoniously, complementary and combined or blended very well together
大展	(dà zhǎn)	*N.*	major exhibition
蒙古族	(měng gǔ zú)	*N.*	Mongolian nationality
領袖	(lǐng xiù)	*N.*	leader
成吉思汗	(chéng jí sī hàn)	*Personal N*	Jenghiz Khan 1167?-1227, unifier of Mongols and great conquerer (whose conquests included all of central Asia and North China)
箴言	(zhēn yán)	*N.*	admonition; a type of didactic literary composition
民族	(mín zú)	*N.*	nationality
文化宮	(wén huà gōng)	*N.*	the cultural palace
組委會	(zǔ wěi huì)	*Abbrev.*	executive committee＝組織委員會
參展	(cān zhǎn)	*VO.*	to be included in the exhibition
整體結構	(zhěng tǐ jié gòu)	*NP.*	the overall pattern, the overall framework
模式	(mó shì)	*N.*	the pattern
各顯技藝	(gè xiǎn jì yì)	*VP.*	each manifesting its own (special) techniques
相得益彰	(xiāng dé yì zhāng)	*Idiom.*	each setting off (complementing) the other to best advantage
薈萃	(huì cuì)	*V.*	to gather the most outstanding ones together

合璧	(hé bì)	VO.	to blend together harmoniously, complementary and combined or blended very well together
大展	(dà zhǎn)	N.	major exhibition
蒙古族	(měng gǔ zú)	N.	Mongolian nationality
领袖	(lǐng xiù)	N.	leader
成吉思汗	(chéng jí sī hàn)	Personal N.	Jenghiz Khan 1167?-1227, unifier of Mongols and great conquerer (whose conquests included all of central Asia and North China)
箴言	(zhēn yán)	N.	admonition; a type of didactic literary composition
民族	(mín zú)	N.	nationality
文化宫	(wén huà gōng)	N.	the cultural palace
组委会	(zǔ wěi huì)	Abbrev.	executive committee = 组织委员会
参展	(cān zhǎn)	VO.	to be included in the exhibition
整体结构	(zhěng tǐ jié gòu)	NP.	the overall pattern, the overall framework
模式	(mó shì)	N.	the pattern
各显技艺	(gè xiǎn jì yì)	VP.	each manifesting its own (special) techniques
相得益彰	(xiāng dé yì zhāng)	Idiom.	each setting off (complementing) the other to best advantage
荟萃	(huì cuì)	V.	to gather the most outstanding ones together

四、報紙閱讀

國際中國書畫博覽會將舉行

《國際中國書畫博覽會》定於 1993年10月16日在北京舉行。博覽會分為 12項展覽、3項大獎賽，內容包括：中國古代書畫珍品展、中國已故當代書畫大師作品展、 現代中國書畫精品展、中外名人書畫展、中國文房四寶、金石篆刻展、中國美術圖書展、國際中國書畫裝裱藝術大獎賽展等。

国际中国书画博览会将举行

《国际中国书画博览会》定于1993年10月16日在北京举行。博览会分为12项展览、3项大奖赛，内容包括：中国古代书画珍品展、中国已故当代书画大师作品展、现代中国书画精品展、中外名人书画展、中国文房四宝、金石篆刻展、中国美术图书展、国际中国书画装裱艺术大奖赛展等。 （京生）

生詞

書畫	(shū huà)	NP.	paintings and calligraphy
博覽會	(bó lǎn huì)	N.	international exposition, exhibition
已故	(yǐ gù)	Adj.	late (used to refer to someone who has passed away)
當代	(dāng dài)	N.	modern time; contemporary
大師	(dà shī)	N.	master
作品	(zuò pǐn)	N.	(artistic or literary) works
文房四寶	(wén fáng sì bǎo)	NP.	the four precious things in a Chinese study (紙 paper, 墨 ink, 筆 brushes, 硯 inkstone, inkslab for grinding and mixing ink)
金石篆刻	(jīn shí zhuàn kè)	NP.	metal and stone inscriptions, inscriptions on ancient bronzes and stone tablets

四、报纸阅读

国际中国书画博览会将举行

《国际中国书画博览会》定于1993年10月16日在北京举行。博览会分为 12项展览、3项大奖赛，内容包括：中国古代书画珍品展、中国已故当代书画大师作品展、现代中国书画精品展、中外名人书画展、中国文房四宝、金石篆刻展、中国美术图书展、国际中国书画装裱艺术大奖赛展等。

国际中国书画博览会将举行

《国际中国书画博览会》定于1993年10月16日在北京举行。博览会分为12项展览、3项大奖赛，内容包括：中国古代书画珍品展、中国已故当代书画大师作品展、现代中国书画精品展、中外名人书画展、中国文房四宝、金石篆刻展、中国美术图书展、国际中国书画装裱艺术大奖赛展等。 （京生）

生词

书画	(shū huà)	NP.	paintings and calligraphy
博览会	(bó lǎn huì)	N.	international exposition, exhibition
已故	(yǐ gù)	Adj.	late (used to refer to someone who has passed away)
当代	(dāng dài)	N.	modern time; contemporary
大师	(dà shī)	N.	master
作品	(zuò pǐn)	N.	(artistic or literary) works
文房四宝	(wén fáng sì bǎo)	NP.	the four precious things in a Chinese study (纸 paper, 墨 ink, 笔 brushes, 砚 inkstone, inkslab for grinding and mixing ink)
金石篆刻	(jīn shí zhuàn kè)	NP.	metal and stone inscriptions, inscriptions on ancient bronzes and stone tablets

| 篆刻 | (zhuàn kè) | *V/N.* | to carve, seal carving |
| 裝裱 | (zhuāng biǎo) | *VP.* | to mount and to frame |

五、幽默小品

何須麻煩

老林從口袋裡拿出一只香蕉，連皮吃了。

老李：「你吃香蕉為甚麼不先剝皮？」

老林：「我早就知道裡面是甚麼了，何必再剝開來看，那多麻煩呢！」

篆刻	(zhuàn kè)	*V/N.*	to carve, seal carving
装裱	(zhuāng biǎo)	*VP.*	to mount and to frame

五、幽默小品

何须麻烦

老林从口袋里拿出一只香蕉，连皮吃了。

老李："你吃香蕉为什么不先剥皮？"

老林："我早就知道里面是什么了，何必再剥开来看，那多麻烦呢！"

課文要點

一、常用文言詞、縮略語與慣用語

1. 餘＝多 (more than)

　例：在野外的華南虎只有五十餘頭。
　　　There are only some fifty Indo-Chinese tigers left in the wild.

2. 約＝大約 (about, approximately, approximate)

　例：美術館建館約六十餘年。
　　　The Hall of Fine Arts is about sixty years old.

3. 喻為＝說成是 (in a manner of speaking; may be said to be)

　例：她畫的畫被喻為國寶。
　　　The paintings she painted are considered as national treasures.

4. 歷程＝經歷的過程 (the course of)

　例：這個影星的成長歷程說明了知識與社會實際需要結合的重要性。
　　　The entire course of that film star growing up demonstrated the importance of combining knowledge with the actual needs of society.

5. 參展＝參加展覽 (to be included in an/the exhibition of)

　例：參展的民間作品約一百餘件。
　　　Over 100 folk art works were included in the exhibition.

课文要点

一、常用文言词、缩略语与惯用语

1. 余 = 多 (more than)

   例: 在野外的华南虎只有五十余头。
   There are only some fifty Indo-Chinese tigers left in the wild.

2. 约 = 大约 (about, approximately, approximate)

   例: 美术馆建馆约六十余年。
   The Hall of Fine Arts is about sixty years old.

3. 喻为 = 说成是 (in a manner of speaking; may be said to be)

   例: 她画的画被喻为国宝。
   The paintings she painted are considered as national treasures.

4. 历程 = 经历的过程 (the course of)

   例: 这个影星的成长历程说明了知识与社会实际需要结合的重要性。
   The entire course of that film star growing up demonstrated the importance of combining knowledge with the actual needs of society.

5. 参展 = 参加展览 (to be included in an/the exhibition of)

   例: 参展的民间作品约一百余件。
   Over 100 folk art works were included in the exhibition.

6. 渾為一體＝不可分割 (＝渾然一體)(a unified entity)

例：他的畫將中西畫法渾為一體。
His paintings combine East and West to form a unified entity.

7. 相得益彰＝互相映襯 (to complement)、對比，因此更加明顯 (to bring out the best in each other)

例：文化可以使不同民族的文化相得益彰。
Exchanges enable people from different ethnic backgrounds to bring out the best in each other.

二、常用短語

1. …被喻為…(to be considered as; to be referred to as)

例：大熊貓是世界上的珍貴動物，也被喻為國寶。
China's pandas are rare animals in the world; they are considered a national treasure.

中央美術館收藏了被喻為國畫之魂的齊白石書畫三百餘幅。
China's Central Musem of Fine Arts has collected and is holding more than 300 works of calligraphy and painting by Qi Baishi, whose works are commonly referred to as "the soul of Chinese Ink Painting."

2. 在…的歷程中 (in the course of)

例：在十多年畫畫的歷程中，這位藝術家起早睡晚，日日堅持創作，終於有了自己獨特的風格。
In the course of more than 10 years of painting, this artist worked hard day and night and finally achieved his own unique style of painting.

6. 浑为一体 = 不可分割 （ = 浑然一体）(a unified entity)

例： 他的画将中西画法浑为一体。

His paintings combine East and West to form a unified entity.

7. 相得益彰 = 互相映衬 (to complement)、 对比， 因此更加明显 (to bring out the best in each other)

例： 文化可以使不同民族的文化相得益彰。

Exchanges enable people from different ethnic backgrounds to bring out the best in each other.

二、 常用短语

1. ⋯被喻为⋯ (to be considered as; to be referred to as)

例： 大熊猫是世界上的珍贵动物， 也被喻为国宝。

China's pandas are rare animals in the world; they are considered a national treasure.

中央美术馆收藏了被喻为国画之魂的齐白石书画三百余幅。

China's Central Musem of Fine Arts has collected and is holding more than 300 works of calligraphy and painting by Qi Baishi, whose works are commonly referred to as "the soul of Chinese Ink Painting."

2. 在⋯的历程中 (in the course of)

例： 在十多年画画的历程中， 这位艺术家起早睡晚， 日日坚持创作， 终于有了自己独特的风格。

In the course of more than 10 years of painting, this artist worked hard day and night and finally achieved his own unique style of painting.

在建黨十年的歷程中，印尼專業集團取得了很大的成績。

In the course of 10 years establishment, the Indonesia Special Trade Incorporation has made great progress.

3. …迎來了…(to face, to see the arrival of)

例：大連又迎來了一個新的春天。

Dalian once again witnessed the arrival of a new spring.

華盛頓美術館迎來了她第六十個生日，全國著名的藝術界人士都寫信或題詞向她祝賀。

The Museum of Fine Arts in Washington witnessed its 60th birthday; notables from artistic circles all expressed their wishes by sending a letter or an inscription.

4. …隆重開幕＝拉開帷幕 (to have a grand opening, to ceremoniously commence)

例：全國經濟發展研究會在上海隆重開幕。

The National Association for Research on Economic Development opened in Shanghai with an impressive ceremony.

第三十九屆威尼斯世界電影節今天在威尼斯隆重開幕。參加烏爾提杯角逐的共有60部電影。

The 39th Venice International Film Festival officially opened today. There will be 60 films competing for theInternational Urti Cup.

5. …受到…的重視 (to be taken seriously, to be highly valued, to receive a lot of attention)

例：中國的民間藝術很多，大多沒有受到應有的重視。

There are many kinds of folk arts in China, few of which, however, receive the attention that they deserve.

在建党十年的历程中，印尼专业集团取得了很大的成绩。

In the course of 10 years establishment, the Indonesia Special Trade Incorporation has made great progress.

3. …迎来了…(to face, to see the arrival of)

    例：大连又迎来了一个新的春天。

    Dalian once again witnessed the arrival of a new spring.

    华盛顿美术馆迎来了她第六十个生日，全国著名的艺术界人士都写信或题词向她祝贺。

    The Museum of Fine Arts in Washington witnessed its 60th birthday; notables from artistic circles all expressed their wishes by sending a letter or an inscription.

4. …隆重开幕 = 拉开帷幕 (to have a grand opening, to ceremoniously commence)

    例：全国经济发展研究会在上海隆重开幕。

    The National Association for Research on Economic Development opened in Shanghai with an impressive ceremony.

    第三十九届威尼斯世界电影节今天在威尼斯隆重开幕。参加乌尔提杯角逐的共有六十部电影。

    The 39th Venice International Film Festival officially opened today. There will be 60 films competing for the International Urti Cup.

5. …受到…的重视 (to be taken seriously, to be highly valued, to receive a lot of attention)

    例：中国的民间艺术很多，大多没有受到应有的重视。

    There are many kinds of folk arts in China, few of which, however, receive the attention that they deserve.

像這樣的民間企業，資金少、技術差，很少受到政府的重視。
The local enterprises like these, generally lacking both funding and technology, are rarely taken seriously by the government.

6. 躋身於…之列 (to be ranked among)

例：這個藝術家很早就躋身於名畫家之列。
This artist was long since ranked among the famous artists.

在二十年創辦企業的歷程中，他採取科學管理，精心辦業，終於使他的公司躋身於世界大公司之列。
During the course of 20 years of managing the enterprise, he has adopted a system of scientific management and has carefully handled the business. As a result of this, his company finally grew to be numbered among the largest in the world.

7. 突破…模式 (to break loose from the pattern of, to suddenly transform/reverse the pattern[s] of, to depart from the patterns of)

例：他的表現手法完全突破了傳統的西方模式。
His way of expressing himself has completely broken away from the traditional western patterns.

王力的語言學理論完全突破了美國19世紀的結構論模式。
The linguistic theory by Wang Li completely transformed the pattern of the structural theory in 19th century America.

像这样的民间企业，资金少、技术差，很少受到政府的重视。

The local enterprises like these, generally lacking both funding and technology, are rarely taken seriously by the government.

6. 跻身于…之列 (to be ranked among)

例：　这个艺术家很早就跻身于名画家之列。

This artist was long since ranked among the famous artists.

在二十年创办企业的历程中，他采取科学管理，精心办业，终于使他的公司跻身于世界大公司之列。

During the course of 20 years of managing the enterprise, he has adopted a system of scientific management and has carefully handled the business. As a result of this, his company finally grew to be numbered among the largest in the world.

7. 突破…模式 (to break loose from the pattern of, to suddenly transform/reverse the pattern[s] of, to depart from the patterns of)

例：　他的表现手法完全突破了传统的西方模式。

His way of expressing himself has completely broken away from the traditional western patterns.

王力的语言学理论完全突破了美国19世纪的结构论模式。

The linguistic theory by Wang Li completely transformed the pattern of the structural theory in 19th century America.

135

第三單元　文化新聞

第四課

髮繡

課文

一、電視新聞

髮繡

　　人類無奇不有，用頭髮繡成人像，可以說是奇中之奇。素描是每個畫家的基本功，但以素描為藍本，再用頭髮將人像繡到絲綢錦緞乃至布匹上就不是每個畫家所擁有的技藝了。他—中國浙江省溫州市人像研究所所長魏竸先先生就擁有這份神奇的創造功力。

　　魏竸先早年就讀於中國南京藝術學院美術系，畢業以後一直從事於水彩畫和刺繡的創作與研究。他的水彩畫清新明麗，刺繡針法嚴謹，色彩斑爛。他與人合作的巨幅彩繡《清明上河圖》可以說是他刺繡生涯中的輝煌巨作。這幅長達十餘米的作品將各種針法和絲線的功能發揮得淋漓盡致。他的作品曾榮獲中國工藝美術百花獎創作大獎，但他並不滿足於這些。他記得幾個世紀以前曾經有人用頭髮來繡樓台亭閣、花鳥魚蟲，那麼能不能來繡人物肖像呢？為此，他買來縷縷青絲，用水洗滌，用醋浸泡，晾乾以後就開始在緞面上刺繡了起來。無數個日日夜夜他就這樣坐在工作台前飛針走線，苦心揣摩。終於，他成功了。成了中國第一位用頭髮刺繡現代人物肖像的藝術家。

第三单元　文化新闻

第四课

发绣

课文

一、电视新闻

发绣

人类无奇不有，用头发绣成人像，可以说是奇中之奇。素描是每个画家的基本功，但以素描为蓝本，再用头发将人像绣到丝绸锦缎乃至布匹上就不是每个画家所拥有的技艺了。他—中国浙江省温州市人像研究所所长魏竞先先生就拥有这份神奇的创造功力。

魏竞先早年就读于中国南京艺术学院美术系，毕业以后一直从事于水彩画和刺绣的创作与研究。他的水彩画清新明丽，刺绣针法严谨，色彩斑斓。他与人合作的巨幅彩绣《清明上河图》可以说是他刺绣生涯中的辉煌巨作。这幅长达十余米的作品将各种针法和丝线的功能发挥得淋漓尽致。他的作品曾荣获中国工艺美术百花奖创作大奖，但他并不满足于这些。他记得几个世纪以前曾经有人用头发来绣楼台亭阁、花鸟鱼虫，那么能不能来绣人物肖像呢？为此，他买来缕缕青丝，用水洗涤，用醋浸泡，晾干以后就开始在缎面上刺绣了起来。无数个日日夜夜他就这样坐在工作台前飞针走线，苦心揣摩。终于，他成功了。成了中国第一位用头发刺绣现代人物肖像的艺术家。

他製成的髮繡肖像天然色澤，立體感強，形象逼真，保存經久，被人們譽為"東方一絕"。幾年來，他創作了眾多的現代名人肖像髮繡：郭沫若、戴高樂、齊白石、畢加索、貝多芬、諾貝爾、愛因斯坦、英國女王、荷蘭女王，一個個維妙維肖，栩栩如生。他為各國領導人和王室成員繡的肖像精品又被當作國禮贈送給了他們本人。為此，黛安娜王妃給予了他高度評價，有的國家領導人還寄來了熱情洋溢的親筆信。又是一個近半年的時間，他精心繡製了中國領導人鄧小平的肖像，並托人敬獻給了本人，表達了他對中國這位改革開放總設計師的深深敬意。

現在，他正在指導學生繡歷代美國總統肖像，準備赴美國舉辦髮繡展覽，為此，他被人們譽為"髮繡外交家"。

生詞

髮繡	(fǎ xiù)	N.	embroidery with hair
人像	(rén xiàng)	N.	portrait
奇中之奇	(qí zhōng zhī qí)	Idiom.	the strangest of the strange
素描	(sù miáo)	N/V.	sketch; to sketch
基本功	(jī běn gōng)	N.	basic skill(s), the essential technique(s)
藍本	(lán běn)	N.	the original version, chief source (upon which later work was based)
絲	(sī)	N.	silk fibers
綢	(chóu)	N.	silk fabric, woven silk
錦	(jǐn)	N.	a rich fabric with raised designs woven or embroidered into it
緞	(duàn)	N.	silk fabric woven in thicker weave with lustrous face and dull back
絲綢錦緞	(sī chóu jǐn duàn)	NP.	silks and brocades
布匹	(bù pǐ)	N.	fabric, cloth
溫州	(wēn zhōu)	Place N.	major coastal city, cultural center in

他制成的发绣肖像天然色泽，立体感强，形象逼真，保存经久，被人们誉为"东方一绝"。几年来，他创作了众多的现代名人肖像发绣：郭沫若、戴高乐、齐白石、毕加索、贝多芬、诺贝尔、爱因斯坦、英国女王、荷兰女王，一个个维妙维肖，栩栩如生。他为各国领导人和王室成员绣的肖像精品又被当作国礼赠送给了他们本人。为此，黛安娜王妃给予了他高度评价，有的国家领导人还寄来了热情洋溢的亲笔信。又是一个近半年的时间，他精心绣制了中国领导人邓小平的肖像，并托人敬献给了本人，表达了他对中国这位改革开放总设计师的深深敬意。

现在，他正在指导学生绣历代美国总统肖像，准备赴美国举办发绣展览，为此，他被人们誉为"发绣外交家"。

生词

发绣	(fǎ xiù)	N.	embroidery with hair
人像	(rén xiàng)	N.	portrait
奇中之奇	(qí zhōng zhī qí)	Idiom.	the strangest of the strange
素描	(sù miáo)	N/V.	sketch; to sketch
基本功	(jī běn gōng)	N.	basic skill(s), the essential technique(s)
蓝本	(lán běn)	N.	the original version, chief source (upon which later work was based)
丝	(sī)	N.	silk fibers
绸	(chóu)	N.	silk fabric, woven silk
锦	(jǐn)	N.	a rich fabric with raised designs woven or embroidered into it
缎	(duàn)	N.	silk fabric woven in thicker weave with lustrous face and dull back
丝绸锦缎	(sī chóu jǐn duàn)	NP.	silks and brocades
布匹	(bù pǐ)	N.	fabric, cloth
温州	(wēn zhōu)	Place N.	major coastal city, cultural center in

			southern Zhejiang province, China
神奇	(shén qí)	*Adj.*	wondrous, amazing, magical, miraculous
功力	(gōng lì)	*N.*	capability, skill
就讀於	(jiù dú yú)	*VP.*	to go to school at
從事於	(cóng shì yú)	*VP.*	to follow the occupation of, to be engaged in, to pursue a career in
水彩畫	(shuǐ cǎi huà)	*N.*	watercolor painting(s)
刺繡	(cì xiu)	*V/N.*	to embroider, embroidery
清新明麗	(qīng xīn míng lì)	*Idiom.*	to be fresh and (luminously) beautiful
針法	(zhēn fǎ)	*N.*	needle work
嚴謹	(yán jǐn)	*Adj.*	tight and well-knit; rigorous, strict (approach to learning, research, etc.)
色彩斑斕	(sè cǎi bān làn)	*Idiom.*	richly colored, full of many rich shades and hues
生涯	(shēng yá)	*N.*	career
輝煌	(huī huáng)	*Adj.*	brilliant, glorious, splendid
絲線	(sī xiàn)	*N.*	silk thread
巨作	(jù zuò)	*Abbrev.*	magnum opus, monumental creation, landmark work＝巨大的作品
發揮	(fā huī)	*V.*	to bring into play, to give free rein to; to develop, to bring into full play
淋漓盡致	(lín lí jìn zhì)	*Idiom.*	thoroughly, most vividly; to greatest effect
工藝美術	(gōng yì měi shù)	*NP.*	arts and crafts
百花獎	(bǎi huā jiǎng)	*N.*	the One Hundred Flower Award
滿足於	(mǎn zú yú)	*VP.*	to be satisfied with
世紀	(shì jì)	*N.*	century
樓台亭閣	(lóu tái tíng gé)	*NP.*	buildings and pavilions (implicitly two storied)
肖像	(xiāo xiàng)	*N.*	portrait (painted or drawn), portraiture
縷縷青絲	(lǚ lǚ qīng sī)	*NP.*	many tresses of black hair (long black

			southern Zhejiang province, China
神奇	(shén qí)	*Adj.*	wondrous, amazing, magical, miraculous
功力	(gōng lì)	*N.*	capability, skill
就读于	(jiù dú yú)	*VP.*	to go to school at
从事于	(cóng shì yú)	*VP.*	to follow the occupation of, to be engaged in, to pursue a career in
水彩画	(shuǐ cǎi huà)	*N.*	watercolor painting(s)
刺绣	(cì xiù)	*V/N.*	to embroider, embroidery
清新明丽	(qīng xīn míng lì)	*Idiom.*	to be fresh and (luminously) beautiful
针法	(zhēn fǎ)	*N.*	needle work
严谨	(yán jǐn)	*Adj.*	tight and well-knit; rigorous, strict (approach to learning, research, etc.)
色彩斑斓	(sè cǎi bān làn)	*Idiom.*	richly colored, full of many rich shades and hues
生涯	(shēng yá)	*N.*	career
辉煌	(huī huáng)	*Adj.*	brilliant, glorious, splendid
丝线	(sī xiàn)	*N.*	silk thread
巨作	(jù zuò)	*Abbrev.*	magnum opus, monumental creation, landmark work = 巨大的作品
发挥	(fā huī)	*V.*	to bring into play, to give free rein to; to develop, to bring into full play
淋漓尽致	(lín lí jìn zhì)	*Idiom.*	thoroughly, most vividly; to greatest effect
工艺美术	(gōng yì měi shù)	*NP.*	arts and crafts
百花奖	(bǎi huā jiǎng)	*N.*	the One Hundred Flower Award
满足于	(mǎn zú yú)	*VP.*	to be satisfied with
世纪	(shì jì)	*N.*	century
楼台亭阁	(lóu tái tíng gé)	*NP.*	buildings and pavilions (implicitly two storied)
肖像	(xiāo xiàng)	*N.*	portrait (painted or drawn), portraiture
缕缕青丝	(lǚ lǚ qīng sī)	*NP.*	many tresses of black hair (long black

			locks of women's hair)
洗滌	(xǐ dí)	*V.*	to wash; to cleanse
醋	(cù)	*N.*	vinegar
浸泡	(jìn pào)	*V.*	to soak
晾乾	(liàng gān)	*V.*	to dry by airing, to hang out to dry, to dry in the sun
飛針走線	(fēi zhēn zǒu xiàn)	*Idiom.*	"to make the needle and thread fly," to do needlework very deftly and rapidly
揣摩	(chuǎi mó)	*V.*	to try to figure out; to arrive at a deep understanding of something, to puzzle out
苦心揣摩	(kǔ xīn chuǎi mó)	*Idiom.*	(here) to painstakingly progress through trial and error
製成	(zhì chéng)	*V.*	to make, to finish
天然色澤	(tiān rán sè zé)	*NP.*	natural color and sheen
立體感	(lì tǐ gǎn)	*N.*	the sense of three-dimensional depth
形象逼真	(xíng xiàng bī zhēn)	*VP.*	image(s) is /are true to life, lifelike in shape and form
保存	(bǎo cún)	*V/N.*	to preserve; preservation
經久	(jīng jiǔ)	*Adj.*	durable, long-lasting
譽為	(yù wéi)	*VP.*	to be renowned as famous for; to be noted for, to be praised as
東方一絕	(dōng fāng yī jué)	*NP.*	something unique to the orient
郭沫若	(guō mò ruò)	*Personal N.*	a prominent Chinese intellectual/writer/political activist
戴高樂	(dài gāo lè)	*Personal N.*	Charles De Gaulle (1890-1970) French general and statesman, first president of the Fifth Republic
畢加索	(bì jiā suǒ)	*Personal N.*	Pablo Picasso (1881-1973) Catalonian painter, sulptor, graphic artist who lived and worked in France after 1900
貝多芬	(bèi duō fēn)	*Personal N.*	Ludwig van Beethoven (1770-1827)

			locks of women's hair)
洗涤	(xǐ dí)	V.	to wash; to cleanse
醋	(cù)	N.	vinegar
浸泡	(jìn pào)	V.	to soak
晾干	(liàng gān)	V.	to dry by airing, to hang out to dry, to dry in the sun
飞针走线	(fēi zhēn zǒu xiàn)	Idiom.	"to make the needle and thread fly," to do needlework very deftly and rapidly
揣摩	(chuǎi mó)	V.	to try to figure out; to arrive at a deep understanding of something, to puzzle out
苦心揣摩	(kǔ xīn chuǎi mó)	Idiom.	(here) to painstakingly progress through trial and error
制成	(zhì chéng)	V.	to make, to finish,
天然色泽	(tiān rán sè zé)	NP.	natural color and sheen
立体感	(lì tǐ gǎn)	N.	the sense of three-dimensional depth
形象逼真	(xíng xiàng bī zhēn)	VP.	image(s) is /are true to life, lifelike in shape and form
保存	(bǎo cún)	V/N.	to preserve; preservation
经久	(jīng jiǔ)	Adj.	durable, long-lasting
誉为	(yù wéi)	VP.	to be renowned as famous for; to be noted for, to be praised as
东方一绝	(dōng fāng yī jué)	NP.	something unique to the orient
郭沫若	(guō mò ruò)	Personal N.	a prominent Chinese intellectual/writer/political activist
戴高乐	(dài gāo lè)	Personal N.	Charles De Gaulle (1890-1970) French general and statesman, first president of the Fifth Republic
毕加索	(bì jiā suǒ)	Personal N.	Pablo Picasso (1881-1973) Catalonian painter, sulptor, graphic artist who lived and worked in France after 1900
贝多芬	(bèi duō fēn)	Personal N.	Ludwig van Beethoven (1770-1827)

			German composer
諾貝爾	(nuò bèi ěr)	*Personal N.*	Alfred Bernhard Nobel (1833-1896), Swedish inventor of dynamite and other explosives, founder and legator of the Nobel Prizes
愛因斯坦	(ài yīn sī tǎn)	*Personal N.*	Albert Einstein (1879-1955), German-born and raised physicist, discovered law of relativity, Nobel prize winner
維妙維肖	(wéi miào wéi xiāo)	*Idiom.*	remarkably true to life
栩栩如生	(xǔ xǔ rú shēng)	*Idiom.*	striking and lifelike
王室成員	(wáng shì chéng yuán)	*NP.*	members of the royal family, royalty
國禮	(guó lǐ)	*N.*	the national gift
高度的	(gāo dù de)	*Adj.*	high
評價	(píng jià)	*V/N.*	to evaluate; evaluation
熱情洋溢	(rè qíng yáng yì)	*Idiom.*	with enthusiasm and warmth
敬獻	(jìng xiàn)	*V.*	to dedicate to
改革開放	(gǎi gé kāi fàng)	*VP.*	to reform and open
總設計師	(zǒng shè jì shī)	*NP.*	the chief designer, chief architect of
指導	(zhǐ dǎo)	*V.*	to guide and supervise
歷代	(lì dài)	*N.*	successive dynasties; down through the ages, throughout the decades
外交家	(wài jiāo jiā)	*N.*	diplomat

			German composer
诺贝尔	(nuò bèi ěr)	*Personal N.*	Alfred Bernhard Nobel (1833-1896), Swedish inventor of dynamite and other explosives, founder and legator of the Nobel Prizes
爱因斯坦	(ài yīn sī tǎn)	*Personal N.*	Albert Einstein (1879-1955), German-born and raised physicist, discovered law of relativity, Nobel prize winner
维妙维肖	(wéi miào wéi xiāo)	*Idiom.*	remarkably true to life
栩栩如生	(xǔ xǔ rú shēng)	*Idiom.*	striking and lifelike
王室成员	(wáng shì chéng yuán)	*NP.*	members of the royal family, royalty
国礼	(guó lǐ)	*N.*	the national gift
高度的	(gāo dù de)	*Adj.*	high
评价	(píng jià)	*V/N.*	to evaluate; evaluation
热情洋溢	(rè qíng yáng yì)	*Idiom.*	with enthusiasm and warmth
敬献	(jìng xiàn)	*V.*	to dedicate to
改革开放	(gǎi gé kāi fàng)	*VP.*	to reform and open
总设计师	(zǒng shè jì shī)	*NP.*	the chief designer, chief architect of
指导	(zhǐ dǎo)	*V.*	to guide and supervise
历代	(lì dài)	*N.*	successive dynasties; down through the ages, throughout the decades
外交家	(wài jiāo jiā)	*N.*	diplomat

二、幽默小品

學習母雞

媽媽："小明，你吃糖為甚麼不分給妹妹吃？你看老母雞找到小蟲子，都給小雞吃。你應該向老母雞學習呀！"

小明："我如果找到小蟲子，也都給妹妹吃。"

二、幽默小品

学习母鸡

妈妈："小明，你吃糖为什么不分给妹妹吃？你看老母鸡找到小虫子，都给小鸡吃你应该向老母鸡学习呀！"

小明："我如果找到小虫子，也都给妹妹吃。"

課文要點

一、慣用語與成語

1. 無奇不有 (there are all kinds of strange things, "truth is stranger than fiction")

例：生活中無奇不有，走失半年的小狗昨天突然又出現在我們的家門口。
Life is always full of surprises. The puppy which had been lost for half a year suddenly showed up again yesterday at the door of our house.

Note: in "無奇不有", the negative particle "不" is used instead of "沒". This is an exception which can only occur in idioms.

2. 奇中之奇 (the strangest among the strange things)

例：世界上無奇不有，可是在雞蛋上走路卻可以說是奇中之奇。
Although there are all kinds of strange things in the world, possibly the strangest among them is to walk on eggs.

3. 絲綢錦緞 (silk and brocade)

例：絲綢錦緞是中國特有的東西。
Silk and brocade are unique to China.

4. 清新明麗 (to be clear, fresh, bright, and beautiful)

例：人稱王維的詩與畫清新明麗，詩中有畫，畫中有詩。
It was said that the poems and paintings of Wang Wei were characterized by their fresh and luminous beauty; there were paintings in his poetry and poetry in his paintings.

课文要点

一、惯用语与成语

1. 无奇不有 (there are all kinds of strange things, "truth is stranger than fiction")

例：生活中无奇不有，走失半年的小狗昨天突然又出现在我们的家门口。

Life is always full of surprises. The puppy which had been lost for half a year suddenly showed up again yesterday at the door of our house.

Note: in "无奇不有", the negative particle "不" is used instead of "没". This is an exception which can only occur in idioms.

2. 奇中之奇 (the strangest among the strange things)

例：世界上无奇不有，可是在鸡蛋上走路却可以说是奇中之奇。

Although there are all kinds of strange things in the world, possibly the strangest among them is to walk on eggs.

3. 丝绸锦缎 (silk and brocade)

例：丝绸锦缎是中国特有的东西。

Silk and brocade are unique to China.

4. 清新明丽 (to be clear, fresh, bright, and beautiful)

例：人称王维的诗与画清新明丽，诗中有画，画中有诗。

It was said that the poems and paintings of Wang Wei were characterized by their fresh and luminous beauty; there were paintings in his poetry and poetry in his paintings.

5. 色彩斑斕 (the splendid color)

　　例: 昨天西安市政府舉辦的花展色彩斑斕，香氣誘人。
　　The flower show opened yesterday by the Xian government is replete with a multiplicity of rich hues and intoxicating fragrances.

6. 輝煌巨作 (magnificent works)

　　例：曹雪芹的《紅樓夢》被普遍認為是中國小説史上的輝煌巨作。
　　The Dream of the Red Chamber by Cao Xueqin is generally regarded as the magnum opus in the history of Chinese fiction.

7. 淋漓盡致 (forceful[ly], telling[ly], compelling[ly], vivid[ly])

8. 維妙維肖 (true to life, exactly like the original)

　　例：電視上的那位演員模仿法國總統戴高樂可以説是維妙維肖、淋漓盡致。
　　That actor's televised impersonation of French President De Gaulle was so striking and vivid that he could be mistaken for De Gaulle himself.

9. 樓台亭閣 (buildings and pavilions)

10. 花鳥蟲魚 (flowers, birds, insects, and fish)

　　例：在傳統的中國畫中，樓台亭閣，花鳥蟲魚是常見的主題。
　　In traditional Chinese ink painting, houses, pavilions, flowers, birds, insects, and fish are frequent motifs.

11. 飛針走線 (to stitch rapidly and skillfully, "to make the needle and thread fly")

　　例：他的母親飛針走線，一晚上為他做了兩件上衣。
　　His mother can make the needle and thread fly. She finished two jackets for him in one night.

143

5. 色彩斑斓 (the splendid color)

例: 昨天西安市政府举办的花展色彩斑斓，香气诱人。
The flower show opened yesterday by the Xian government is replete with a multiplicity of rich hues and intoxicating fragrances.

6. 辉煌巨作 (magnificent works)

例: 曹雪芹的《红楼梦》被普遍认为是中国小说史上的辉煌巨作。
The Dream of the Red Chamber by Cao Xueqin is generally regarded as the magnum opus in the history of Chinese fiction.

7. 淋漓尽致 (forceful[ly], telling[ly], compelling[ly], vivid[ly])

8. 维妙维肖 (true to life, exactly like the original)

例: 电视上的那位演员模仿法国总统戴高乐可以说是维妙维肖、淋漓尽致。
That actor's televised impersonation of French President De Gaulle was so striking and vivid that he could be mistaken for De Gaulle himself.

9. 楼台亭阁 (buildings and pavilions)

10. 花鸟虫鱼 (flowers, birds, insects, and fish)

例: 在传统的中国画中，楼台亭阁，花鸟虫鱼是常见的主题。
In traditional Chinese ink painting, houses, pavilions, flowers, birds, insects, and fish are frequent motifs.

11. 飞针走线 (to stitch rapidly and skillfully, "to make the needle and thread fly")

例: 他的母亲飞针走线，一晚上为他做了两件上衣。
His mother can make the needle and thread fly. She finished two jackets for him in one night.

12. 東方一絕 (one of the wonders of the orient)

13. 保存經久 (to be kept forever, to be enduring, long-lasting)

14. 天然色澤 (natural color)

例：中國的景泰藍製品天然色澤，保存經久，可以說是東方一絕。
Chinese Cloisonne not only possesses natural colors and sheen, but also is very long-lasting. It can be termed one of the wonders of the East.

15. 立體感強 (strong sense of three-dimensionality)

16. 形象逼真 (in appearance very true to life; a striking likeness)

例：他創造的人物畫兒形象逼真，立體感強。看過之後令人經久不忘。
His figure paintings are very lifelike and three-dimensional, leaving a lasting impression on the viewer.

17. 苦心揣摩 (to arrive at deeper understanding through painstaking and persistent efforts)

例：中國名畫家齊白石經過一生的苦心揣摩，終於畫出了形象逼真的小動物。
The famous Chinese artist Qi Baishi eventually succeeded in painting the most lifelike images of small animals after a life of hard practice and experimentation.

12. 东方一绝 (one of the wonders of the orient)

13. 保存经久 (to be kept forever, to be enduring, long-lasting)

14. 天然色泽 (natural color)

例：中国的景泰兰制品天然色泽，保存经久，可以说是东方一绝。
Chinese Cloisonne not only possesses natural colors and sheen, but also is very long-lasting . It can be termed one of the wonders of the East.

15. 立体感强 (strong sense of three-dimensionality)

16. 形象逼真 (in appearance very true to life; a striking likeness)

例：他创造的人物画儿形象逼真，立体感强。看过之后令人经久不忘。
His figure paintings are very lifelike and three-dimensional, leaving a lasting impression on the viewer.

17. 苦心揣摩 (to arrive at deeper understanding through painstaking and persistent efforts)

例：中国名画家齐白石经过一生的苦心揣摩，终于画出了形象逼真的小动物。
The famous Chinese artist Qi Baishi eventually succeeded in painting the most lifelike images of small animals after a life of hard practice and experimentation.

二、常用短語

1. 以⋯為藍本 (based on the original version of, to use something as the basis of)

> 例：他以自己的江南家鄉為藍本創造了很多名畫。
>
> He created a great many famous paintings modeled on the original version provided by his hometown in Jiangnan [the lower Yangtze region].
>
> 這個公司以遼寧電冰箱為藍本設計了好幾個不同的產品。
>
> This company designed several different products based on the Liaoning refrigerator model.

2. ⋯就讀於⋯ (to go to school at)

> 例：他的父親年輕時就讀於美國的西北大學。
>
> When he was young, his father went to Northwestern University in the U.S.
>
> 四年以前我就讀於一所美國中西部的大學。
>
> Four years ago I enrolled at a university in the Mid-west (USA).

3. ⋯從事於⋯ (to engage in)

> 例：孫中山很早就從事於政治活動。
>
> Sun Yatsen began to engage in political activities from his early years.
>
> 齊白石早年從事於木工。
>
> Qi Baishi engaged in carpentry during his early years.

4. ⋯滿足於⋯ (to be satisfied with)

> 例：她從不滿足於她的好成績，每天還要看很多功課以外的書。
>
> She never just settles for her good grades; she is always reading a lot of books in addition to her assignments.

二、常用短语

1. 以…为蓝本 (based on the original version of, to use something as the basis of)

例： 他以自己的江南家乡为蓝本创造了很多名画。
He created a great many famous paintings modeled on the original version provided by his hometown in Jiangnan [the lower Yangtze region].

这个公司以辽宁电冰箱为蓝本设计了好几个不同的产品。
This company designed several different products based on the Liaoning refrigerator model.

2. …就读于… (to go to school at)

例： 他的父亲年轻时就读于美国的西北大学。
When he was young, his father went to Northwestern University in the U.S.

四年以前我就读于一所美国中西部的大学。
Four years ago I enrolled at a university in the Mid-west (USA).

3. …从事于… (to engage in)

例： 孙中山很早就从事于政治活动。
Sun Yatsen began to engage in political activities from his early years.

齐白石早年从事于木工。
Qi Baishi engaged in carpentry during his early years.

4. …满足于… (to be satisfied with)

例： 她从不满足于她的好成绩，每天还要看很多功课以外的书。
She never just settles for her good grades; she is always reading a lot of books in addition to her assignments.

這位藝術家從不滿足於他的現有作品，總是在不斷地改進和提高。
This artist is never satisfied with his present works. He is constantly revising and improving them.

5. …給予…高度的評價 (to speak highly about)

例：《紐約時報》對他在上周貿易會談中所起的作用給予了高度的評價。
"The New York Times" gave him high marks for the role he played in the trade talks last week.

該公司的總經理對這一產品給予了高度的評價。
That company's general manager speaks highly of this product.

6. …被當作… (to be treated as; to be used as)

例：中國的一對大熊貓被當作國禮送給了華盛頓動物園。
A pair of Chinese giant pandas was presented to the Washington Zoo as a national gift [gift from the Chinese government and people].

這部電影被當作教育影片放給中學生看。
This film is shown to middle/secondary school students as an educational film.

这位艺术家从不满足于他的现有作品， 总是在不断地改进和提高。
This artist is never satisfied with his present works. He is constantly revising and improving them.

5. …给予…高度的评价 (to speak highly about)

例： 《纽约时报》对他在上周贸易会谈中所起的作用给予了高度的评价。
"The New York Times" gave him high marks for the role he played in the trade talks last week.

该公司的总经理对这一产品给予了高度的评价。
That company's general manager speaks highly of this product.

6. …被当作… (to be treated as; to be used as)

例： 中国的一对大熊猫被当作国礼送给了华盛顿动物园。
A pair of Chinese giant pandas was presented to the Washington Zoo as a national gift [gift from the Chinese government and people].

这部电影被当作教育影片放给中学生看。
This film is shown to middle/secondary school students as an educational film.

小課文

媽媽為甚麼要這樣？

一、看電視小課文、回答問題

    1. 這個廣告反映了中國的一個甚麼問題？

    2. 你覺得這個女學生的母親能不能理解她女兒為甚麼不高興？為甚麼？

    3. 你覺得人需要privacy嗎？為甚麼？

    4. 要是你是那個女學生，你會對母親說甚麼？

二、用你自己的話把這個故事寫下來，講給大家聽

小课文

妈妈为什么要这样？

一、看电视小课文、回答问题

    1. 这个广告反映了中国的一个什么问题？

    2. 你觉得这个女学生的母亲能不能理解她女儿为什么不高兴？为什么？

    3. 你觉得人需要privacy吗？为什么？

    4. 要是你是那个女学生，你会对母亲说什么？

二、用你自己的话把这个故事写下来，讲给大家听

中國歌曲

聞雞起舞

看　日出在高高太行山
山　山中有武林的好漢
汗　汗水它練就我的心
心　心中已充滿激情
聽　天邊的金雞在齊鳴
鳴　鳴出了武林功夫經
經　經經常常出沒山川
穿　穿行在八千里路

同是龍的血脈
不必講究門派
日出輕風飛來
神州功夫更風采
日出東山　聞雞起舞
青龍寶劍嗖嗖掀起四方八丈土
雲梯百步　山中一條路
手出少林拳　腳蹬武當步
站要如松　坐要如鐘
喊哧咯嚓唰啦啦
穿行落山風
中華兒男　流血不流淚
黃河邊上走出多少武林老前輩

看　日出在高高太行山
山　山中有武林的好漢
汗　汗水它練就我的心
心　心中已充滿激情
聽　天邊的金雞在齊鳴
鳴　鳴出了武林功夫經
經　經經常常出沒山川
穿　穿行在八千里路

生詞

太行山	(tài háng shān)	Taihang Mountain
武林	(wǔ lín)	the field of martial art

中国歌曲

闻鸡起舞

看　日出在高高太行山
山　山中有武林的好汉
汗　汗水它练就我的心
心　心中已充满激情
听　天边的金鸡在齐鸣
鸣　鸣出了武林功夫经
经　经经常常出没山川
穿　穿行在八千里路

同是龙的血脉
不必讲究门派
日出轻风飞来
神州功夫更风采
日出东山　闻鸡起舞
青龙宝剑嗖嗖掀起四方八丈土
云梯百步　山中一条路
手出少林拳　脚登武当步
站要如松　坐要如钟
喊咻喀嚓唰啦啦
穿行落山风
中华儿男　流血不流泪
黄河边上走出多少武林老前辈

看　日出在高高太行山
山　山中有武林的好汉
汗　汗水它练就我的心
心　心中已充满激情
听　天边的金鸡在齐鸣
鸣　鸣出了武林功夫经
经　经经常常出没山川
穿　穿行在八千里路

生词

太行山	(tài háng shān)	Taihang Mountain
武林	(wǔ lín)	the field of martial art

好漢	(hǎo hàn)	good fellow, brave man
金雞	(jīn jī)	golden cock
齊鳴	(qí míng)	to crow in unison
功夫	(gōng fū)	Kongfu, skill, training
經	(jīng)	"tao", a way of doing things
出沒	(chū mò)	to be in and out of (a place)
山川	(shān chuān)	mountains and rivers
血脈	(xiě mài)	blood veins
講究	(jiǎng jīu)	to be picky about
門派	(mén pài)	school, faction, sect
神州	(shén zhōu)	majestic land
聞雞起舞	(wén jī qǐ wǔ)	to begin to exercise at dawn
寶劍	(bǎo jiàn)	the precious sword
丈	(zhàng)	Chinese measurement, a unit of lenghth = 3.33 meters
雲梯	(yún tī)	the ladder reaching to the sky
少林拳	(shào lín quán)	a school of martial art originated in Shaolin Temple in Henan Province
松	(sōng)	pine tree
鐘	(zhōng)	bell

好汉	(hǎo hàn)	good fellow, brave man
金鸡	(jīn jī)	golden cock
齐鸣	(qí míng)	to crow in unison
功夫	(gōng fū)	Kongfu, skill, training
经	(jīng)	"tao", a way of doing things
出没	(chū mò)	to be in and out of (a place)
山川	(shān chuān)	mountains and rivers
血脉	(xiě mài)	blood veins
讲究	(jiǎng jīu)	to be picky about
门派	(mén pài)	school, faction, sect
神州	(shén zhōu)	majestic land
闻鸡起舞	(wén jī qǐ wǔ)	to begin to exercise at dawn
宝剑	(bǎo jiàn)	the precious sword
丈	(zhàng)	Chinese measurement, a unit of lenghth = 3.33 meters
云梯	(yún tī)	the ladder reaching to the sky
少林拳	(shào lín quán)	a school of martial art originated in Shaolin Temple in Henan Province
松	(sōng)	pine tree
钟	(zhōng)	bell

Unit 4: Sports News

第四單元 體育新聞

第一課

中國運動員在殘疾人奧運會上再奪金牌

課文

一、簡介

體育新聞是中國新聞聯播中必有的節目。體育新聞主要報道各種重大的國內國際比賽的開幕、閉幕情況以及比賽結果等。本單元介紹的就是幾種常見的體育新聞報道。

生詞

| 體育 | (tǐ yù) | N. | sports; physical training, physical education |

第四单元　体育新闻

第一课

中国运动员在残疾人奥运会上再夺金牌

课文

一、简介

体育新闻是中国新闻联播中必有的节目。体育新闻主要报道各种重大的国内国际比赛的开幕、闭幕情况以及比赛结果等。本单元介绍的就是几种常见的体育新闻报道。

生词

体育	(tǐ yù)	N.	sports; physical training, physical education

二、對話

（一）

張小玲：世界殘疾人奧運會已經舉辦了多少次了？

周學之：到現在為止，大概有九次了。

張小玲：殘奧會有哪些體育項目呢？

周學之：有田徑、游泳、乒乓球、 排球、馬拉松賽跑等。

張小玲：那參賽的選手也要經過檢查嗎？ 萬一他們要不是殘疾人怎麼辦呢？

周學之：參加殘奧會要經過一套嚴格的檢查制度，不是殘疾人絕不讓參加比賽。

問題： 殘奧會舉辦了几次？ 有哪些體育項目？

生詞

殘疾人	(cán jī rén)	*N.*	handicapped people
到現在為止	(dào xiàn zài wéi zhǐ)	*Prep P.*	up to now＝到目前
田徑	(tián jìng)	*N.*	track and field
游泳	(yóu yǒng)	*V/N.*	to swim; swimming
乒乓球	(pīng pāng qíu)	*N.*	table tennis
排球	(pái qíu)	*N.*	volleyball
馬拉松	(mǎ lā sōng)	*N.*	Marathon
參賽	(cān sài)	*VO.*	to participate in competition
選手	(xuǎn shǒu)	*N.*	contestant; player

（二）

周學之：你最喜歡的體育項目是甚麼？

張小玲：當然是乒乓球了。因為這是我從小就從事的運動。

151

二、对话

（一）

张小玲：世界残疾人奥运会已经举办了多少次了？

周学之：到现在为止，大概有九次了。

张小玲：残奥会都有哪些体育项目呢？

周学之：有田径、游泳、乒乓球、排球、马拉松赛跑等。

张小玲：那参赛的选手也要经过检查吗？万一他们要不是残疾人怎么办呢？

周学之：参加残奥会要经过一套严格的检查制度，不是残疾人绝不让参加比
赛。

问题：残奥会举办了几次？有哪些体育项目？

生词

残疾人	(cán jī rén)	*N.*	handicapped people
到现在为止	(dào xiàn zài wéi zhǐ)	*Prep P.*	up to now = 到目前
田径	(tián jìng)	*N.*	track and field
游泳	(yóu yǒng)	*V/N.*	to swim; swimming
乒乓球	(pīng pāng qíu)	*N.*	table tennis
排球	(pái qíu)	*N.*	volleyball
马拉松	(mǎ lā sōng)	*N.*	Marathon
参赛	(cān sài)	*VO.*	to participate in competition
选手	(xuǎn shǒu)	*N.*	contestant; player

（二）

周学之：你最喜欢的体育项目是什么？

张小玲：当然是乒乓球了。因为这是我从小就从事的运动。

周學之：聽你這麼說，好像很自信嘛。

張小玲：不敢吹牛。我參加過中國體育代表隊去丹麥、瑞典、荷蘭比賽。我在這幾個地方分別獲得過三枚金牌、兩枚銀牌和一枚銅牌。

周學之：好傢伙，真了不起。

問題：為甚麼張小玲很自信？

生詞

從事	(cóng shì)	*V.*	to go in for, to engage in
自信	(zì xìn)	*Adj/N.*	self-confident; self-confidence
吹牛	(chuī níu)	*VO.*	to toot one's own horn, to brag
丹麥	(dān mài)	*Place N.*	Denmark
瑞典	(ruì diǎn)	*Place N.*	Sweden
荷蘭	(hé lán)	*Place N.*	Holland, the Netherlands
枚	(méi)	*Classifier.*	classifier for medals＝塊
金牌	(jīn pái)	*N.*	gold medal
銀牌	(yín pái)	*N.*	silver medal
銅牌	(tóng pai)	*N.*	bronze medal
奧運會	(ào yùn huì)	*Abbrev.*	Olympic Games＝奧林匹克運動會
了不起	(liǎo bù qǐ)	*Idiom.*	great

（三）

張小玲：在美國，殘疾人的生活怎麼樣？

周學之：我覺得他們到處都受到照顧和保護。比方說，現在多數的建築都有殘疾人入口處，停車場也有專門為殘疾人提供的停車處等。

張小玲：那麼他們的工作機會呢？

周学之：听你这么说，好像很自信嘛。

张小玲：不敢吹牛。我参加过中国体育代表队去丹麦、瑞典、荷兰比赛。我
      在这几个地方分别获得过三枚金牌、两枚银牌和一枚铜牌。

周学之：好家伙，真了不起。

问题：为什么张小玲很自信？

生词

从事	(cóng shì)	*V.*	to go in for, to engage in
自信	(zì xìn)	*Adj/N.*	self-confident; self-confidence
吹牛	(chuī niú)	*VO.*	to toot one's own horn, to brag
丹麦	(dān mài)	*Place N.*	Denmark
瑞典	(ruì diǎn)	*Place N.*	Sweden
荷兰	(hé lán)	*Place N.*	Holland, the Netherlands
枚	(méi)	*Classifier.*	classifier for medals = 块
金牌	(jīn pái)	*N.*	gold medal
银牌	(yín pái)	*N.*	silver medal
铜牌	(tóng pái)	*N.*	bronze medal
奥运会	(ào yùn huì)	*Abbrev.*	Olympic Games = 奥林匹克运动会
了不起	(liǎo bù qǐ)	*Idiom.*	great

（三）

张小玲：在美国，残疾人的生活怎么样？

周学之：我觉得他们到处都受到照顾和保护。比方说，现在多数的建筑都有
      残疾人入口处，停车场也有专门为残疾人提供的停车处等。

张小玲：那么他们的工作机会呢？

周學之： 我想多數的殘疾人可以像正常人那樣上學、上班，選擇自己喜歡的
課程，做自己喜歡做的事。只要他們不怕艱難險阻，有頑強毅力，
多半也可以在社會上獲得成功。

問題： 美國殘疾人的生活和工作機會怎麼樣？

生詞

照顧	(zhào gù)	V.	to take care of; look after
入口處	(rù kǒu chù)	N.	entrance
停車場	(tíng chē chǎng)	N.	parking spot, parking lot
艱難險阻	(jiān nán xiǎn zǔ)	Idiom.	hardship and obstacles
頑強毅力	(wán qiáng yì lì)	Idiom.	strong will

三、電視新聞

中國運動員在殘疾人奧運會再奪金牌

在第九屆殘疾人奧運會上，中國選手於9月10號又獲得兩枚金牌。

中國殘疾人體育代表團在9月10號的田徑比賽中取得了兩塊金牌、一塊
銀牌、一塊銅牌。到目前中國隊已獲得了10枚金牌，並10次打破了8項世界紀
錄。

生詞

| 運動員 | (yùn dòng yuán) | N. | athlete |
| 奪 | (duó) | V. | to carry off (prize, medal), to capture, to successfully compete and win |

周学之：我想多数的残疾人可以像正常人那样上学、上班，选择自己喜欢的

课程，做自己喜欢做的事。只要他们不怕艰难险阻，有顽强毅力，

多半也可以在社会上获得成功。

问题：美国残疾人的生活和工作机会怎么样？

生词

照顾	(zhào gù)	*V.*	to take care of; look after
入口处	(rù kǒu chù)	*N.*	entrance
停车场	(tíng chē chǎng)	*N.*	parking spot, parking lot
艰难险阻	(jiān nán xiǎn zǔ)	*Idiom.*	hardship and obstacles
顽强毅力	(wán qiáng yì lì)	*Idiom.*	strong will

三、电视新闻

中国运动员在残疾人奥运会再夺金牌

在第九届残疾人奥运会上，中国选手于9月10号又获得两枚金牌。

中国残疾人体育代表团在9月10号的田径比赛中取得了两块金牌、一块银牌、一块铜牌。到目前中国队已获得了 10枚金牌，并10次打破了8项世界纪录。

生词

运动员	(yùn dòng yuán)	*N.*	athlete
夺	(duó)	*V.*	to carry off (prize, medal), to capture, to successfully compete and win

到目前	(dào mù qián)	*Prep P.*	up to now＝到現在為止
項	(xiàng)	*Classifier.*	event (s), classifier for athletic contests
打破	(dǎ pò)	*V.*	to break (the record of); to smash
世界紀錄	(shì jiè jì lù)	*NP.*	the world record

四、報紙閱讀

残疾人奥运会比赛结束
我国选手共获11枚金牌

本报巴塞罗那9月13日电 新华社记者**肖梓树**、本报记者**陈兴贵**报道：第九届残疾人奥运会的15个项目的比赛今天全部结束，共决出483枚金牌、481枚银牌和519枚铜牌。

中国运动员在前几天的比赛中夺得11枚金牌。张小玲和杨毅在今天下午进行的女子乒乓球单打比赛中，又获得1枚银牌和1枚铜牌。周学元和石铁音还获得100米蝶泳和蛙泳两枚铜牌。这样使中国的银牌和铜牌总数分别增至7枚。

中国的金牌总数和丹麦、韩国一样，排在第11位，但奖牌总数排在第18位。

美国残疾人选手展示了强劲实力，共获得76枚金牌、52枚银牌和48枚铜牌，居金牌和奖牌总数的首位。德国实现了保持金牌和奖牌总数第2位的愿望，金牌和奖牌总数分别为60枚和169枚。英国和法国分别居金牌第3和第4位，金牌总数各为38枚和36枚。东道主西班牙运动员表现出色，以34枚金牌居第5位。

第九届残奥会是举办残疾人奥运会以来规模最大、参赛运动员最多的残疾人体育盛会。在这届盛会中，世界各国和地区的运动员展示了自信、自强的精神和战胜艰难险阻的顽强毅力。

今天下午进行了本届残疾人奥运会的最后一个比赛项目——男子马拉松赛。巴塞罗那20多万人在街道两旁为参赛者加油。在有45名选手参加的TW3，4级的比赛中，美国的西斯科·豪特尔、瑞典的赖内尔·库斯查尔、荷兰的特赫奥和瑞典的弗雷伊分获金牌。其中弗雷伊的成绩为1小时27分53秒。

明晚将举行隆重的闭幕式。

到目前	(dào mù qián)	*Prep P.*	up to now = 到现在为止
项	(xiàng)	*Classifier.*	event (s), classifier for athletic contests
打破	(dǎ pò)	*V.*	to break (the record of); to smash
世界纪录	(shì jiè jì lù)	*NP.*	the world record

四、报纸阅读

残疾人奥运会比赛结束
我国选手共获11枚金牌

本报巴塞罗那9月13日电　新华社记者**肖梓树**、本报记者**陈兴贵**报道：第九届残疾人奥运会的15个项目的比赛今天全部结束，共决出483枚金牌、481枚银牌和519枚铜牌。

中国运动员在前几天的比赛中夺得11枚金牌。张小玲和杨毅在今天下午进行的女子乒乓球单打比赛中，又获得1枚银牌和1枚铜牌。周学元和石铁音还获得100米蝶泳和蛙泳两枚铜牌。这样使中国的银牌和铜牌总数分别增至7枚。

中国的金牌总数和丹麦、韩国一样，排在第11位，但奖牌总数排在第18位。

美国残疾人选手展示了强劲实力，共获得76枚金牌、52枚银牌和48枚铜牌，居金牌和奖牌总数的首位。德国实现了保持金牌和奖牌总数第2位的愿望，金牌和奖牌总数分别为60枚和169枚。英国和法国分别居金牌第3和第4位，金牌总数各为38枚和36枚。东道主西班牙运动员表现出色，以34枚金牌居第5位。

第九届残奥会是举办残疾人奥运会以来规模最大、参赛运动员最多的残疾人体育盛会。在这届盛会中，世界各国和地区的运动员展示了自信、自强的精神和战胜艰难险阻的顽强毅力。

今天下午进行了本届残疾人奥运会的最后一个比赛项目——男子马拉松赛。巴塞罗那20多万人在街道两旁为参赛者加油。在有45名选手参加的TW3，4级的比赛中，美国的西斯科·豪特尔、瑞典的赖内尔·库斯查尔、荷兰的特赫奥和瑞典的弗雷伊分获金牌。其中弗雷伊的成绩为1小时27分53秒。

明晚将举行隆重的闭幕式。

殘疾人奧運會比賽結束
我國選手共獲11枚金牌

　　本報巴塞羅那9月13日電　新華社記者肖梓樹、本報記者陳興貴報道：第九屆殘疾人奧運會的15個項目的比賽今天全部結束，共決出483枚金牌、481枚銀牌和519枚銅牌。

　　中國運動員在前幾天的比賽中奪得11枚金牌。張小玲和楊毅在今天下午進行的女子乒乓球單打比賽中，又獲得1枚銀牌和1枚銅牌。周學元和石鐵音還獲得100米蝶泳和蛙泳兩枚銅牌。這樣使中國的銀牌和銅牌總數分別增至7枚。中國的金牌總數和丹麥、韓國一樣，排在第11位，但獎牌總數排在第18位。

　　美國殘疾人選手展示了強勁實力，共獲得76枚金牌、52枚銀牌和48枚銅牌，居金牌和獎牌總數的首位。德國實現了保持金牌和獎牌總數第2位的願望，金牌和獎牌總數分別為60枚和169枚。英國和法國分別居金牌第3和第4位，金牌總數各為38枚和36枚。東道主西班牙運動員表現出色，以34枚金牌居第5位。

　　第九屆殘奧會是舉辦殘疾人奧運會以來規模最大、參賽運動員最多的殘疾人體育盛會。在這屆盛會中，世界各國和地區的運動員展示了自信、自強的精神和戰勝艱難險阻的頑強毅力。

　　今天下午進行了本屆殘疾人奧運會的最後一個比賽項目—男子馬拉松賽。巴塞羅那20多萬人在街道兩旁為參賽者加油。在有45名選手參加的TW 3,4級的比賽中，美國的西斯科．豪特爾、瑞典的賴內爾．庫斯查爾、荷蘭的特赫奧和瑞典的弗雷伊分獲金牌。其中弗雷伊的成績為1小時27分53秒。

　　明晚將舉行隆重的閉幕式。

残疾人奥运会比赛结束
我国选手共获11枚金牌

　　本报巴塞罗那9月13日电　　新华社记者肖梓树、本报记者陈兴贵报道：第九届残疾人奥运会的15个项目的比赛今天全部结束，共决出483枚金牌、481枚银牌和519枚铜牌。

　　中国运动员在前几天的比赛中夺得11枚金牌。张小玲和杨毅在今天下午进行的女子乒乓球单打比赛中，又获得1枚银牌和1枚铜牌。周学元和石铁音还获得100米蝶泳和蛙泳两枚铜牌。这样使中国的银牌和铜牌总数分别增至7枚。中国的金牌总数和丹麦、韩国一样，排在第11位，但奖牌总数排在第18位。

　　美国残疾人选手展示了强劲实力，共获得76枚金牌、52枚银牌和48枚铜牌，居金牌和奖牌总数的首位。德国实现了保持金牌和奖牌总数第2位的愿望，金牌和奖牌总数分别为60枚和169枚。英国和法国分别居金牌第3和第4位，金牌总数各为38枚和36枚。东道主西班牙运动员表现出色，以34枚金牌居第5位。

　　第九届残奥会是举办残疾人奥运会以来规模最大、参赛运动员最多的残疾人体育盛会。在这届盛会中，世界各国和地区的运动员展示了自信、自强的精神和战胜艰难险阻的顽强毅力。

　　今天下午进行了本届残疾人奥运会的最后一个比赛项目—男子马拉松赛。巴塞罗那20多万人在街道两旁为参赛者加油。在有45名选手参加的TW 3,4级的比赛中，美国的西斯科·豪特尔、瑞典的赖内尔·库斯查尔、荷兰的特赫奥和瑞典的弗雷伊分获金牌。其中弗雷伊的成绩为1小时27分53秒。

　　明晚将举行隆重的闭幕式。

生詞

決出	(jué chū)	*V.*	as decided by the outcome of a competition
張小玲	(zhāng xiǎo líng)	*Personal N.*	Zhang Xiaoling
楊毅	(yáng yì)	*Personal N.*	Yang Yi
單打	(dān dǎ)	*N.*	singles (athletic competition)
周學之	(zhōu xué zhī)	*Personal N.*	Zhou Xuezhi
石鐵音	(shí tiě yīn)	*Personal N.*	Shi Tieyin
蝶泳	(dié yǒng)	*N.*	butterfly style swimming
韓國	(hán guó)	*Place N.*	South Korea
排在	(pái zài)	*VP.*	to be ranked at
獎牌	(jiǎng pái)	*N.*	medal
展示	(zhǎn shì)	*V.*	to demonstrate; to show
強勁	(qiáng jìn)	*Adj.*	strong
實力	(shí lì)	*N.*	actual strength, real power
總數	(zǒng shù)	*N.*	total number
首位	(shǒu wèi)	*N.*	top ranked, first position＝第一位
居	(jū)	*V.*	排在
東道主	(dōng dào zhǔ)	*N.*	host, host country
出色	(chū sè)	*Adj.*	outstanding
殘奧會	(cán ào huì)	*Abbrev.*	the Special Olympics＝殘疾人奧林匹克運動會
自強	(zì qiáng)	*VP.*	to strengthen oneself
戰勝	(zhàn shèng)	*V.*	to overcome
加油	(jiā yóu)	*V.*	to cheer for; go, team! (lit. "step on the gas")
西斯科．豪特爾	(xī sī kē háo tè ěr)	*Personal N.*	the name of an American athlete
賴內爾．庫斯查爾	(lài nèi ěr kù sī chá ěr)	*Personal N.*	the name of a Swedish athlete

生词

决出	(jué chū)	*V.*	as decided by the outcome of a competition
张小玲	(zhāng xiǎo líng)	*Personal N.*	Zhang Xiaoling
杨毅	(yáng yì)	*Personal N.*	Yang Yi
单打	(dān dǎ)	*N.*	singles (athletic competition)
周学之	(zhōu xué zhī)	*Personal N.*	Zhou Xuezhi
石铁音	(shí tiě yīn)	*Personal N.*	Shi Tieyin
蝶泳	(dié yǒng)	*N.*	butterfly style swimming
韩国	(hán guó)	*Place N.*	South Korea
排在	(pái zài)	*VP.*	to be ranked at
奖牌	(jiǎng pái)	*N.*	medal
展示	(zhǎn shì)	*V.*	to demonstrate; to show
强劲	(qiáng jìn)	*Adj.*	strong
实力	(shí lì)	*N.*	actual strength, real power
总数	(zǒng shù)	*N.*	total number
首位	(shǒu wèi)	*N.*	top ranked, first position = 第一位
居	(jū)	*V.*	排在
东道主	(dōng dào zhǔ)	*N.*	host, host country
出色	(chū sè)	*Adj.*	outstanding
残奥会	(cán ào huì)	*Abbrev.*	the Special Olympics = 残疾人奥林匹克运动会
自强	(zì qiáng)	*VP.*	to strengthen oneself
战胜	(zhàn shèng)	*V.*	to overcome
加油	(jiā yóu)	*V.*	to cheer for; go, team! (lit. "step on the gas")
西斯科·豪特尔	(xī sī kē háo tè ěr)	*Personal N.*	the name of an American athlete
赖内尔·库斯查尔	(lài nèi ěr kù sī chá ěr)	*Personal N.*	the name of a Swedish athlete

特赫奧	(tè hè ào)	*Personal N.*	the name of a Dutch athlete
費雷伊	(fèi léi yī)	*Personal N.*	the name of a Swedish athlete
閉幕式	(bì mù shì)	*N.*	closing ceremony

五、幽默

睡得很累

　　"你昨晚在沙發上睡得還好嗎？"女主人關切地問。

　　"還不壞，"她兒子的同學彬彬有禮地回答："我每隔一小時就起來休息一下。"

特赫奥	(tè hè ào)	*Personal N.*	the name of a Dutch athlete
费雷伊	(fèi léi yī)	*Personal N.*	the name of a Swedish athlete
闭幕式	(bì mù shì)	*N.*	closing ceremony

五、幽默

睡得很累

"你昨晚在沙发上睡得还好吗？"
女主人关切地问。

"还不坏，" 她儿子的同学彬彬有礼地回答："我每隔一小时就起来休息一下。"

課文要點

一、常用文言詞、縮略語與慣用語

1. 至＝到 (up to)

例：這個比賽必須有五至十人參加。
This competition/contest requires 5 to 10 participants.

2. 以＝用 (with)

例：中國選手以五比三再奪乒乓球金牌。
The Chinese competitors clinched the gold medal again with a score of 5 to 3.

3. 居＝排在 (rank at)

例：這個美術館收藏的畫居全國首位。
This art museum's painting collection is ranked first in the nation.

4. 分獲＝分別獲得 (to obtain separately)

例： 這兩個企業分獲最佳產品獎和最佳管理獎。
These two enterprises obtained the honors for best product and the honors for best management, respectively.

5. 田徑＝田賽和徑賽 (track and field contests)

例：田徑賽在奧運會上很受觀眾的歡迎。
The track and field competitions in the Olympics are very popular with the spectators.

课文要点

一、常用文言词、缩略语与惯用语

1. 至 = 到 (up to)

例: 这个比赛必须有五至十人参加。

This competition/contest requires 5 to 10 participants.

2. 以 = 用 (with)

例: 中国选手以五比三再夺乒乓球金牌。

The Chinese competitors clinched the gold medal again with a score of 5 to 3.

3. 居 = 排在 (rank at)

例: 这个美术馆收藏的画居全国首位。

This art museum's painting collection is ranked first in the nation.

4. 分获 = 分别获得 (to obtain separately)

例: 这两个企业分获最佳产品奖和最佳管理奖。

These two enterprises obtained the honors for best product and the honors for best management, respectively.

5. 田径 = 田赛和径赛 (track and field contests)

例: 田径赛在奥运会上很受观众的欢迎。

The track and field competitions in the Olympics are very popular with the spectators.

7. 參賽者＝參加比賽的人＝選手 (participants, contestants)

例：殘奧會的參賽者來自世界各國。

The participants in the Special Olympics are from all over the world.

8. 殘奧會＝殘疾人奧林匹克運動會 (the Special Olympics, i.e., the Olympic Games for athletes with a disability)

二、常用短語

1. …打破…世界紀錄 (to break the world record in)

例：中國選手郭建華打破了男子跳高世界紀錄。

The Chinese athlete, Guo Jianhua, broke the world record in the men's high jump.

上屆奧林匹克運動會上，美國男子游泳選手打破了好幾項世界紀錄。

At the last Olympic Games, American men swimmers broke quite a few world records.

2. 居…的首位 (to be ranked at the top of)

例：中國的輕工產品出口現在差不多居世界首位。

The products of China's light industry come close to ranking number 1 in the world.

日本電冰箱的質量居世界首位。

The quality of Japanese refrigerators is ranked first in the world.

3. …的成績為… (the record [score] is)

例：芝加哥公牛隊(Chicago Bulls) 跟洛杉磯湖人隊 (L.A. Lakers) 的比賽成績為 103:98。

The final score of the basketball game between Chicago Bulls and L.A. Lakers was 103 to 98.

7. 参赛者 = 参加比赛的人 = 选手 (participants, contestants)

例: 残奥会的参赛者来自世界各国。
The participants in the Special Olympics are from all over the world.

8. 残奥会 = 残疾人奥林匹克运动会 (the Special Olympics, i.e., the Olympic Games for athletes with a disability)

二、 常用短语

1. …打破…世界纪录 (to break the world record in)

例: 中国选手郭建华打破了男子跳高世界纪录。
The Chinese athlete, Guo Jianhua, broke the world record in the men's high jump.

上届奥林匹克运动会上， 美国男子游泳选手打破了好几项世界纪录。
At the last Olympic Games, American men swimmers broke quite a few world records.

2. 居…的首位 (to be ranked at the top of)

例: 中国的轻工产品出口现在差不多居世界首位。
The products of China's light industry come close to ranking number 1 in the world.

日本电冰箱的质量居世界首位。
The quality of Japanese refrigerators is ranked first in the world.

3. …的成绩为… (the record [score] is)

例: 芝加哥公牛队(Chicago Bulls) 跟洛衫矶湖人队 (L.A. Lakers) 的比赛成绩为 103:98。
The final score of the basketball game between Chicago Bulls and L.A. Lakers was 103 to 98.

這屆奧運會男子百米最好成績為 9 秒 86 。

The best time in the men's 100 meter sprint in these Olympic Games was 9.86 seconds.

4. 實現…的願望 (to realize the wish [dream] of)

例：有一個中國殘疾人用腳寫字，寫出了很多小說，終於實現了他當小說家的願望。

There is a handicapped person in China who has written a lot of fiction with his feet. Finally, he fulfilled his dream of becoming a novelist.

為了實現願望，很多亞州運動員正在加緊訓練，準備參加下一屆的奧運會。

In order to fulfill their dreams, many Asian athletes are training intensively in preparation for taking part in the next Olympics.

5. …分別為… (to be... respectively)

例：中國隊和美國隊獲得的金牌數分別為 9 和 14 枚。

The gold medals collected by China and the U.S. were 9 and 14 respectively.

這屆奧運會德國隊獲得的金牌和銀牌分別為 19 和 26 枚。

The gold and silver medals captured by Germans at this Olympic Games were 19 and 26 respectively.

6. 展示了…精神 (to demonstrate the spirit of)

例：參加殘疾人奧運會的運動員向世界人民展示了他們為生活頑強奮鬥的精神。

The athletes attending the Special Olympics demonstrate to the world the indomitable spirit with which they live their lives.

这届奥运会男子百米最好成绩为 9 秒 86 。

The best time in the men's 100 meter sprint in these Olympic Games was 9.86 seconds.

4. 实现…的愿望 (to realize the wish [dream] of)

例: 有一个中国残疾人用脚写字，写出了很多小说，终于实现了他当小说家的愿望。

There is a handicapped person in China who has written a lot of fiction with his feet. Finally, he fulfilled his dream of becoming a novelist.

为了实现愿望，很多亚州运动员正在加紧训练，准备参加下一届的奥运会。

In order to fulfill their dreams, many Asian athletes are training intensively in preparation for taking part in the next Olympics.

5. …分别为… (to be ... respectively)

例: 中国队和美国队获得的金牌数分别为 9 和 14 枚。

The gold medals collected by China and the U.S. were 9 and 14 respectively.

这届奥运会德国队获得的金牌和银牌分别为 19 和 26 枚。

The gold and silver medals captured by Germans at this Olympic Games were 19 and 26 respectively.

6. 展示了…精神 (to demonstrate the spirit of)

例: 参加残疾人奥运会的运动员向世界人民展示了他们为生活顽强奋斗的精神。

The athletes attending the Special Olympics demonstrate to the world the indomitable spirit with which they live their lives.

瑞典人民向全世界人民展示了他們愛好和平反對戰爭的精神。

The Swedish people have demonstrated to the world their spirit of cherishing peace and opposing war.

7. 為⋯加油 (to cheer on, to root for)

例：我們全家都到街上去為跑馬拉松的運動員加油。

Our entire family went out to the street to cheer on the marathon runners.

為運動員加油會使他們獲得更好的成績。

Cheering for the athletes will help them achieve even more.

8. 舉行（開幕式、閉幕式）(to hold the opening or closing ceremony)

例：昨天東亞運動會在上海體育館舉行隆重的開幕式。

Yesterday the grand opening ceremony for the East Asia Games was held in Shanghai Stadium .

下一屆奧林匹克運動會將在美國亞特蘭大舉行。

The next Olympic Games will be held in Atlanta, U.S.A.

瑞典人民向全世界人民展示了他们爱好和平反对战争的精神。
The Swedish people have demonstrated to the world their spirit of cherishing peace and opposing war.

7. 为···加油 (to cheer on, to root for)

例: 我们全家都到街上去为跑马拉松的运动员加油。
Our entire family went out to the street to cheer on the marathon runners.

为运动员加油会使他们获得更好的成绩。
Cheering for the athletes will help them achieve even more.

8. 举行（开幕式、闭幕式）(to hold the opening or closing ceremony)

例: 昨天东亚运动会在上海体育馆举行隆重的开幕式。
Yesterday the grand opening ceremony for the East Asia Games was held in Shanghai Stadium.

下一届奥林匹克运动会将在美国亚特兰大举行。
The next Olympic Games will be held in Atlanta, U.S.A.

第四單元　體育新聞

第二課

一九九二年中國體壇碩果累累
首屆東亞運動會將在中國上海舉行

課文

一、簡介

　　本課的兩條新聞雖然在日期和內容上有些過時，但是它們在不同程度上集中反映了中國體育新聞的常用詞彙和基本結構，對理解體育新聞有很大的幫助。

生詞

過時	(guò shí)	*Adj.*	to be out-of-date, outdated
不同程度	(bù tóng chéng dù)	*NP.*	to different degrees; to a certain extent
集中	(jí zhōng)	*Adv.*	collectively, typically
常用詞彙	(cháng yòng cí huì)	*NP.*	commonly used vocabulary
基本結構	(jī běn jié gòu)	*NP.*	basic structure

第四单元 体育新闻

第二课

一九九二年中国体坛硕果累累
首届东亚运动会将在中国上海举行

课文

一、简介

本课的两条新闻虽然在日期和内容上有些过时，但是它们在不同程度上集中反映了中国体育新闻的常用词汇和基本结构，对理解体育新闻有很大的帮助。

生词

过时	(guò shí)	*Adj.*	to be out-of-date, outdated
不同程度	(bù tóng chéng dù)	*NP.*	to different degrees; to a certain extent
集中	(jí zhōng)	*Adv.*	collectively, typically
常用词汇	(cháng yòng cí huì)	*NP.*	commonly used vocabulary
基本结构	(jī běn jié gòu)	*NP.*	basic structure

162

二、對話

（一）

唐小風：你會用中文說哪些體育項目呢？

段劍虹：我會說很多了。比如：田徑、體操、長跑、短跑、馬拉松賽跑、跳高、 跳遠等。

唐小風：那游泳呢？

段劍虹：游泳有自由泳、混合泳、蛙泳、蝶泳等。

唐小風：那球類呢？

段劍虹：球類有乒乓球、籃球、排球、足球、還有保齡球。

唐小風：看來我們真學了不少體育詞彙。

問題： 你記得哪些所學過的體育詞彙？

生詞

長跑	（cháng pǎo）	*N.*	long-distance running
短跑	（duǎn pǎo）	*N.*	dash, sprint
體操	（tǐ cāo）	*N.*	gymnastics
跳高	（tiào gāo）	*N.*	high jump
跳遠	（tiào yuǎn）	*N.*	long jump
自由泳	（zì yóu yǒng）	*N.*	free-style swimming
混合泳	（hǔn hé yǒng）	*N.*	medley (event) swimming (swimming different styles during one race)
籃球	（lán qíu）	*N.*	basketball
足球	（zú qíu）	*N.*	soccer
保齡球	（bǎo líng qíu）	*N.*	bowling

二、对话

（一）

唐小凤：你会用中文说哪些体育项目呢？

段剑虹：我会说很多。比如：田径、体操、长跑、短跑、马拉松赛跑、跳高、跳远等。

唐小凤：那游泳呢？

段剑虹：游泳有自由泳、混合泳、蛙泳、蝶泳等。

唐小凤：那球类呢？

段剑虹：球类有乒乓球、篮球、排球、足球、还有保龄球。

唐小凤：看来我们真学了不少体育词汇。

问题：你记得哪些所学过的体育词汇？

生词

长跑	(cháng pǎo)	N.	long-distance running
短跑	(duǎn pǎo)	N.	dash, sprint
体操	(tǐ cāo)	N.	gymnastics
跳高	(tiào gāo)	N.	high jump
跳远	(tiào yuǎn)	N.	long jump
自由泳	(zì yóu yǒng)	N.	free-style swimming
混合泳	(hǔn hé yǒng)	N.	medley (event) swimming (swimming different styles during one race)
篮球	(lán qíu)	N.	basketball
足球	(zú qíu)	N.	soccer
保龄球	(bǎo líng qíu)	N.	bowling

(二)

段劍虹： 韓國和朝鮮是指一個國家還是兩個國家？

唐小風： 我想應該是兩個國家。在歷史上，這兩個國家本來是一個國家，有
一段時期叫韓國，有一段時期叫朝鮮。但是由於政治原因，這兩個
國家現在分為兩個，一個叫朝鮮人民共和國，一個叫大韓民國。一
個在北邊，一個在南邊。人們把在北邊的國家叫朝鮮，把在南邊的
國家叫韓國。

段劍虹：對了，我記得上屆奧運會的東道主就是韓國。它的首都是漢城，對
不對？

問題： 談談韓國和朝鮮的來歷。

生詞

朝鮮	(cháo xiǎn)	*Place N.*	North Korea
時期	(shí qī)	*N.*	period
漢城	(hàn chéng)	*Place N.*	Seoul
來歷	(lái lì)	*N.*	Origin, background, past history

(三)

段劍虹： 體育比賽有很多術語，要是聽不懂就沒有法子了解比賽的情況。

唐小風： 對了。比方説，田徑比賽中有小組賽，然後有半決賽，最後是決
賽。

段劍虹： 舉重比賽也採用同樣的方法。但運動員是根據他們的體重來分小組
參加比賽的。比方説，抓舉有50公斤級也有150公斤級。這里説的是

（二）

段剑虹： 韩国和朝鲜是指一个国家还是两个国家？

唐小风： 我想应该是两个国家。在历史上，这两个国家本来是一个国家，有一段时期叫韩国，有一段时期叫朝鲜。但是由于政治原因，这两个国家现在分为两个，一个叫朝鲜人民共和国，一个叫大韩民国。一个在北边，一个在南边。人们在把北边的国家叫朝鲜，把在南边的国家叫韩国。

段剑虹： 对了，我记得上届奥运会的东道主就是韩国。它的首都是汉城，对不对？

问题： *谈谈韩国和朝鲜的来历。*

生词

朝鲜	(cháo xiǎn)	*Place N.*	North Korea
时期	(shí qī)	*N.*	period
汉城	(hàn chéng)	*Place N.*	Seoul
来历	(lái lì)	*N.*	Origin, background, past history

（三）

段剑虹： 体育比赛有很多术语，要是听不懂就没有法子了解比赛的情况。

唐小风： 对了。比方说，田径比赛中有小组赛，然后有半决赛，最后是决赛。

段剑虹： 举重比赛也采用同样的方法。但运动员是根据他们的体重来分小组参加比赛的。比方说，抓举有50公斤级也有150公斤级。这里说的是抓舉運動員的體重。他們的體重決定他們在哪個小組參加比賽。

唐小風： 比賽的目的是要角逐出冠軍、亞軍。 冠軍通常得金牌，亞軍得銀牌，第三名得銅牌。

段劍虹： 看來這些體育名詞還真有用啊！

問題： 體育比賽中所用的術語有哪些？

生詞

團體賽	(tuán tǐ sài)	N.	team competition
半決賽	(bàn jué sài)	N.	semi-final(s)
決賽	(jué sài)	N.	final contest or match, finals, deciding match
舉重	(jǔ zhòng)	N.	weight-lifting
抓舉	(zhuā jǔ)	N.	snatch (in weight-lifting)
冠軍	(guàn jūn)	N.	championship
亞軍	(yà jūn)	N.	runner-up, 2nd place

三、電視新聞

1992年中國體壇碩果累累 新聞（一）

1992年中國體壇碩果累累。中國運動員在1992年共奪得89個世界冠軍，其中29個屬於奧運會項目，是歷年來獲得奧運會項目冠軍最多的一年。

中國選手在世界大賽中還奪得52個亞軍和45個第3名。在國內外比賽中，共有29人，4個隊，103次打破40項世界紀錄。

1992年是奧運會年，中國選手在第16屆冬季奧運會實現了零的突破。在第25屆夏季奧運會上奪得16枚金牌，22枚銀牌和16枚銅牌。

165

抓举运动员的体重。他们的体重决定他们在哪个小组参加比赛。

唐小风： 比赛的目的是要角逐出冠军、亚军。冠军通常得金牌，亚军得银牌，第三名得铜牌。

段剑虹： 看来这些体育名词还真有用啊！

问题: 体育比赛中所用的术语有哪些？

生词

团体赛	(tuán tǐ sài)	N.	team competition
半决赛	(bàn jué sài)	N.	semi-final(s)
决赛	(jué sài)	N.	final contest or match, finals, deciding match
举重	(jǔ zhòng)	N.	weight-lifting
抓举	(zhuā jǔ)	N.	snatch (in weight-lifting)
冠军	(guàn jūn)	N.	championship
亚军	(yà jūn)	N.	runner-up, 2nd place

三、电视新闻

1992年中国体坛硕果累累　新闻（一）

1992年中国体坛硕果累累。中国运动员在1992年共夺得89个世界冠军，其中29个属于奥运会项目，是历年来获得奥运会项目冠军最多的一年。

中国选手在世界大赛中还夺得52个亚军和45个第3名。在国内外比赛中，共有29人，4个队，103次打破40项世界纪录。

1992年是奥运会年，中国选手在第16届冬季奥运会实现了零的突破。在第25届夏季奥运会上夺得16枚金牌，22枚银牌和16枚铜牌。

生詞

體壇	(tǐ tán)	N.	the field of sports, sports world, realm of athletics
碩果	(shuò guǒ)	N.	great achievement, impressive fruits of success
累累	(lěi lěi)	Adj.	plenty, many
屬於	(shǔ yú)	V.	belong to
實現	(shí xiàn)	V.	to achieve, to bring about, to realize (a victory or goal)
夏季	(xià jì)	N.	summer season; summer
奪得	(duó dé)	V.	to obtain through competition, to carry off (the prize, honor, etc.)

首屆東亞運動會將在中國上海舉行 新聞（二）

　　首屆東亞運動會新聞報道座談會1月14號在北京舉行。

　　據會議透露，首屆東亞運動會將於1993年5月9號至18號在中國上海舉行。屆時將有來自東亞地區的韓國、蒙古、朝鮮、日本、香港及中國等9個國家和地區的6,000多人參加這次盛會。其中各國運動員為2,100多名，將分別參加田徑、游泳、體操等12個項目的角逐。前往東亞運動會採訪的新聞記者預計有1,200多名。

生詞

座談會	(zuò tán huì)	N.	talk(s), discussion meeting, forum
屆時	(jiè shí)	Adv.	at the appointed hour; when the time comes, at that time
前往	(qián wǎng)	V.	to proceed to, to go to, to head out for (place, event)
新聞記者	(xīn wén jì zhě)	N.	journalist, reporter, news reporter
預計	(yù jì)	V.	to estimate

生词

体坛	(tǐ tán)	N.	the field of sports, sports world, realm of athletics
硕果	(shuò guǒ)	N.	great achievement, impressive fruits of success
累累	(lěi lěi)	Adj.	plenty, many
属于	(shǔ yú)	V.	belong to
实现	(shí xiàn)	V.	to achieve, to bring about, to realize (a victory or goal)
夏季	(xià jì)	N.	summer season; summer
夺得	(duó dé)	V.	to obtain through competition, to carry off (the prize, honor, etc.)

首届东亚运动会将在中国上海举行 新闻（二）

　　首届东亚运动会新闻报道座谈会1月14号在北京举行。

　　据会议透露，首届东亚运动会将于1993年5月9号至18号在中国上海举行。届时将有来自东亚地区的韩国、蒙古、朝鲜、日本、香港及中国等9个国家和地区的6,000多人参加这次盛会。其中各国运动员为2,100多名，将分别参加田径、游泳、体操等12个项目的角逐。前往东亚运动会采访的新闻记者预计有1,200多名。

生词

座谈会	(zuò tán huì)	N.	talk(s), discussion meeting, forum
届时	(jiè shí)	Adv.	at the appointed hour; when the time comes, at that time
前往	(qián wǎng)	V.	to proceed to, to go to, to head out for (place, event)
新闻记者	(xīn wén jì zhě)	N.	journalist, reporter, news reporter
预计	(yù jì)	V.	to estimate

四、報紙閱讀

东亚运动会全面展开角逐
我选手杨斌摘取首枚金牌

本报上海5月10日电 记者**李泓冰**报道：首届东亚运动会的比赛今天全面展开。第1天9枚金牌为中、日、韩、中国台北队分获，东道主在举重、游泳、体操赛中夺得5金。

我国选手杨斌在54公斤级举重中摘取首枚金牌。韩国运动员全炳宽在59公斤级举重中以295公斤的总成绩和抓举135公斤的成绩创造了两项新的亚洲纪录，并获冠军。

游泳池内，中国选手庄泳、陈剑虹、王大力分获女子100米自由泳、男子100米蛙泳和男子200米自由泳的金牌。在女子400米个人混合泳决赛中，中国名将林莉以6秒之差输给日本17岁的前原仁美，前原仁美获冠军，成绩是4分42秒84。

今天最大冷门爆在唯一没有观众的项目——保龄球赛场内。中国台北队曾获5次世界冠军的马英杰马失前蹄，在男子单人比赛中跌至第6名，前3名均为日本选手，女子单人冠军是中国台北队的陈玉琴。

中国队还夺得今天的最后一枚金牌——以较大优势登上男子体操团体冠军领奖台。

在今天的足球比赛中，韩国队以12：0大胜澳门队，中国队以6：1胜蒙古队，朝鲜队2：0胜日本队。中国台北队在女篮比赛中，因最后5秒罚球未中，以83：84的1分之差输给日本队。

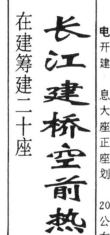

在建筹建二十座

长江建桥空前热

据新华社武汉5月10日电 （记者**李永升**）长江的开放开发带来了前所未有的建桥热。

来自沿江8个省市的信息表明，目前长江上新建成大桥2座，正在兴建的大桥5座，已经立项筹建的6座，正在进行可行性研究的4座，正在酝酿或作中长期规划的还有5座。

据了解，在建和筹建的20座大桥总长度将超过100公里，总投资200亿元左右。

東亞運動會全面展開角逐
我選手楊斌摘取首枚金牌

　　本報上海5月10日電　　記者李泓冰報道：首屆東亞運動會的比賽今天全面展開。第1天9枚金牌為中、日、韓、中國台北隊分獲，東道主在舉重、游泳、體操賽中奪得5金。

　　我國選手楊斌在54公斤級舉重中摘取首枚金牌。韓國運動員全炳寬在 59公斤級舉重中以295公斤的總成績和抓舉 135公斤的成績創造了兩項新的亞洲紀錄，並獲冠軍。

四、报纸阅读

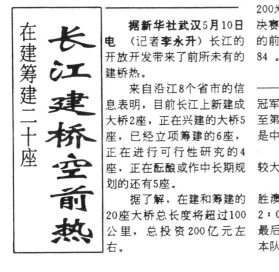

东亚运动会全面展开角逐
我选手杨斌摘取首枚金牌

本报上海5月10日电 记者李泓冰报道：首届东亚运动会的比赛今天全面展开。第1天9枚金牌为中、日、韩、中国台北队分获，东道主在举重、游泳、体操赛中夺得5金。

我国选手杨斌在54公斤级举重中摘取首枚金牌。韩国运动员全炳宽在59公斤级举重中以295公斤的总成绩和抓举135公斤的成绩创造了两项新的亚洲纪录，并获冠军。

游泳池内，中国选手庄泳、陈剑虹、王大力分获女子100米自由泳、男子100米蛙泳和男子200米自由泳的金牌。在女子400米个人混合泳决赛中，中国名将林莉以6秒之差输给日本17岁的前原仁美，前原仁美获冠军，成绩是4分42秒84。

今天最大冷门爆在唯一没有观众的项目——保龄球赛场内。中国台北队曾获5次世界冠军的马英杰马失前蹄，在男子单人比赛中跌至第6名，前3名均为日本选手，女子单人冠军是中国台北队的陈玉琴。

中国队还夺得今天的最后一枚金牌——以较大优势登上男子体操团体冠军领奖台。

在今天的足球比赛中，韩国队以12：0大胜澳门队，中国队以6：1胜蒙古队，朝鲜队2：0胜日本队。中国台北队在女篮比赛中，因最后5秒罚球未中，以83：84的1分之差输给日本队。

据新华社武汉5月10日电 （记者李永开）长江的开放开发带来了前所未有的建桥热。

来自沿江8个省市的信息表明，目前长江上新建成大桥2座，正在兴建的大桥5座，已经立项筹建的6座，正在进行可行性研究的4座，正在酝酿或作中长期规划的还有5座。

据了解，在建和筹建的20座大桥总长度将超过100公里，总投资200亿元左右。

在建筹建二十座

长江建桥空前热

东亚运动会全面展开角逐
我选手杨斌摘取首枚金牌

　　本报上海5月10日电　　记者李泓冰报道：首届东亚运动会的比赛今天全面展开。第1天9枚金牌为中、日、韩、中国台北队分获，东道主在举重、游泳、体操赛中夺得5金。

　　我国选手杨斌在54公斤级举重中摘取首枚金牌。韩国运动员全炳宽在59公斤级举重中以295公斤的总成绩和抓举135公斤的成绩创造了两项新的亚洲纪录，并获冠军。

游泳池內，中國選手莊泳、陳劍虹、王大力分獲女子100米自由泳、男子100米蛙泳和男子200米自由泳的金牌。在女子400米個人混合泳決賽中，中國名將林莉以6秒之差輸給日本17歲的前原仁美，前原仁美獲冠軍，成績4分42秒84。

今天最大的冷門爆在唯一沒有觀眾的項目—保齡球賽場內。中國台北隊曾獲5次世界冠軍的馬英傑馬失前蹄，在男子單人比賽中跌至第6名，前3名均為日本選手，女子單人冠軍是中國台北隊的陳玉琴。

中國隊還奪得今天的最後一枚金牌—以較大優勢登上男子體操團體冠軍領獎台。

在今天的足球比賽中，韓國隊以12:0大勝澳門隊，中國隊以6:1勝蒙古隊，朝鮮隊2:0勝日本隊。中國台北隊在女籃比賽中，因最後5秒罰球未中，以83:84的1分之差輸給日本隊。

生詞

楊斌	(yáng bīn)	*Personal N.*	Yang Bin, the name of a Chinese weight-lifter
摘取	(zhāi qǔ)	*V.*	to pick up; to take, to capture (prize, award)
全炳寬	(quán bǐng kuān)	*Personal N.*	the name of a South Korean weight-lifter
游泳池	(yóu yǒng chí)	*N.*	swimming pool
莊泳	(zhuāng yǒng)	*Personal N.*	Zhuang Yong, a famous Chinese swimmer
陳劍虹	(chén jiàn hóng)	*Personal N.*	Chen Jianhong, the name of a Chinese swimmer
王大力	(wáng dà lì)	*Personal N.*	Wang Dali, the name of a Chinese swimmer

　　游泳池内，中国选手庄泳、陈剑虹、王大力分获女子100米自由泳、男子100米蛙泳和男子200米自由泳的金牌。在女子400米个人混合泳决赛中，中国名将林莉以6秒之差输给日本17岁的前原仁美，前原仁美获冠军，成绩4分42秒84。

　　今天最大的冷门爆在唯一没有观众的项目—保龄球赛场内。中国台北队曾获5次世界冠军的马英杰马失前蹄，在男子单人比赛中跌至第6名，前3名均为日本选手，女子单人冠军是中国台北队的陈玉琴。

　　中国队还夺得今天的最后一枚金牌—以较大优势登上男子体操团体冠军领奖台。

　　在今天的足球比赛中，韩国队以12:0大胜澳门队，中国队以6:1胜蒙古队，朝鲜队2:0胜日本队。中国台北队在女篮比赛中，因最后5秒罚球未中，以83:84的1分之差输给日本队。

生词

杨斌	(yáng bīn)	*Personal N.*	Yang Bin, the name of a Chinese weight-lifter
摘取	(zhāi qǔ)	*V.*	to pick up; to take, to capture (prize, award)
全炳宽	(quán bǐng kuān)	*Personal N.*	the name of a South Korean weight-lifter
游泳池	(yóu yǒng chí)	*N.*	swimming pool
庄泳	(zhuāng yǒng)	*Personal N.*	Zhuang Yong, a famous Chinese swimmer
陈剑虹	(chén jiàn hóng)	*Personal N.*	Chen Jianhong, the name of a Chinese swimmer
王大力	(wáng dà lì)	*Personal N.*	Wang Dali, the name of a Chinese swimmer

名將	(míng jiàng)	*N.*	famous star
林莉	(lín lì)	*Personal N.*	Lin Li, the name of a Chinese swimmer
前原仁美	(qián yuán rén měi)	*Personal N.*	the name of a Japanese medley swimmer
冷門	(lěng mén)	*N.*	unexpected result; dark horse
爆	(bào)	*V.*	to burst out, to surprise everyone
賽場	(sài chǎng)	*N.*	court, site of contest (here; bowling alley)
馬英傑	(mǎ yīng jié)	*Personal N.*	Ma Yingjie, the name of a bowling star from Taiwan
馬失前蹄	(mǎ shī qián tí)	*Idiom.*	the horse lost its footing; i.e., to suffer an unexpected reversal
跌至	(diē zhì)	*V.*	to fall to
陳玉琴	(chén yù qín)	*Personal N.*	Chen Yuqin, the name of a bowling star from Taiwan
優勢	(yōu shì)	*N.*	dominant position, favorable position
團體	(tuán tǐ)	*N.*	team
領獎台	(lǐng jiǎng tái)	*N.*	the awards platform or podium
澳門	(ào mén)	*Place N.*	Macau
罰球	(fá qíu)	*N.*	penalty shot
未中	(wèi zhōng)	*V.*	fail to hit/score (the goal, the target, basket, etc.)

169

名将	(míng jiàng)	*N.*	famous star
林莉	(lín lì)	*Personal N.*	Lin Li, the name of a Chinese swimmer
前原仁美	(qián yuán rén měi)	*Personal N.*	the name of a Japanese medley swimmer
冷门	(lěng mén)	*N.*	unexpected result; dark horse
爆	(bào)	*V.*	to burst out, to surprise everyone
赛场	(sài chǎng)	*N.*	court, site of contest (here; bowling alley)
马英杰	(mǎ yīng jié)	*Personal N.*	Ma Yingjie, the name of a bowling star from Taiwan
马失前蹄	(mǎ shī qián tí)	*Idiom.*	the horse lost its footing; i.e., to suffer an unexpected reversal
跌至	(diē zhì)	*V.*	to fall to
陈玉琴	(chén yù qín)	*Personal N.*	Chen Yuqin, the name of a bowling star from Taiwan
优势	(yōu shì)	*N.*	dominant position, favorable position
团体	(tuán tǐ)	*N.*	team
领奖台	(lǐng jiǎng tái)	*N.*	the awards platform or podium
澳门	(ào mén)	*Place N.*	Macau
罚球	(fá qíu)	*N.*	penalty shot
未中	(wèi zhōng)	*V.*	fail to hit/score (the goal, the target, basket, etc.)

五、幽默小品

再找個爸爸

　　父親："你看看人家的小超，他和你一樣年紀，可是從來沒有被爸爸打過。你說，你以後應該怎麼辦？"

　　兒子："我要再找個好爸爸。"

五、幽默小品

再找个爸爸

父亲：　"你看看人家的小超，他和你一样年纪，可是从来没有被爸爸打过。你说，你以后应该怎么办？"

儿子：　"我要再找个好爸爸。"

課文要點

一、常用文言詞、縮略語與慣用語

1. 屆時＝到時 (at this time, at the appointed hour; when the time comes)

　　例：今天下午的交易會請屆時參加。

　　　　Please attend this afternoon's trade fair on time.

2. 未（中）＝沒有（中）(unable to hit the target)

　　例：他發球未中，所以丟了一分。

　　　　Because his serve was out-of-bounds, he lost a point.

3. 之（差）＝的（差別）(the difference is)

例：由於一分之差，她沒有拿到銀牌。

　　　　She missed taking a silver medal by only one point.

4. （體）壇＝（體育）界 (the sports world)

　　例：他是體壇最有名的運動員之一。

　　　　He is one of the most famous athletes in the sports world.

5. 馬失前蹄＝馬沒有控制好前蹄，指沒有想到的差錯 (the horse's front hooves stumbled, i.e., to experience an unexpected reversal)

　　例：最好的運動員也有馬失前蹄的時候。

　　　　Even the best athlete will suffer unexpected loss.

课文要点

一、常用文言词、缩略语与惯用语

1. 届时 = 到时 (at this time, at the appointed hour; when the time comes)

例：今天下午的交易会请届时参加。
Please attend this afternoon's trade fair on time.

2. 未（中）= 没有（中）(unable to hit the target)

例：他发球未中，所以丢了一分。
Because his serve was out-of-bounds, he lost a point.

3. 之（差）= 的（差别）(the difference is)

例：由于一分之差，她没有拿到银牌。
She missed taking a silver medal by only one point.

4. （体）坛 = （体育）界 (the sports world)

例：他是体坛最有名的运动员之一。
He is one of the most famous athletes in the sports world.

5. 马失前蹄 = 马没有控制好前蹄，指没有想到的差错 (the horse's front hooves stumbled, i.e., to experience an unexpected reversal)

例：最好的运动员也有马失前蹄的时候。
Even the best athlete will suffer unexpected loss.

6. 碩果累累＝收穫很大 (very successful)

例：今年中國的工業碩果累累。
China's industrial development has progressed greatly.

7. 舉重 (weightlifting)

8. 體操 (gymnastics)

9. 54公斤級舉重 (54 kilogram weightlifting)

10. 抓舉 (snatch)

11. 自由泳 (free style swimming)

12. 混合泳 (mixed style swimming)

13. 保齡球 (bowling)

二、常用短語

1. 據…透露 (according to ...who released that...)

例：據美國《時代》周刊透露美國總統曾跟印尼總統有過一個秘密會談。
It is divulged by Time Magazine that the U.S. President had previously held a secret meeting with the President of Indonesia.

據《經濟日報》透露，中國的經濟政策在近幾個月會有一個新的改變。
According to information disclosed by the Economics Daily, China's economic policy will have some new changes in the next several months.

6. 硕果累累 = 收获很大 (very successful)

例: 今年中国的工业硕果累累。
China's industrial development has progressed greatly.

7. 举重 (weightlifting)

8. 体操 (gymnastics)

9. 54公斤级举重 (54 kilogram weightlifting)

10. 抓举 (snatch)

11. 自由泳 (free style swimming)

12. 混合泳 (mixed style swimminɡ)

13. 保龄球 (bowling)

二、常用短语

1. 据…透露 (according to ...who released that...)

例: 据美国《时代》周刊透露美国总统曾跟印尼总统有过一个秘密会谈。
It is divulged by Time Magazine that the U.S. President had previously held a secret meeting with the President of Indonesia.

据《经济日报》透露，中国的经济政策在近几个月会有一个新的改变。
According to information disclosed by the Economics Daily, China's economic policy will have some new changes in the next several months.

2. 於…(time) 在…(place)舉行 (to hold a meeting or a conference, etc. at [place expression] at [time expression])

例：中文教師協會年會將於11月在波士頓舉行。
The Chinese Teacher's Association will hold its annual meeting in November in Boston.

由市政府舉辦的文化交流會將在本市電影宮舉行。
The cultural exchange convention sponsored by the city government will be held in the municipal film center.

3. 前往… (to come to)

例：屆時，將有數百名中文教師前往波士頓參加年會。
On this occasion, hundreds of Chinese teachers will travel to Boston to attend the annual meeting.

這次在廣州招開的盛會將有數千名地方政府和企業界人士參加。
This large scale meeting held in Guangzhou will be attended by thousands of local government officials and entrepreneurs.

4. 奪得（獲得）（冠軍、亞軍）(to win [obtain] a championship or runner-up, etc.)

例：在這次體操比賽中，意大利選手米勒奪得冠軍。
In this gymnastics meet, the gold medal went to an Italian athlete, Miller.

奪得這次運動會冠軍和亞軍的分別是瑞典隊和丹麥隊。
The championship and number two spot for this sports meet went to the teams from Switzerland and Denmark, respectively.

5. 實現了…的突破 (to break the record of; to achieve the result of)

例：在去年的冬季奧運會上，很多國家都實現了零的突破。
At the Winter Olympic Games last year, quite a few countries broke into the winning column (for taking a medal).

2. 于…(time) 在…(place)举行 (to hold a meeting or a conference, etc. at [place expression] at [time expression])

例: 中文教师协会年会将于11月在波士顿举行。

The Chinese Teacher's Association will hold its annual meeting in November in Boston.

由市政府举办的文化交流会将在本市电影宫举行。

The cultural exchange convention sponsored by the city government will be held in the municipal film center.

3. 前往… (to come to)

例: 届时，将有数百名中文教师前往波士顿参加年会。

On this occasion, hundreds of Chinese teachers will travel to Boston to attend the annual meeting.

这次在广州招开的盛会将有数千名地方政府和企业界人士参加。

This large scale meeting held in Guangzhou will be attended by thousands of local government officials and entrepreneurs.

4. 夺得（获得）（冠军、亚军）(to win [obtain] a championship or runner-up, etc.)

例: 在这次体操比赛中，意大利选手米勒夺得冠军。

In this gymnastics meet, the gold medal went to an Italian athlete, Miller.

夺得这次运动会冠军和亚军的分别是瑞典队和丹麦队。

The championship and number two spot for this sports meet went to the teams from Switzerland and Denmark, respectively.

5. 实现了…的突破 (to break the record of; to achieve the result of)

例: 在去年的冬季奥运会上，很多国家都实现了零的突破。

At the Winter Olympic Games last year, quite a few countries broke into the winning column (for taking a medal).

由於在經濟管理上開展產、供、銷一條龍，今年很多集體企業在創匯上實現了三十萬美元的突破。

Because of the implementation of the management system of combining production, supply, and sales into one, many collective enterprises have achieved record earnings in excess of 30,000 U.S. dollars.

6. 摘取⋯(to win an award, a medal...)

　例：在奧運會上摘取一枚金牌是我最大的願望。

　　My fondest dream is to win a medal at the Olympic Games.

　那個抓舉運動員最大的願望就是摘取一枚獎牌，把它獻給他的母親。

　That weight lifter's greatest wish is to win a medal and dedicate it to his mother.

7. 以⋯（時間、比分）輸給（勝了）...(to lose to [or to win] someone by a certain margin of points or score)

　例：我們學校的籃球隊昨天以 80:78 勝了明德籃球隊。

　　Our school's basketball team beat the Middlebury team by a score of 80 to 78 yesterday.

　在保齡球比賽中，加州的殘疾人運動員以 5:4 勝了紐約殘疾人運動員。

　In the bowling contest, the handicapped bowler from California outpaced the bowler from New York by a score of 5 games to 4.

174

由于在经济管理上开展产、供、销一条龙，今年很多集体企业在创汇上实现了三十万美元的突破。

Because of the implementation of the management system of combining production, supply, and sales into one, many collective enterprises have achieved record earnings in excess of 30,000 U.S. dollars.

6. 摘取···(to win an award, a medal...)

例：在奥运会上摘取一枚金牌是我最大的愿望。
My fondest dream is to win a medal at the Olympic Games.

那个抓举运动员最大的愿望就是摘取一枚奖牌，把它献给他的母亲。
That weight lifter's greatest wish is to win a medal and dedicate it to his mother.

7. 以···（时间、比分）输给（胜了）···(to lose to [or to win] someone by a certain margin of points or score)

例：我们学校的篮球队昨天以80:78胜了明德篮球队。
Our school's basketball team beat the Middlebury team by a score of 80 to 78 yesterday.

在保龄球比赛中，加州的残疾人运动员以5:4胜了纽约残疾人运动员。
In the bowling contest, the handicapped bowler from California outpaced the bowler from New York by a score of 5 games to 4.

第四單元 體育新聞

第三課

飛越長城

課文[1]

一、電視新聞

飛越長城

男：哎，小文，你還曾經記得我們報道過的飛越長城的柯受良先生嗎？

女：是的，他被稱為中國的"特技王"是吧？

男：是的。

女：在1992年11月成功地一次性飛過了萬里長城。

男：柯受良先生來自香港，他懷著我們中華民族自強不息的精神完成了這次歷史性的飛越。

女：而且他的飛越還被人們稱為"東方的奇觀"。

男：他還是世界上第一個飛越長城的人。

女：接下來的體壇縱橫欄目。我們就一起去看一看這壯觀的飛越場面。

---

[1]本課宜作為補充教材，幫助學生理解體育現場報道。課文開始的對話部分在錄像帶中省略。另外課文中省略了現場直播口語中的重復詞。

第四单元 体育新闻

第三课

飞越长城

课文[1]

一、电视新闻

飞越长城

男：哎，小文，你还曾经记得我们报道过的飞越长城的柯受良先生吗？

女：是的，他被称为中国的"特技王"是吧？

男：是的。

女：在1992年11月成功地一次性飞过了万里长城。

男：柯受良先生来自香港，他怀着我们中华民族自强不息的精神完成了这次历史性的飞越。

女：而且他的飞越还被人们称为"东方的奇观"。

男：他还是世界上第一个飞越长城的人。

女：接下来的体坛纵横栏目。我们就一起去看一看这壮观的飞越场面。

---

[1]本课宜作为补充教材，帮助学生理解体育现场报道。课文开始的对话部分在录像带中省略。另外课文中省略了现场直播口语中的重复词。

　　柯受良先生是一個專門從事特技表演的特技演員，在東南亞一帶享有很高的盛譽，人稱“特技王小飛”，現在我們看到的就是金山嶺長城。在他們決定11月15日飛越長城之前幾天，這里下起了鵝毛大雪。無疑這對施工、搭架子、以及11月15日的飛越在很多方面造成了很大的壓力。這個缺口是 30米整。11月15日這天天氣突然變好，這無疑是個很好的徵兆。柯受良先生的很多好朋友，大陸、台灣、香港，特別是演藝界的一些著名演員也來這里為他助威，祝願他能完成第一次飛越長城的壯舉。

　　各位注意看，這位騎在摩托車上的就是柯受良先生，跟在他後面的是他的學生和弟子，他們在柯受良先生的指導下完成了很多電影里面的高、精、難、險的特技表演和動作。柯受良今年 39歲，從事特技表演已經有18年的歷史。這一次他為甚麼選擇在 11月15日這個氣候並不是很好的情況下飛越長城呢？這在後面我們會向各位介紹的。現在他的弟子們和主辦單位都在預祝他能夠完成這次壯舉。站在了飛越台上，工人們拆下了最後一道能夠連接安全地帶的鐵管，大家看到那輛車就是他要使用的那部車。這個車里只有一點點兒汽油，因為如果汽油多，剎不住車就會有很大的危險。

　　現在他正在試車。站在最高平台上的是他的兩個助手。在飛越前，柯受良先生和我們講，他由一檔起速，變成二檔，三檔，直至四檔，任何一次都不能有錯，如果出現錯誤，就有可能掉下去。對面的平台上只有 50米長，所以搭了一個防護網。現在已經做好了一切準備，他就要進行飛越了。

　　走，好！他勝利地完成了這次飛越。盡管是搭了這麼厚的防護牆，事後，柯受良先生的右肩還是受了一些輕傷，因為他飛越起來的速度，在空中只有一秒鐘左右，下地之後剎車是根本來不及的，所以用了這樣一個防護網。防護網只能減輕一些衝擊力量，可是畢竟我們正常人是承受不了的。從

　　柯受良先生是一个专门从事特技表演的特技演员，在东南亚一带享有很高的盛誉，人称"特技王小飞"，现在我们看到的就是金山岭长城。在他们决定11月15日飞越长城之前几天，这里下起了鹅毛大雪。无疑这对施工、搭架子、以及11月15日的飞越在很多方面造成了很大的压力。这个缺口是 30米整。11月15日这天天气突然变好，这无疑是个很好的征兆。柯受良先生的很多好朋友，大陆、台湾、香港，特别是演艺界的一些著名演员也来这里为他助威，祝愿他能完成第一次飞越长城的壮举。

　　各位注意看，这位骑在摩托车上的就是柯受良先生，跟在他后面的是他的学生和弟子，他们在柯受良先生的指导下完成了很多电影里面的高、精、难、险的特技表演和动作。柯受良今年 39岁，从事特技表演已经有18年的历史。这一次他为什么选择在 11月15日这个气候并不是很好的情况下飞越长城呢？这在后面我们会向各位介绍的。现在他的弟子们和主办单位都在预祝他能够完成这次壮举。站在了飞越台上，工人们拆下了最后一道能够连接安全地带的铁管，大家看到那辆车就是他要使用的那部车。这个车里只有一点点儿汽油，因为如果汽油多，刹不住车就会有很大的危险。

　　现在他正在试车。站在最高平台上的是他的两个助手。在飞越前，柯受良先生和我们讲，他由一档起速，变成二档，三档，直至四档，任何一次都不能有错，如果出现错误，就有可能掉下去。对面的平台上只有 50米长，所以搭了一个防护网。现在已经做好了一切准备，他就要进行飞越了。

　　走，好！他胜利地完成了这次飞越。尽管是搭了这么厚的防护墙，事后，柯受良先生的右肩还是受了一些轻伤，因为他飞越起来的速度，在空中只有一秒钟左右，下地之后刹车是根本来不及的，所以用了这样一个防护网。防护网只能减轻一些冲击力量，可是毕竟我们正常人是承受不了的。从事這個職業需要堅強的信念和極強的心理素質。你看，他的女兒為他獻上了鮮花。好，讓我們再看一遍慢動作。…二檔，三檔，四檔！再看看正面拍攝。

當柯受良先生，也就是小飛完成了這次飛越長城的壯舉之後，我們當晚在他居住的地方對他進行了一次採訪，他向我們觀眾解答了一些大家都很想知道和了解的問題。

問：那一天天氣預報有六級大風，下面還有一點雪…

柯：對，還飄了一點雪，很漂亮，很壯觀。為甚麼我會選在這個時候飛，其實我已經跟國家體委、國家雜誌社在一年半以前就籌備這個事情。當我在新加坡的時候，打開報紙一看，聽説有個英國人要飛萬里長城，我們中國人的東西為甚麼給外國人飛？那我就在很短的時間， 9月份就趕緊上來北京在接洽這個事情，那我們就決定在河北省金山嶺來飛。當然，我一定要做，中國人是第一，讓世界看，我們也做得到特技。有這麼多觀眾，整個山頭都是人，那種中國人…大家好像連著心團結起來…在現場要飛之前那種感覺和士氣很重要。

問：當我們快要結束採訪的時候，柯受良先生將他特技表演集錦的錄像帶送給了我們，這是他在完成飛越大峽谷的動作，這是他在跨越兩條高速公路。經常看電影的同志們可能會注意到，這部影片是成龍導演並主演的“警察故事”的片斷，由於柯受良先生經常在一些影片中準確無誤地表演了特技表演動作，所以他贏得了諸多導演和演員的尊重。所以此次長城飛越的時候，他們都是自己花的錢來北京來為他助威。

經過準確的丈量，柯受良先生此次飛越長城的跨度是： 58.85米，並且已經申報了吉尼斯世界紀錄。

事这个职业需要坚强的信念和极强的心理素质。你看，他的女儿为他献上了鲜花。好，让我们再看一遍慢动作。…二档，三档，四档！再看看正面拍摄。

当柯受良先生，也就是小飞完成了这次飞越长城的壮举之后，我们当晚在他居住的地方对他进行了一次采访，他向我们观众解答了一些大家都很想知道和了解的问题。

问：那一天天气预报有六级大风，下面还有一点雪…

柯：对，还飘了一点雪，很漂亮，很壮观。为什么我会选在这个时候飞，其实我已经跟国家体委、国家杂志社在一年半以前就筹备这个事情。当我在新加坡的时候，打开报纸一看，听说有个英国人要飞万里长城，我们中国人的东西为什么给外国人飞？那我就在很短的时间，9月份就赶紧上来北京在接洽这个事情，那我们就决定在河北省金山岭来飞。当然，我一定要做，中国人是第一，让世界看，我们也做得到特技。有这么多观众，整个山头都是人，那种中国人…大家好象连着心团结起来…在现场要飞之前那种感觉和士气很重要。

问：当我们快要结束采访的时候，柯受良先生将他特技表演集锦的录像带送给了我们，这是他在完成飞越大峡谷的动作，这是他在跨越两条高速公路。经常看电影的同志们可能会注意到，这部影片是成龙导演并主演的"警察故事"的片断，由于柯受良先生经常在一些影片中准确无误地表演了特技表演动作，所以他赢得了诸多导演和演员的尊重。所以此次长城飞越的时候，他们都是自己花的钱来北京来为他助威。

经过准确的丈量，柯受良先生此次飞越长城的跨度是：58.85米，并且已经申报了吉尼斯世界纪录。

生詞

特技	(tè jì)	*N.*	stunts, tricks; stunts and special effects (in movies, photography, TV production)
特技王	(tè jì wáng)	*NP.*	the king of stunts
懷著	(huái zhe)	*V.*	to cherish, imbued with the spirit of
自強不息	(zì qiáng bù xī)	*Idiom.*	to make unceasing efforts to improve oneself
東方的奇觀	(dōng fāng de qí guān)	*NP.*	one of the wonders of the Orient
體壇縱橫	(tǐ tán zòng héng)	*N.*	sports review
欄目	(lán mù)	*N.*	column
壯觀	(zhuàng guān)	*Adj.*	splendid scene
場面	(chǎng miàn)	*N.*	scene
享有	(xiǎng yǒu)	*V.*	to enjoy (fame, rights, prestige)
盛譽	(shèng yù)	*N.*	great fame
稱	(chēng)	*V.*	to be called, to be addressed as
金山嶺	(jīn shān lǐng)	*Place N.*	Mount Jinshan
鵝毛大雪	(é máo dà xuě)	*Idiom.*	heavy snow
無疑	(wú yí)	*Adv.*	doubtless
施工	(shī gōng)	*VO.*	to be under construction
搭架子	(dā jià zi)	*VO.*	to build a framework
缺口	(quē kǒu)	*N.*	breach, gap
徵兆	(zhēng zhào)	*N.*	omen, portent, sign
演藝界	(yǎn yì jiè)	*NP.*	the show business
助威	(zhù wēi)	*VO.*	to cheer on, to lend their moral support
壯舉	(zhuàng jǔ)	*N.*	splendid deeds
摩托車	(mó tuō chē)	*N.*	motorcycle
弟子	(dì zǐ)	*N.*	follower(s), disciple(s)
精	(jīng)	*Adj.*	skillful, accurate
主辦單位	(zhǔ bàn dān wèi)	*NP.*	sponsoring institution
鐵管	(tiě guǎn)	*N.*	iron pipe
汽油	(qì yóu)	*N.*	gas

生词

特技	(tè jì)	N.	stunts, tricks; stunts and special effects (in movies, photography, TV production)
特技王	(tè jì wáng)	NP.	the king of stunts
怀着	(huái zhe)	V.	to cherish, imbued with the spirit of
自强不息	(zì qiáng bù xī)	Idiom.	to make unceasing efforts to improve oneself
东方的奇观	(dōng fāng de qí guān)	NP.	one of the wonders of the Orient
体坛纵横	(tǐ tán zhòng héng)	N.	sports review
栏目	(lán mù)	N.	column
壮观	(zhuàng guān)	Adj.	splendid scene
场面	(chǎng miàn)	N.	scene
享有	(xiǎng yǒu)	V.	to enjoy (fame, rights, prestige)
盛誉	(shèng yù)	N.	great fame
称	(chēng)	V.	to be called, to be addressed as
金山岭	(jīn shān lǐng)	Place N.	Mount Jinshan
鹅毛大雪	(é máo dà xuě)	Idiom.	heavy snow
无疑	(wú yí)	Adv.	doubtless
施工	(shī gōng)	VO.	to be under construction
搭架子	(dā jià zi)	VO.	to build a framework
缺口	(quē kǒu)	N.	breach, gap
征兆	(zhēng zhào)	N.	omen, portent, sign
演艺界	(yǎn yì jiè)	NP.	the show business
助威	(zhù wēi)	VO.	to cheer on, to lend their moral support
壮举	(zhuàng jǔ)	N.	splendid deeds
摩托车	(mó tuō chē)	N.	motorcycle
弟子	(dì zǐ)	N.	follower(s), disciple(s)
精	(jīng)	Adj.	skillful, accurate
主办单位	(zhǔ bàn dān wèi)	NP.	sponsoring institution
铁管	(tiě guǎn)	N.	iron pipe
汽油	(qì yóu)	N.	gas

檔	(dǎng)	N.	gear
起速	(qǐ sù)	VO.	to accelerate, to start to accelerate
搭	(dā)	V.	to put up
防護網	(fáng hù wǎng)	N.	protection net
右肩	(yòu jiān)	N.	the right shoulder
輕傷	(qīng shāng)	NP.	light wound
剎車	(shā chē)	VO.	to brake, to put on the brakes of a vehicle
衝擊力量	(chōng jī lì liàng)	NP.	momentum
畢竟	(bì jìng)	Adv.	after all
鮮花	(xiān huā)	N.	fresh flower
慢動作	(màn dòng zuò)	NP.	slow motion
正面	(zhèng miàn)	N.	the front
天氣預報	(tiān qì yù bào)	NP.	weather broadcasting
六級大風	(liu jí dà fēng)	NP.	a force six wind
籌備	(chóu bèi)	V.	to prepare
接洽	(jiē qià)	V.	to contact, make arrangement
士氣	(shì qì)	N.	morale
集錦	(jí jǐn)	N.	collection of outstanding examples
大峽谷	(dà xiá gǔ)	Place N.	the grand canyon
高速公路	(gāo sù gōng lù)	N.	highway
片斷	(piàn duàn)	N.	excerpts
準確無誤	(zhǔn què wú wù)	Idiom.	accurate and precise
贏得	(yíng dé)	V.	to win
諸多	(zhū duō)	Adj.	many
跨度	(kuà dù)	N.	gap

档	(dǎng)	N.	gear
起速	(qǐ sù)	VO.	to accelerate, to start to accelerate
搭	(dā)	V.	to put up
防护网	(fáng hù wǎng)	N.	protection net
右肩	(yòu jiān)	N.	the right shoulder
轻伤	(qīng shāng)	NP.	light wound
刹车	(shā chē)	VO.	to brake, to put on the brakes of a vehicle
冲击力量	(chōng jī lì liàng)	NP.	momentum
毕竟	(bì jìng)	Adv.	after all
鲜花	(xiān huā)	N.	fresh flower
慢动作	(màn dòng zuò)	NP.	slow motion
正面	(zhèng miàn)	N.	the front
天气预报	(tiān qì yù bào)	NP.	weather broadcasting
六级大风	(liu jí dà fēng)	NP.	a force six wind
筹备	(chóu bèi)	V.	to prepare
接洽	(jiē qià)	V.	to contact, make arrangement
士气	(shì qì)	N.	morale
集锦	((jí jǐn)	N.	collection of outstanding examples
大峡谷	(dà xiá gǔ)	Place N.	the grand canyon
高速公路	(gāo sù gōng lù)	N.	highway
片断	(piàn duàn)	N.	excerpts
准确无误	(zhǔn què wú wù)	Idiom.	accurate and precise
赢得	(yíng dé)	V.	to win
诸多	(zhū duō)	Adj.	many
跨度	(kuà dù)	N.	gap

二、幽默小品

大家都笑

太太：“今天我到市場買菜，有個人摔得四腳朝天，大家都笑。只有我一個人沒有笑。”

丈夫：“想不到你這麼有同情心。”

太太：“摔倒的那個人就是我。”

二、幽默小品

大家都笑

太太： "今天我到市场买菜，有个人摔得四脚朝天，大家都笑。只有我一个人没有笑。"

丈夫： "想不到你这么有同情心。"

太太： "摔倒的那个人就是我。"

課文要點

一、常用縮略語

體委＝中國體育委員會 (China's Sports Committee)

二、常用短語

1. …懷著…的精神（的心） (with the spirit of [with curiosity])

例：這個動物園的工人懷著對國家高度負責的精神精心飼養大熊貓。
The animal keepers of the zoo take good care of the pandas with the understanding that their responsibility is related to the honor of the country.

我懷著一顆好奇心來到倫敦電冰箱廠。
I came to visit the London refrigerator factory with curiosity.

2. …專門從事… (to specialize in; to specially engage in)

例：我的朋友專門從事買賣帆船的生意。
My friend specializes in buying and selling sailboats.

李明這幾年專門從事多功能、豪華型的產品出口貿易。
In recent years, Li Ming has engaged in exporting multifunctional, deluxe products.

3. …享有盛譽 (to enjoy the fame of)

例：魏競先的髮繡肖像在國內外都享有很高的盛譽。
The portraits embroidered with hair by Wei Jingxian enjoy great fame both domestically and internationally.

181

课文要点

一、常用缩略语

体委 = 中国体育委员会 (China's Sports Committee)

二、常用短语

1. …怀着…的精神（的心）(with the spirit of [with curiosity])

例：这个动物园的工人怀着对国家高度负责的精神精心饲养大熊猫。

The animal keepers of the zoo take good care of the pandas with the understanding that their responsibility is related to the honor of the country.

我怀着一颗好奇心来到伦敦电冰箱厂。

I came to visit the London refrigerator factory with curiosity.

2. …专门从事… (to specialize in; to specially engage in)

例：我的朋友专门从事买卖帆船的生意。

My friend specializes in buying and selling sailboats.

李明这几年专门从事多功能、豪华型的产品出口贸易。

In recent years, Li Ming has engaged in exporting multifunctional, deluxe products.

3. …享有盛誉 (to enjoy the fame of)

例：魏竞先的发绣肖像在国内外都在享有很高的盛誉。

The portraits embroidered with hair by Wei Jingxian enjoy great fame both domestically and internationally.

中國的絹花在國外也享有盛譽。

The silk flowers of China are also famous in other countries.

4. 為⋯助威 (to cheer for, to boost the morale of)

例：前天，我們都去為學校的乒乓球隊助威。

The day before yesterday, we all went to root for our school's ping pong team.

巴賽羅那的市民為西班牙的奧運健兒助威。

The citizens of Barcelona cheered for Spain's Olympic athletes.

5. ⋯完成⋯的壯舉 (to achieve/fulfill the great feat of)

例：中國奧運健兒完成了贏得17塊金牌的歷史壯舉，今天回到中國。

The Olympic athletes of China fulfilled the historic winning of 17 gold medals and returned to China yesterday.

柯先生經過短期準備，終於完成了飛越長城的壯舉。

After short period of preperation, Mr. Ke finally fulfilled the great feat of crossing the Great Wall.

6. 在⋯的指導下⋯ (under the guidance of , under the supervision of)

例：在專業人員的指導下，他們成功地生產出很多多功能的家用電器。

Under the guidance of the experts, they succeeded in producing many multifunctional domestic appliances.

在我的老師的指導下，我終於完成了我的畢業論文。

I finally finished my senior thesis under the guidance of my professor.

7. 已經有⋯年的歷史 (to have a history of... for ... years)

中国的绢花在国外也享有盛誉。

The silk flowers of China are also famous in other countries.

4. 为…助威 (to cheer for, to boost the morale of)

例: 前天，我们都去为学校的乒乓球队助威。

The day before yesterday, we all went to root for our school's ping pong team.

巴赛罗那的市民为西班牙的奥运健儿助威。

The citizens of Barcelona cheered for Spain's Olympic athletes.

5. …完成…的壮举 (to achieve/fulfill the great feat of)

例: 中国奥运健儿完成了赢得17块金牌的历史壮举，今天回到中国。

The Olympic athletes of China fulfilled the historic winning of 17 gold medals and returned to China yesterday.

柯先生经过短期准备，终於完成了飞越长城的壮举。

After short period of preperation, Mr. Ke finally fulfilled the great feat of crossing the Great Wall.

6. 在…的指导下… (under the guidance of , under the supervision of)

例: 在专业人员的指导下，他们成功地生产出很多多功能的家用电器。

Under the guidance of the experts, they succeeded in producing many multifunctional domestic appliances.

在我的老师的指导下，我终於完成了我的毕业论文。

I finally finished my senior thesis under the guidance of my professor.

例：他當總統已經有六年的歷史了。
He has been a president for 6 years.

這家航空公司已經有二十年的歷史了。
This airline has had a history of 20 years.

8. 為…獻上… (to present flowers to)

例：當印度客人到達機場的時候，兒童們為他們獻上了鮮花。
When Indian guests arrived at the airport, the children presented flowers to them.

在中外合資的洽談會上，公司的經理為客人獻上一杯酒。
At the Chinese-foreign joint venture talk, the head of the company toasted each of the guests with a glass of wine.

9. 對…進行採訪 (to have an interview with)

例：ABC 的記者對我們的州長進行了採訪。
The ABC correspondents interviewed our governer.

你可以去中南海對中國政府要人進行採訪嗎？
Can you go to Zhongnanhai and interview high ranking Chinese government officials？

7. 已经有…年的历史 (to have a history of... for ... years)

例: 他当总统已经有六年的历史了。
He has been a president for 6 years.

这家航空公司已经有二十年的历史了。
This airline has had a history of 20 years.

8. 为…献上… (to present flowers to)

例: 当印度客人到达机场的时候，儿童们为他们献上了鲜花。
When Indian guests arrived at the airport, the children presented flowers to them.

在中外合资的洽谈会上，公司的经理为客人献上一杯酒。
At the Chinese-foreign joint venture talk, the head of the company toasted each of the guests with a glass of wine.

9. 对…进行采访 (to have an interview with)

例: ABC 的记者对我们的州长进行了采访。
The ABC correspondents interviewed our governer.

你可以去中南海对中国政府要人进行采访吗？
Can you go to Zhongnanhai and interview high ranking Chinese government officials ?

小課文

不拘小節的人

一、看電視小課文、回答問題

    1. 廣告中的青年做了甚麼事情？

    2. 為甚麼他的同事都很不高興？

    3. 從廣告中你看到中國人的工作條件怎麼樣？

    4. 這里 "不拘小節" 是甚麼意思？

二、寫作

    寫一個小故事描述廣告中的 "不拘小節" 的人。

小课文

不拘小节的人

一、看电视小课文、回答问题

1. 广告中的青年做了什么事情？

2. 为什么他的同事都很不高兴？

3. 从广告中你看到中国人的工作条件怎么样？

4. 这里 "不拘小节" 是什么意思？

二、写作

写一个小故事描述广告中的 "不拘小节" 的人。

輕輕地告訴你

讓我輕輕地告訴你
天上的星星在等待
分享你的寂寞，你的歡樂
還有甚麼不能說
讓我慢慢地靠近你
伸出雙手你還有我
給你我的幻想，我的祝福
生命陽光最溫暖
啦啦啦……
不要問我太陽有多高
我會告訴你我有多真
不要問我星星有幾顆
我會告訴你很多
不要問我太陽有多高
我會告訴你我有多真
不要問我星星有幾顆
我會告訴你很多，很多

讓我輕輕地告訴你
天上的星星在等待
分享你的寂寞，你的歡樂
還有甚麼不能說
讓我慢慢的靠近你
伸出雙手你還有我
給你我的幻想，我的祝福
生命陽光最溫暖
啦啦啦……
不要問我太陽有多高
我會告訴你我有多真
不要問我星星有幾顆
我會告訴你很多
不要問我太陽有多高
我會告訴你我有多真
不要問我星星有幾顆
我會告訴你很多，很多

中国歌曲

轻轻地告诉你

让我轻轻地告诉你
天上的星星在等待
分享你的寂寞，你的欢乐
还有什么不能说
让我慢慢地靠近你
伸出双手你还有我
给你我的幻想，我的祝福
生命阳光最温暖
啦啦啦……
不要问我太阳有多高
我会告诉你我有多真
不要问我星星有几颗
我会告诉你很多
不要问我太阳有多高
我会告诉你我有多真
不要问我星星有几颗
我会告诉你很多，很多

让我轻轻地告诉你
天上的星星在等待
分享你的寂寞，你的欢乐
还有什么不能说
让我慢慢的靠近你
伸出双手你还有我
给你我的幻想，我的祝福
生命阳光最温暖
啦啦啦……
不要问我太阳有多高
我会告诉你我有多真
不要问我星星有几颗
我会告诉你很多
不要问我太阳有多高
我会告诉你我有多真
不要问我星星有几颗
我会告诉你很多，很多

Appendix I: Vocabulary Index

生詞表

Vocabulary Index[1]

愛因斯坦	àiyīnsītǎn	*Personal N.*	Albert Einstein (1879-1955), German-born and raised physicist, discovered law of relativity, Nobel prize winner; U3L4
按	àn	*Prep.*	according to; U1L3
按比例	ànbǐlì	*Prep P*	proportionally; U2L2
安全	ānquán	*Adv/N.*	safely; safety; U2L1
澳門	àomén	*Place N.*	Macau; U4L2
澳星	àoxīng	*Abbrev.*	澳大利亞的衛星, the Australian Satellite (a communications satellite launched by China for Australia); U1L1
奧運	àoyùn	*Abbrev.*	the Olympic Games＝奧運會＝奧林匹克運動會; U1L1
奧運會	àoyùnhuì	*Abbrev.*	Olympic Games＝奧林匹克運動會; U4L1
巴格達	bāgédá	*Place N.*	Bagdad (Baghdad); U1L3
罷工	bàgōng	*VO.*	to go on strike; U2L1
百花獎	bǎihuājiǎng	*N.*	the One Hundred Flower Award; U3L4
白酒	báijiǔ	*N.*	colorless spirits, usually 40-50% alcohol, distilled from sorghum, corn, wheat or other grains; U2L3
擺攤	bǎitān	*VO.*	to set up a booth; U2L4
百縣千鄉	bǎixiànqiānxiāng	*Idiom.*	hundreds of counties, thousands of small towns and villages; U2L4
巴勒斯坦	bālèsītǎn	*Place N.*	Palestine; U2L2
班機	bānjī	*N.*	flight; U2L1

---

[1] The index is arranged alphabetically according to the Pinyin system. On each line, first listed is the Chinese character, then its pinyin and grammatical category, and finally its English translation. The Unit and Lesson where the vocabulary entry first appears is provided at the end.

生词表

Vocabulary Index[1]

爱因斯坦	àiyīnsītǎn	*Personal N.*	Albert Einstein (1879-1955), German-born and raised physicist, discovered law of relativity, Nobel prize winner; U3L4
按	àn	*Prep.*	according to; U1L3
按比例	ànbǐlì	*Prep P.*	proportionally; U2L2
安全	ānquán	*Adv/N.*	safely; safety; U2L1
澳门	àomén	*Place N.*	Macau; U4L2
澳星	àoxīng	*Abbrev.*	澳大利亚的卫星, the Australian Satellite (a communications satellite launched by China for Australia); U1L1
奥运	àoyùn	*Abbrev.*	the Olympic Games = 奥运会 = 奥林匹克运动会; U1L1
奥运会	àoyùnhuì	*Abbrev.*	Olympic Games = 奥林匹克运动会; U4L1
巴格达	bāgédá	*Place N.*	Bagdad (Baghdad); U1L3
罢工	bàgōng	*VO.*	to go on strike; U2L1
百花奖	bǎihuājiǎng	*N.*	the One Hundred Flower Award; U3L4
白酒	báijiǔ	*N.*	colorless spirits, usually 40-50% alcohol, distilled from sorghum, corn, wheat or other grains; U2L3
摆摊	bǎitān	*VO.*	to set up a booth; U2L4
百县千乡	bǎixiànqiānxiāng	*Idiom.*	hundreds of counties, thousands of small towns and villages; U2L4
巴勒斯坦	bālèsītǎn	*Place N.*	Palestine; U2L2
班机	bānjī	*N.*	flight; U2L1

[1] The index is arranged alphabetically according to the Pinyin system. On each line, first listed is the Chinese character, then its pinyin and grammatical category, and finally its English translation. The Unit and Lesson where the vocabulary entry first appears is provided at the end.

半決賽	bànjuésài	N.	semi-final(s); U4L2
爆	bào	V.	to burst out, to surprise everyone; U4L2
保存	bǎocún	V/N.	to preserve; preservation; U3L4
報道	bàodào	V/N.	to report; report; U1L2
暴跌	bàodiē	VP.	to drop sharply, to plunge, to plummet; U1L1
報告	bàogào	N/V.	report; to report; U1L1
保管	bǎoguǎn	V/N.	to store, to preserve; storage, preservation; U3L3
保護	bǎohù	V.	to protect; U3L2
包括	bāokuò	V.	to include; U3L3
保齡球	bǎolíngqíu	N.	bowling; U4L2
保密	bǎomì	Adj/Adv.	secretive; secretively; U1L3
巴塞羅那	bāsàiluónà	Place N.	Barcelona; U3L2
北斑鷹	běibānyīng	N.	northern spotted owl; U3L2
貝多芬	bèiduōfēn	Personal N.	Ludwig van Beethoven (1770-1827) German composer; U3L4
本台	běntái	N.	one's own station; our own broadcasting station; this station; U1L2
閉	bì	V.	to close (eyes, mouth, gate, etc.); U1L3
表演	biǎoyǎn	V/N.	to perform, performance; U3L1
畢加索	bìjiāsuǒ	Personal N.	Pablo Picasso (1881-1973) Catalonian painter, sulptor, graphic artist who lived and worked in France after 1900; U3L4
畢竟	bìjìng	Adv.	after all; U4L3
閉幕	bìmù	VO.	to close, to conclude; U3L1
閉幕式	bìmùshì	N.	closing ceremony; U4L1
畢業晚會	bìyèwǎnhuì	NP.	graduation party; U3L1
博覽會	bólánhuì	N.	international exposition, exhibition; U3L3
博物館	bówùguǎn	N.	museum; U3L3
部	bù	Classifier.	a classifier for movies; U3L1
步伐	bùfá	N.	steps, pace, speed; U1L4
不及格	bùjígé	V.	fail to pass; U2L3
布匹	bùpǐ	N.	fabric, cloth; U3L4
不同程度	bùtóngchéngdù	NP.	to different degrees; to a certain extent; U4L2
哺育	bǔyù	V.	to nurse; to feed; to nurture; U3L2

半决赛	bànjuésài	*N.*	semi-final(s); U4L2
爆	bào	*V.*	to burst out, to surprise everyone; U4L2
保存	bǎocún	*V/N.*	to preserve; preservation; U3L4
报道	bàodào	*V/N.*	to report; report; U1L2
暴跌	bàodiē	*VP.*	to drop sharply, to plunge, to plummet; U1L1
报告	bàogào	*N/V.*	report; to report; U1L1
保管	bǎoguǎn	*V/N.*	to store, to preserve; storage, preservation; U3L3
保护	bǎohù	*V.*	to protect; U3L2
包括	bāokuò	*V.*	to include; U3L3
保龄球	bǎolíngqíu	*N.*	bowling; U4L2
保密	bǎomì	*Adj/Adv.*	secretive; secretively; U1L3
巴塞罗那	bāsàiluónà	*Place N.*	Barcelona; U3L2
北斑鹰	běibānyīng	*N.*	northern spotted owl; U3L2
贝多芬	bèiduōfēn	*Personal N.*	Ludwig van Beethoven (1770-1827) German composer; U3L4
本台	běntái	*N.*	one's own station; our own broadcasting station; this station; U1L2
闭	bì	*V.*	to close (eyes, mouth, gate, etc.); U1L3
表演	biǎoyǎn	*V/N.*	to perform, performance; U3L1
毕加索	bìjiāsuǒ	*Personal N.*	Pablo Picasso (1881-1973) Catalonian painter, sulptor, graphic artist who lived and worked in France after 1900; U3L4
毕竟	bìjìng	*Adv.*	after all; U4L3
闭幕	bìmù	*VO.*	to close, to conclude; U3L1
闭幕式	bìmùshì	*N.*	closing ceremony; U4L1
毕业晚会	bìyèwǎnhuì	*NP.*	graduation party; U3L1
博览会	bólánhuì	*N.*	international exposition, exhibition; U3L3
博物馆	bówùguǎn	*N.*	museum; U3L3
部	bù	*Classifier.*	a classifier for movies; U3L1
步伐	bùfá	*N.*	steps, pace, speed; U1L4
不及格	bùjígé	*V.*	fail to pass; U2L3
布匹	bùpǐ	*N.*	fabric, cloth; U3L4
不同程度	bùtóngchéngdù	*NP.*	to different degrees; to a certain extent; U4L2
哺育	bǔyù	*V.*	to nurse; to feed; to nurture; U3L2

部長	bùzhǎng	*Title/rank*	minister; U1L3
不足	bùzú	*Adj/Adv.*	less than; insufficient to/for; U3L2
猜測	cāicè	*V/N.*	to speculate about; to guess; speculation; conjecture (s), guesses; U1L3
採訪	cǎifǎng	*V.*	to gather information, to cover the story; U1L3
採取	cǎiqǔ	*V.*	to adopt (a policy, a plan), to take (action); U1L3
踩在	cǎizài	*V.*	to step on; U2L1
殘奧會	cánàohuì	*Abbrev.*	the special Olympics＝殘疾人奧林匹克運動會; U4L1
藏	cáng	*V.*	to collect, to hold (of a museum's collection); U3L3
殘疾人	cánjírén	*N.*	handicapped people; U4L1
參賽	cānsài	*VO.*	to participate in competition; U4L1
參展	cānzhǎn	*VO.*	to be included in the exhibition; U3L3
場	chǎng	*Classifier.*	showing (of films), screening(s); U3L1
長春	chángchūn	*Place N.*	Changchun, capital city of Jilin Province; U3L1
長春杯	chángchūnbēi	*Title.*	the Changchun Cup (top award in a film festival); U3L1
廠房	chǎngfáng	*N.*	factory shop, workshop, factory bldg., factory floor; U2L3
場面	chǎngmiàn	*N.*	scene; U4L3
長跑	chángpǎo	*N.*	long-distance running; U4L2
嘗試	chángshì	*N.*	attempt, trial run; U2L4
常用詞彙	chángyòngcíhuì	*NP.*	commonly used vocabulary; U4L2
產品	chǎnpǐn	*N.*	product; U2L2
產品形象	chǎnpǐnxíngxiàng	*NP.*	product lines, appearance of products; U2L2
產銷	chǎnxiāo	*V/N.*	to produce and sell; production and sales; U2L2
產值	chǎnzhí	*N.*	value of output, total value of what was produced; U2L2
產仔	chǎnzǐ	*VO.*	＝產下幼仔, to give birth to a baby animal; U3L2
超過	chāoguò	*V.*	to exceed; U2L1
朝鮮	cháoxiǎn	*Place N.*	North Korea; U4L2

部长	bùzhǎng	Title/rank	minister; U1L3
不足	bùzú	Adj/Adv.	less than; insufficient to/for; U3L2
猜测	cāicè	V/N.	to speculate about; to guess; speculation; conjecture (s), guesses; U1L3
采访	cǎifǎng	V.	to gather information, to cover the story; U1L3
采取	cǎiqǔ	V.	to adopt (a policy, a plan), to take (action); U1L3
踩在	cǎizài	V.	to step on; U2L1
残奥会	cánàohuì	Abbrev.	the special Olympics = 残疾人奥林匹克运动会; U4L1
藏	cáng	V.	to collect, to hold (of a museum's collection); U3L3
残疾人	cánjírén	N.	handicapped people; U4L1
参赛	cānsài	VO.	to participate in competition; U4L1
参展	cānzhǎn	VO.	to be included in the exhibition; U3L3
场	chǎng	Classifier.	showing (of films), screening(s); U3L1
长春	chángchūn	Place N.	Changchun, capital city of Jilin Province; U3L1
长春杯	chángchūnbēi	Title.	the Changchun Cup (top award in a film festival); U3L1
厂房	chǎngfáng	N.	factory shop, workshop, factory bldg., factory floor; U2L3
场面	chǎngmiàn	N.	scene; U4L3
长跑	chángpǎo	N.	long-distance running; U4L2
尝试	chángshì	N.	attempt, trial run; U2L4
常用词汇	chángyòngcíhuì	NP.	commonly used vocabulary; U4L2
产品	chǎnpǐn	N.	product; U2L2
产品形象	chǎnpǐnxíngxiàng	NP.	product lines, appearance of products; U2L2
产销	chǎnxiāo	V/N.	to produce and sell; production and sales; U2L2
产值	chǎnzhí	N.	value of output, total value of what was produced; U2L2
产仔	chǎnzǎi	VO.	= 产下幼仔, to give birth to a baby animal; U3L2
超过	chāoguò	V.	to exceed; U2L1
朝鲜	cháoxiǎn	Place N.	North Korea; U4L2

乘	chéng	V.	to take (a vehicle), to ride on; U2L4
稱	chēng	V.	to be called, to be addressed as; U4L3
成材	chéngcái	VO.	to become useful (people, materials); U2L4
成都	chéngdū	Place N.	provincial capital of Sichuan; U3L2
懲罰	chéngfá	V.	to punish; U1L3
成活	chénghuó	V.	to survive, to be born successfully, to be born alive and to survive; U3L2
成交	chéngjiāo	VO.	to clinch a deal; U2L2
成績表	chéngjìbiǎo	N.	report card, grade booklet; U1L3
成吉思汗	chéngjísīhàn	Personal N+Title.	Jenghiz Khan 1167?-1227, unifier of Mongols and great conquerer whose conquests included all of central Asia and North China; U3L3
成就	chéngjiù	N.	achievement (s); accomplishment (s); U1L1
成立	chénglì	V.	to establish; U2L1
誠實	chéngshí	Adj.	honest; U1L1
呈現	chéngxiàn	V.	to present (an appearance); to show forth; U2L2
陳劍虹	chénjiànhóng	Personal N.	Chen Jianhong, the name of a Chinese swimmer; U4L2
陳列	chénliè	V.	to display; to show; U3L3
陳玉琴	chényùqín	Personal N.	Chen Yuqin, the name of a bowling star from Taiwan; U4L2
衝擊力量	chōngjílìliàng	NP.	momentum; U4L3
衝突	chōngtú	N/V.	conflict; to conflict; U1L2
綢	chóu	N.	silk fabric, woven silk; U3L4
籌備	chóubèi	V.	to prepare; U4L3
籌備組	chóubèizǔ	NP.	preparatory committee; U3L3
籌建	chóujiàn	V.	to plan to establish; U2L2
揣摩	chuǎimó	V.	to try to figure out; to arrive at a deep understanding of something, to puzzle out; U3L4
傳到	chuándào	V.	to pass on to, to convey to; U3L2
創匯	chuànghuì	VO.	to earn foreign currency; U2L2
床頭櫃	chuángtóuguì	N.	night stand, bedside table; U2L2

乘	chéng	V.	to take (a vehicle), to ride on; U2L4
称	chēng	V.	to be called, to be addressed as; U4L3
成材	chéngcái	VO.	to become useful (people, materials); U2L4
成都	chéngdū	Place N.	provincial capital of Sichuan; U3L2
惩罚	chéngfá	V.	to punish; U1L3
成活	chénghuó	V.	to survive, to be born successfully, to be born alive and to survive; U3L2
成交	chéngjiāo	VO.	to clinch a deal; U2L2
成绩表	chéngjìbiǎo	N.	report card, grade booklet; U1L3
成吉思汗	chéngjísīhàn	Personal N.+Title.	Jenghiz Khan 1167?-1227, unifier of Mongols and great conquerer whose conquests included all of central Asia and North China; U3L3
成就	chéngjiù	N.	achievement (s); accomplishment (s); U1L1
成立	chénglì	V.	to establish; U2L1
诚实	chéngshí	Adj.	honest; U1L1
呈现	chéngxiàn	V.	to present (an appearance); to show forth; U2L2
陈剑虹	chénjiànhóng	Personal N.	Chen Jianhong, the name of a Chinese swimmer; U4L2
陈列	chénliè	V.	to display; to show; U3L3
陈玉琴	chényùqín	Personal N.	Chen Yuqin, the name of a bowling star from Taiwan; U4L2
冲击力量	chōngjīlìliàng	NP.	momentum; U4L3
冲突	chōngtú	N/V.	conflict; to conflict; U1L2
绸	chóu	N.	silk fabric, woven silk; U3L4
筹备	chóubèi	V.	to prepare; U4L3
筹备组	chóubèizǔ	NP.	preparatory committee; U3L3
筹建	chóujiàn	V.	to plan to establish; U2L2
揣摩	chuǎimó	V.	to try to figure out; to arrive at a deep understanding of something, to puzzle out; U3L4
传到	chuándào	V.	to pass on to, to convey to; U3L2
创汇	chuànghuì	VO.	to earn foreign currency; U2L2
床头柜	chuángtóuguì	N.	night stand, bedside table; U2L2

創造	chuàngzào	V/N.	to create; creation; to make a record of; U3L2
創作	chuàngzuò	N/V.	creation; to create; U3L3
傳統	chuántǒng	N/Adj.	tradition; traditional; U3L3
吹牛	chuīníu	VO.	to toot one's own horn, to brag; U4L1
出口	chūkǒu	V/N.	to export; exports; U2L2
處理	chǔlǐ	V.	to handle, to deal with; U1L2
出色	chūsè	Adj.	outstanding; U4L1
出售	chūshòu	V.	to sell; U1L3
次	cì	Classifier.	(this) time, (this) round, (this) session; U1L4
詞彙量	cíhuìliàng	N.	quantity of vocabulary, vocabulary range; U1L3
刺繡	cìxìu	V/N.	to embroider, embroidery; U3L4
從事	cóngshì	V.	to go in for, to engage in; U4L1
從事於	cóngshìyú	VP.	to follow the occupation of, to be engaged in, to pursue a career in; U3L4
從未	cóngwèi	Adv.	never; U1L3
醋	cù	N.	vinegar; U3L4
促進	cùjìn	V.	to promote; U1L2
措施	cuòshī	N.	measures; method; U3L2
搭	dā	V.	to put up; U4L3
達	dá	V.	to reach; to be as high as; U2L2
達到	dádào	V.	to arrive, to reach; U1L4
大都會	dàdūhuì	N.	metropolitan; U3L3
大都會博物館	dàdūhuìbówùguǎn	N.	The Metropolitan Museum of Art; U3L3
打官司	dǎguānsī	VO.	to sue someone, to bring a suit against, to take legal action against; U3L1
大規模	dàguīmó	NP.	(on) a large scale; U1L3
大規模殺傷武器	dàguīmóshāshāngwǔqì	NP.	weapons of mass destruction; U1L3
代辦處	dàibànchù	N.	agency; U2L3
代表團	dàibiǎotuán	N.	delegation; U1L2
代表性	dàibiǎoxìng	N.	characteristics; U3L3
戴高樂	dàigāolè	Personal N.	Charles De Gaulle (1890-1970) French general and stateman, first president of the Fifth Republic; U3L4
搭架子	dājiàzi	VO.	to build a framework; U4L3
大類	dàlèi	N.	major kind, major type; U3L1

创造	chuàngzào	V/N.	to create; creation; to make a record of; U3L2
创作	chuàngzuò	N/V.	creation; to create; U3L3
传统	chuántǒng	N/Adj.	tradition; traditional; U3L3
吹牛	chuīniú	VO.	to toot one's own horn, to brag; U4L1
出口	chūkǒu	V/N.	to export; exports; U2L2
处理	chǔlǐ	V.	to handle, to deal with; U1L2
出色	chūsè	Adj.	outstanding; U4L1
出售	chūshòu	V.	to sell; U1L3
次	cì	Classifier.	(this) time, (this) round, (this) session; U1L4
词汇量	cíhuìliàng	N.	quantity of vocabulary, vocabulary range; U1L3
刺绣	cìxiù	V/N.	to embroider, embroidery; U3L4
从事	cóngshì	V.	to go in for, to engage in; U4L1
从事于	cóngshìyú	VP.	to follow the occupation of, to be engaged in, to pursue a career in; U3L4
从未	cóngwèi	Adv.	never; U1L3
醋	cù	N.	vinegar; U3L4
促进	cùjìn	V.	to promote; U1L2
措施	cuòshī	N.	measures; method; U3L2
搭	dā	V.	to put up; U4L3
达	dá	V.	to reach; to be as high as; U2L2
达到	dádào	V.	to arrive, to reach; U1L4
大都会	dàdūhuì	N.	metropolitan; U3L3
大都会博物馆	dàdūhuìbówùguǎn	N.	The Metropolitan Museum of Art; U3L3
打官司	dǎguānsi	VO.	to sue someone, to bring a suit against, to take legal action against; U3L1
大规模	dàguimó	NP.	(on) a large scale; U1L3
大规模杀伤武器	dàguimóshāshāngwǔqì	NP.	weapons of mass destruction; U1L3
代办处	dàibànchù	N.	agency; U2L3
代表团	dàibiǎotuán	N.	delegation; U1L2
代表性	dàibiǎoxìng	N.	characteristics; U3L3
戴高乐	dàigāolè	Personal N.	Charles De Gaulle (1890-1970) French general and stateman, first president of the Fifth Republic; U3L4
搭架子	dājiàzi	VO.	to build a framework; U4L3
大类	dàlèi	N.	major kind, major type; U3L1

大陸	dàlù	N.	Mainland China; U1L4
單打	dāndǎ	N.	singles (athletic competition); U4L1
檔	dǎng	N.	gear; U4L3
當代	dāngdài	N.	modern time; comtemporary; U3L3
當地	dāngdì	N.	local; U2L4
丹麥	dānmài	Place N.	Denmark; U4L1
誕生	dànshēng	V.	to be born; U3L2
單位	dānwèi	N.	unit (as in 'work unit', administrative unit, organization); U2L4
到達	dàodá	V.	to arrive; U1L1
到目前	dàomùqián	Prep P.	up to now＝到現在為止; U4L1
到現在為止	dàoxiànzàiwéizhǐ	Prep P.	up to now, 到目前; U4L1
導演	dǎoyǎn	N.	director; U3L1
打破	dǎpò	V.	to break (the record of); to smash; U4L1
打入	dǎrù	V.	to break into; U2L2
大師	dàshī	N.	master; U3L3
大峽谷	dàxiágǔ	Place N.	the grand canyon; U4L3
大型	dàxíng	N/Adj.	large scale; large, large-sized; on a large scale; U2L2
大熊貓	dàxióngmāo	N.	giant panda; U3L2
大約	dàyuē	Adv.	approximately; U2L1
大展	dàzhǎn	N.	major exhibition; U3L3
大中型	dàzhōngxíng	NP.	large-size and middle-size; U2L2
登台獻藝	dēngtáixiànyì	VP.	to perform on stage; U3L1
電報	diànbào	N.	telegram; U2L4
電冰箱	diànbīngxiāng	N.	refrigerator; U2L2
典禮	diǎnlǐ	N.	ceremony; U2L4
電視觀眾	diànshìguānzhòng	NP.	TV viewers, the viewing public, the viewers; U1L1
電視迷	diànshìmí	N.	TV fan, "TV junkie"; U1L1
殿堂	diàntáng	N.	palace; hall; U3L3
電影城	diànyǐngchéng	N.	movie city; U3L1
電影宮	diànyǐnggōng	N.	movie theater, film palace; U3L1
電影節	diànyǐngjié	NP.	film festival; U3L1
調查	diàochá	N/V.	survey (s), investigation; to investigate, to take a survey; U3L2
釣魚台	diàoyútái	Place N.	the most prestigious complex of VIP state guest residences in

大陆	dàlù	N.	Mainland China; U1L4
单打	dāndǎ	N.	singles (athletic competition); U4L1
档	dǎng	N.	gear; U4L3
当代	dāngdài	N.	modern time; comtemporary; U3L3
当地	dāngdì	N.	local; U2L4
丹麦	dānmài	Place N.	Denmark; U4L1
诞生	dànshēng	V.	to be born; U3L2
单位	dānwèi	N.	unit (as in 'work unit', administrative unit, organization); U2L4
到达	dàodá	V.	to arrive; U1L1
到目前	dàomùqián	Prep P.	up to now, = 到现在为止; U4L1
到现在为止	dàoxiànzàiwéizhǐ	Prep P.	up to now, 到目前; U4L1
导演	dǎoyǎn	N.	director; U3L1
打破	dǎpò	V.	to break (the record of); to smash; U4L1
打入	dǎrù	V.	to break into; U2L2
大师	dàshī	N.	master; U3L3
大峡谷	dàxiágǔ	Place N.	the grand canyon; U4L3
大型	dàxíng	N/Adj.	large scale; large, large-sized; on a large scale; U2L2
大熊猫	dàxióngmāo	N.	giant panda; U3L2
大约	dàyuē	Adv.	approximately; U2L1
大展	dàzhǎn	N.	major exhibition; U3L3
大中型	dàzhōngxíng	NP.	large-size and middle-size; U2L2
登台献艺	dēngtáixiànyì	VP.	to perform on stage; U3L1
电报	diànbào	N.	telegram; U2L4
电冰箱	diànbīngxiāng	N.	refrigerator; U2L2
典礼	diǎnlǐ	N.	ceremony; U2L4
电视观众	diànshìguānzhòng	NP.	TV viewers, the viewing public, the viewers; U1L1
电视迷	diànshìmí	N.	TV fan, "TV junkie"; U1L1
殿堂	diàntáng	N.	palace; hall; U3L3
电影城	diànyǐngchéng	N.	movie city; U3L1
电影宫	diànyǐnggōng	N.	movie theater, film palace; U3L1
电影节	diànyǐngjié	NP.	film festival; U3L1
调查	diàochá	N/V.	survey (s), investigation; to investigate, to take a survey; U3L2
钓鱼台	diàoyútái	Place N.	the most prestigious complex of VIP state guest residences in

			Beijing; U1L4
蝶泳	diéyǒng	N.	butterfly style swimming; U4L1
跌至	diēzhì	V.	to fall to; U4L2
地方	dìfāng	N.	locality; local area; U2L2
地面	dìmiàn	N.	ground; U2L1
定點	dìngdiǎn	N.	fixed place; U2L3
頂峰	dǐngfēng	N.	peak, summit, pinnacle; U1L4
地區	dìqū	N.	district; area; U2L2
第一手	dìyīshǒu	N.	first-hand; U2L4
弟子	dìzǐ	N.	follower(s), disciple(s); U4L3
東方的奇觀	dōngfāngdeqíguān	NP.	one of the wonders of the Orient; U4L3
東方一絕	dōngfāngyījué	NP.	something unique to the Orient; U3L4
東南亞	dōngnányà	Place N.	Southeast Asia; U2L2
動物	dòngwù	N.	animal; U3L2
動物園	dòngwùyuán	N.	zoo; U3L2
董希文	dǒngxīwén	Personal N.	Dong Xiwen, a well known professor of oil painting and artist, Central Academy of Fine Arts; U3L3
緞	duàn	N.	silk fabric woven in thicker weave with lustrous face and dull back; U3L4
鍛煉	duànliàn	V.	to build up strength and will power; to temper (steel); to exercise, to train; U2L4
鍛煉成材	duànliànchéngcái	Idiom.	to be tempered and molded into a useful person; U2L4
短跑	duǎnpǎo	N.	dash, sprint; U4L2
斷然	duànrán	Adv.	flatly, categorically; U1L1
對抗	duìkàng	V/N.	to resist, to oppose, to confront; resistance, confrontation; U1L3
對外	duìwài	Adj.	open to foreigners; U2L3
獨聯體	dúliántǐ	Place N.	The Commonwealth of Independent States; U2L3
奪	duó	V.	to carry off (prize, medal), to capture, to successfully compete and win; U4L1
奪得	duódé	V.	to obtain through competition, to carry off (the prize, honor, etc.); U4L2
多功能	duōgōngnéng	Adj.	multifunctional; U2L2
獨特	dútè	Adj.	special; unique; U3L3

			Beijing; U1L4
蝶泳	diéyǒng	*N.*	butterfly style swimming; U4L1
跌至	diēzhì	*V.*	to fall to; U4L2
地方	dìfāng	*N.*	locality; local area; U2L2
地面	dìmiàn	*N.*	ground; U2L1
定点	dìngdiǎn	*N.*	fixed place; U2L3
顶峰	dǐngfēng	*N.*	peak, summit, pinnacle; U1L4
地区	dìqū	*N.*	district; area; U2L2
第一手	dìyīshǒu	*N.*	first-hand; U2L4
弟子	dìzǐ	*N.*	follower(s), disciple(s); U4L3
东方的奇观	dōngfāngdeqíguān	*NP.*	one of the wonders of the Orient; U4L3
东方一绝	dōngfāngyìjué	*NP.*	something unique to the Orient; U3L4
东南亚	dōngnányà	*Place N.*	Southeast Asia; U2L2
动物	dòngwù	*N.*	animal; U3L2
动物园	dòngwùyuán	*N.*	zoo; U3L2
董希文	dǒngxīwén	*Personal N.*	Dong Xiwen, a well known professor of oil painting and artist, Central Academy of Fine Arts; U3L3
缎	duàn	*N.*	silk fabric woven in thicker weave with lustrous face and dull back; U3L4
锻炼	duànliàn	*V.*	to build up strength and will power; to temper (steel); to exercise, to train; U2L4
锻炼成材	duànliànchéngcái	*Idiom.*	to be tempered and molded into a useful person; U2L4
短跑	duǎnpǎo	*N.*	dash, sprint; U4L2
断然	duànrán	*Adv.*	flatly, categorically; U1L1
对抗	duìkàng	*V/N.*	to resist, to oppose, to confront; resistance, confrontation; U1L3
对外	duìwài	*Adj.*	open to foreigners; U2L3
独联体	dúliántǐ	*Place N.*	The Commonwealth of Independent States; U2L3
夺	duó	*V.*	to carry off (prize, medal), to capture, to successfully compete and win; U4L1
夺得	duódé	*V.*	to obtain through competition, to carry off (the prize, honor, etc.); U4L2
多功能	duōgōngnéng	*Adj.*	multifunctional; U2L2
独特	dútè	*Adj.*	special; unique; U3L3

鵝毛大雪	émáodàxuě	Idiom.	heavy snow; U4L3
發揮	fāhuī	V.	to bring into play, to give free rein to; to develop, to bring into full play; U3L4
番	fān	Classifier.	= (here) 些; U1L4
防護網	fánghùwǎng	N.	protection net; U4L3
紡織品	fǎngzhīpǐn	N.	textile products; U2L2
繁榮	fánróng	N/Adj.	prosperity; to be flourishing, booming (of economy, city, etc.); U1L4
繁殖	fánzhí	V.	to breed; to reproduce; U3L2
罰球	fáqiú	N.	penalty shot; U4L2
發射	fāshè	V/N.	to launch; the launching of; U1L1
發射試驗隊	fāshèshìyànduì	NP.	"launch crew"; U1L1
髮繡	fàxiù	N.	embroidery with hair; U3L4
飛返	fēifǎn	V.	to fly back; U2L1
費雷伊	fèiléiyī	Personal N.	the name of a Swedish athlete; U4L1
飛行	fēixíng	V.	to fly; U2L1
飛針走線	fēizhēnzǒuxiàn	Idiom.	"to make the needle and thread fly," to do needlework very deftly and rapidly; U3L4
非洲	fēizhōu	Place N.	Africa; U3L2
分別	fēnbié	Adv.	respectively, separately; U1L1
分配	fēnpèi	V.	to assign (a job, a part, etc.); U2L4
副部長	fùbùzhǎng	Title/rank	Deputy Minister, (the) deputy minister; U1L4
服務	fúwù	N/V.	service; to serve; U2L3
服務公司	fúwùgōngsī	NP.	service agency; U2L3
賦予	fùyǔ	V.	to entrust to, to bestow on, to endow with; U1L4
複雜	fùzá	Adj.	complicated; complex; U2L4
負責	fùzé	V.	to be responsible; U2L3
負責人	fùzérén	N.	responsible person; person in charge; U1L3
福州	fúzhōu	Place N.	provincial capital of Fujian; U3L2
副主席	fùzhúxí	Title/rank.	the vice chairman; U1L2
改革	gǎigé	N/V.	reform, to reform; U2L2
改革開放	gǎigékāifàng	VP.	to reform and open; U3L4
港台地區	gǎngtáidìqū	Abbrev.	Hong Kong and Taiwan areas=

鹅毛大雪	émáodàxué	*Idiom.*	heavy snow; U4L3
发挥	fāhuī	*V.*	to bring into play, to give free rein to; to develop, to bring into full play; U3L4
番	fān	*Classifier.*	= (here) 些; U1L4
防护网	fánghùwǎng	*N.*	protection net; U4L3
纺织品	fǎngzhīpǐn	*N.*	textile products; U2L2
繁荣	fánróng	*N/Adj.*	prosperity; to be flourishing, booming (of economy, city, etc.); U1L4
繁殖	fánzhí	*V.*	to breed; to reproduce; U3L2
罚球	fáqiú	*N.*	penalty shot; U4L2
发射	fāshè	*V/N.*	to launch; the launching of; U1L1
发射试验队	fāshèshìyànduì	*NP.*	"launch crew"; U1L1
发绣	fàxiù	*N.*	embroidery with hair; U3L4
飞返	fēifǎn	*V.*	to fly back; U2L1
费雷伊	fèiléiyī	*Personal N.*	the name of a Swedish athlete; U4L1
飞行	fēixíng	*V.*	to fly; U2L1
飞针走线	fēizhēnzǒuxiàn	*Idiom.*	"to make the needle and thread fly," to do needlework very deftly and rapidly; U3L4
非洲	fēizhōu	*Place N.*	Africa; U3L2
分别	fēnbié	*Adv.*	respectively, separately; U1L1
分配	fēnpèi	*V.*	to assign (a job, a part, etc.); U2L4
副部长	fùbùzhǎng	*Title/rank.*	Deputy Minister, (the) deputy minister; U1L4
服务	fúwù	*N/V.*	service; to serve; U2L3
服务公司	fúwùgōngsī	*NP.*	service agency; U2L3
赋予	fùyǔ	*V.*	to entrust to, to bestow on, to endow with; U1L4
复杂	fùzá	*Adj.*	complicated; complex; U2L4
负责	fùzé	*V.*	to be responsible; U2L3
负责人	fùzérén	*N.*	responsible person; person in charge; U1L3
福州	fúzhōu	*Place N.*	provincial capital of Fujian; U3L2
副主席	fùzhǔxí	*Title/rank.*	the vice chairman; U1L2
改革	gǎigé	*N/V.*	reform, to reform; U2L2
改革开放	gǎigékāifàng	*VP.*	to reform and open; U3L4
港台地区	gǎngtáidìqū	*Abbrev.*	Hong Kong and Taiwan areas =

			香港跟台灣地區; U3L1
鋼鐵	gāngtiě	N.	iron and steel; U2L2
高度	gāodù	N.	high degree of; U3L3
高度的	gāodùde	Adj.	high; U3L4
高峰	gāofēng	N.	peak, summit; pinnacle＝頂峰; U1L4
高速公路	gāosùgōnglù	N.	highway; U4L3
高校	gāoxiào	Abbrev.	universities and colleges, technical institutions; institutions of higher education＝高等學校; U2L4
各顯技藝	gèxiǎnjìyì	VP.	each manifesting its own (special) techniques; U3L3
共產主義	gòngchǎnzhǔyì	N.	communism, communist; U2L4
工程	gōngchéng	N.	an undertaking, a project; engineering or construction project(s); U2L4
攻關	gōngguán	VO.	to tackle key problems; U3L2
公斤	gòngjīn	Classifier.	kilogram; U3L2
鞏俐	gǒnglì	Personal N.	personal name: a famous Chinese female star, plays the lead role in "Red Sorghum", "Raise the Red Lantern", "Judou", "Qiuju", etc.; U3L1
功力	gōnglì	N.	capability, skill; U3L4
貢獻	gòngxiàn	N.	contribution; U2L3
工藝美術	gōngyìměishù	NP.	arts and crafts; U3L4
供應	gòngyìng	V/N.	to supply, to provide; supply; U2L3
工藝品	gōngyìpǐn	N.	handicrafts; U2L3
購買	gòumǎi	V.	to purchase; U2L3
廣東路	guǎngdōnglù	Place N.	Canton Road; U3L1
冠軍	guànjūn	N.	championship; U4L2
管理	guǎnlǐ	V/N.	to manage; to take care of; management of; U2L2
官員	guānyuán	N.	officials; U1L2
觀眾	guānzhòng	N.	spectators, (the) audience, the public, the listener; U1L1
古代	gǔdài	N.	ancient time; U3L3
規定	guīdìng	V.	to regulate; to set the rule; U3L2
規模	guīmó	N.	scale, scope; U1L3
貴州	guìzhōu	Place N.	a province in South China; U2L3
貴子	guìzǐ	N.	"honorable son"; U3L2

			香港跟台湾地区; U3L1
钢铁	gāngtiě	*N.*	iron and steel; U2L2
高度	gāodù	*N.*	high degree of; U3L3
高度的	gāodùde	*Adj.*	high; U3L4
高峰	gāofēng	*N.*	peak, summit; pinnacle = 顶峰; U1L4
高速公路	gāosùgōnglù	*N.*	highway; U4L3
高校	gāoxiào	*Abbrev.*	universities and colleges, technical institutions; institutions of higher education = 高等学校; U2L4
各显技艺	gèxiǎnjìyì	*VP.*	each manifesting its own (special) techniques; U3L3
共产主义	gòngchǎnzhǔyì	*N.*	communism, communist; U2L4
工程	gōngchéng	*N.*	an undertaking, a project; engineering or construction project(s); U2L4
攻关	gōngguān	*VO.*	to tackle key problems; U3L2
公斤	gōngjīn	*Classifier.*	kilogram; U3L2
巩俐	gǒnglì	*Personal N.*	personal name: a famous Chinese female star, plays the lead role in "Red Sorghum", "Raise the Red Lantern", "Judou", "Qiuju", etc.; U3L1
功力	gōnglì	*N.*	capability, skill; U3L4
贡献	gòngxiàn	*N.*	contribution; U2L3
工艺美术	gōngyìměishù	*NP.*	arts and crafts; U3L4
供应	gòngyìng	*V/N.*	to supply, to provide; supply; U2L3
工艺品	gōngyìpǐn	*N.*	handicrafts; U2L3
购买	gòumǎi	*V.*	to purchase; U2L3
广东路	guǎngdōnglù	*Place N.*	Canton Road; U3L1
冠军	guànjūn	*N.*	championship; U4L2
管理	guǎnlǐ	*V/N.*	to manage; to take care of; management of; U2L2
官员	guānyuán	*N.*	officials; U1L2
观众	guānzhòng	*N.*	spectators, (the) audience, the public, the listener; U1L1
古代	gǔdài	*N.*	ancient time; U3L3
规定	guīdìng	*V.*	to regulate; to set the rule; U3L2
规模	guīmó	*N.*	scale, scope; U1L3
贵州	guìzhōu	*Place N.*	a province in South China; U2L3
贵子	guìzǐ	*N.*	"honorable son"; U3L2

谷牧	gǔmù	Personal N.	Gu Mu, high ranking member of CCP and an important Chinese government official; U1L2
過渡	guòdù	Adj/N.	transitional; transition; U1L4
國家級	guójiājí	N.	at the national level; U3L2
國際性	guójìxìng	N/Adj.	internationality; international; U3L1
國禮	guólǐ	N.	the national gift; U3L4
郭沫若	guōmòruò	Personal N.	a prominent Chinese intellectual/writer/political activist; U3L4
國內外	guónèiwài	NP.	domestic and international; U1L1
過時	guòshí	Adj.	to be out-of-date, outdated; U4L2
國之瑰寶	guózhīguíbǎo	NP.	national treasures (art works, antiquities, masterpices,etc.); U3L3
故事片	gùshìpiān	N.	feature film; U3L1
海南	háinán	Place N.	Hainan, an island province off the coast of South China; U1L1
海灣戰爭	háiwǎnzhànzhēng	N.	Gulf War (Persian Gulf War, first half of 1992); U1L3
漢城	hànchéng	Place N.	Seoul; U4L2
航空公司	hángkōnggōngsī	NP.	airline company; U2L1
韓國	hánguó	Place N.	South Korea; U4L1
航線	hángxiàn	N.	air (or shipping) route; U2L1
寒冷	hánlěng	Adj.	bitter cold; U3L2
豪華	háohuá	Adj.	luxurious; deluxe; U2L2
豪華型	háohuáxíng	N.	deluxe model; U2L2
好萊塢	Hǎoláiwū	Place N.	Hollywood; U3L1
好勢頭	háoshìtóu	Idiom.	"a good sign", the outlook is very promising; excellent prospects (for); U2L2
哈薩克	hāsàkè	N.	Kazak; U3L3
哈薩克斯坦	hāsàkèsītǎn	Place N.	Kazakhstan; U2L3
合璧	hébì	VO.	to blend together harmoniously, complementary and combined or blended very well together; U3L3
核查	héchá	V.	to check; U1L3
核查小組	hécháxiǎozú	NP.	inspection team; U1L3
黑猩猩	hēixīngxīng	N.	chimpanzee; U3L2
荷蘭	hélán	Place N.	Holland, the Netherlands; U4L1

谷牧	gǔmù	Personal N.	Gu Mu, high ranking member of CCP and an important Chinese government official; U1L2
过渡	guòdù	Adj/N.	transitional; transition; U1L4
国家级	guójiājí	N.	at the national level; U3L2
国际性	guójìxìng	N/Adj.	internationality; international; U3L1
国礼	guólǐ	N.	the national gift; U3L4
郭沫若	guómòruò	Personal N.	a prominent Chinese intellectual/writer/political activist; U3L4
国内外	guónèiwài	NP.	domestic and international; U1L1
过时	guòshí	Adj.	to be out-of-date, outdated; U4L2
国之瑰宝	guózhīguībǎo	NP.	national treasures (art works, antiquities, masterpices,etc.); U3L3
故事片	gùshìpiān	N.	feature film; U3L1
海南	hǎinán	Place N.	Hainan, an island province off the coast of South China; U1L1
海湾战争	hǎiwānzhànzhēng	N.	Gulf War (Persian Gulf War, first half of 1992); U1L3
汉城	hànchéng	Place N.	Seoul; U4L2
航空公司	hángkōnggōngsī	NP.	airline company; U2L1
韩国	hánguó	Place N.	South Korea; U4L1
航线	hángxiàn	N.	air (or shipping) route; U2L1
寒冷	hánlěng	Adj.	bitter cold; U3L2
豪华	háohuá	Adj.	luxurious; deluxe; U2L2
豪华型	háohuáxíng	N.	deluxe model; U2L2
好莱坞	Hǎoláiwū	Place N.	Hollywood; U3L1
好势头	hǎoshìtóu	Idiom.	"a good sign", the outlook is very promising; excellent prospects (for); U2L2
哈萨克	hāsàkè	N.	Kazak; U3L3
哈萨克斯坦	hāsàkèsītǎn	Place N.	Kazakhstan; U2L3
合璧	hébì	VO.	to blend together harmoniously, complementary and combined or blended very well together; U3L3
核查	héchá	V.	to check; U1L3
核查小组	hécháxiǎozǔ	NP.	inspection team; U1L3
黑猩猩	hēixīngxīng	N.	chimpanzee; U3L2
荷兰	hélán	Place N.	Holland, the Netherlands; U4L1

和平	hépíng	N.	peace; U1L2
合資	hézī	NP.	joint venture(s); U2L3
合作	hézuò	V/N.	to cooperate; cooperation; U1L2
後果	hòuguǒ	N.	result, consequence; U2L1
華	huá	Abbrev.	the People's Republic of China ＝中國、中華人民共和國; U1L2
懷疑	huáiyí	V.	to suspect, to have doubts about; U2L1
懷著	huáizhē	V.	to cherish, imbued with the spirit of; U4L3
華南虎	huánánhǔ	N.	Indo-Chinese tiger; U3L2
環境	huánjìng	N.	environment; U3L2
歡迎	huānyíng	V/N.	to welcome, welcome; U1L1
薈萃	huìcuì	V.	to gather the most outstanding ones together; U3L3
回歸	huíguī	V/N.	to revert to; reversion; U1L4
輝煌	huīhuáng	Adj.	brilliant, glorious, splendid; U3L4
匯率	huìlǜ	N.	exchange rate; U1L1
會談	huìtán	N.	talks, face to face discussions; U1L4
混合泳	hùnhéyǒng	N.	medley (event) swimming (swimming different styles during one race); U4L2
渾為一體	húnwéiyìtǐ	VP.	to merge into a single whole/entity (＝渾然一體); U3L3
獲	huò	V.	to obtain; U3L1
獲得	huòdé	V.	to achieve; to abtain, to earn, to gain; U1L1
夥計	huǒjì	N.	waiter; servant; U1L4
活潑	huópō	Adj.	active; lively; U3L2
加工	jiāgōng	V/N.	to process; processing; U2L2
加工區	jiāgōngqū	N.	zone specializing in manufacturing; U2L2
加緊	jiājǐn	V.	to speed up, to intensify; U3L1
加快	jiākuài	V.	to speed up, to accelerate; U1L4
肩膀	jiānbǎng	N.	shoulder; U3L1
檢查	jiǎnchá	V/N.	to examine, to inspect; inspection; U1L3
健兒	jiànér	N.	top athletes; valiant warriors; U1L1

和平	hépíng	N.	peace; U1L2
合资	hézī	NP.	joint venture(s); U2L3
合作	hézuò	V/N.	to cooperate; cooperation; U1L2
后果	hòuguǒ	N.	result, consequence; U2L1
华	huá	Abbrev.	the People's Republic of China = 中国、中华人民共和国; U1L2
怀疑	huáiyí	V.	to suspect, to have doubts about; U2L1
怀著	huáizhě	V.	to cherish, imbued with the spirit of; U4L3
华南虎	huánánhǔ	N.	Indo-Chinese tiger; U3L2
环境	huánjìng	N.	environment; U3L2
欢迎	huānyíng	V/N.	to welcome, welcome; U1L1
荟萃	huìcuì	V.	to gather the most outstanding ones together; U3L3
回归	huíguī	V/N.	to revert to; reversion; U1L4
辉煌	huíhuáng	Adj.	brilliant, glorious, splendid; U3L4
汇率	huìlǜ	N.	exchange rate; U1L1
会谈	huìtán	N.	talks, face to face discussions; U1L4
混合泳	hùnhéyóng	N.	medley (event) swimming (swimming different styles during one race); U4L2
浑为一体	húnwéiyītǐ	VP.	to merge into a single whole/entity (= 浑然一体); U3L3
获	huò	V.	to obtain; U3L1
获得	huòdé	V.	to achieve; to abtain, to earn, to gain; U1L1
伙计	huǒjì	N.	waiter; servant; U1L4
活泼	huópō	Adj.	active; lively; U3L2
加工	jiāgōng	V/N.	to process; processing; U2L2
加工区	jiāgōngqū	N.	zone specializing in manufacturing; U2L2
加紧	jiājǐn	V.	to speed up, to intensify; U3L1
加快	jiākuài	V.	to speed up, to accelerate; U1L4
肩膀	jiānbǎng	N.	shoulder; U3L1
检查	jiǎnchá	V/N.	to examine, to inspect; inspection; U1L3
健儿	jiànér	N.	top athletes; valiant warriors; U1L1

降低	jiàngdī	*V.*	to drop, to reduce; U1L1
姜恩柱	jiāngēnzhù	*Personal N.*	Jiang Enzhu; U1L4
獎勵	jiǎnglì	*N/V.*	award(s), reward(s); to encourage and reward; U3L1
降落	jiàngluò	*V.*	to land; U2L1
獎牌	jiǎngpái	*N.*	medal; U4L1
建館	jiànguǎn	*VO.*	to establish or to open a hall/a gallery/a public building; U3L3
江澤民	jiāngzémín	*Personal N.*	Jiang Zemin; U1L1
簡介	jiǎnjiè	*N.*	introduction; U1L1
艱難險阻	jiānnánxiǎnzǔ	*Idiom.*	hardship and obstacles; U4L1
建議	jiànyì	*N/V.*	suggestions; to suggest, to make a proposal; U3L2
建築	jiànzhù	*N.*	building, structure, edifice; architecture; U3L1
酵酒	jiàojǐu	*NP.*	naturally fermented alcoholic beverages; U2L3
交流	jiāolíu	*V/N.*	to exchange, exchange; U1L2
交通	jiāotòng	*N.*	transportation; U2L1
交易團	jiāoyìtuán	*N.*	the trade delegation; U3L1
加強	jiāqiáng	*V.*	to strengthen; U1L2
加油	jiāyóu	*V.*	to cheer for; go, team! (lit. "step on the gas"); U4L1
基本功	jīběngōng	*N.*	basic skill(s), the essential technique(s); U3L4
基本結構	jīběnjiégòu	*NP.*	basic structure; U4L2
基地	jīdì	*N.*	base; source; U2L2
屆	jiè	*Classifier.*	session; U3L1
結合	jíéhé	*V.*	to combine; U2L3
節目	jiémù	*N.*	program (TV); U1L1
接洽	jiēqià	*V.*	to contact, make arrangement; U4L3
節日	jiérì	*N.*	holidays, festival; U3L1
屆時	jièshí	*Adv.*	at the appointed hour; when the time comes, at that time; U4L2
街市	jiēshì	*V.*	street fair; U2L4
節選	jiéxuǎn	*N.*	excerpt; U3L1
結業	jiéyè	*N.*	graduation; U2L4
傑作	jiézuò	*N.*	outstanding work; U3L3
機構	jīgòu	*N.*	institution; organization; administrative organization; U2L3
集錦	jíjín	*N.*	collection of outstanding examples; U4L3

降低	jiàngdī	V.	to drop, to reduce; U1L1
姜恩柱	jiāngēnzhù	Personal N.	Jiang Enzhu; U1L4
奖励	jiǎnglì	N/V.	award(s), reward(s); to encourage and reward; U3L1
降落	jiàngluò	V.	to land; U2L1
奖牌	jiǎngpái	N.	medal; U4L1
建馆	jiànguǎn	VO.	to establish or to open a hall/a gallery/a public building; U3L3
江泽民	jiāngzémín	Personal N.	Jiang Zemin; U1L1
简介	jiǎnjiè	N.	introduction; U1L1
艰难险阻	jiānnánxiǎnzǔ	Idiom.	hardship and obstacles; U4L1
建议	jiànyì	N/V.	suggestions; to suggest, to make a proposal; U3L2
建筑	jiànzhù	N.	building, structure, edifice; architecture; U3L1
酵酒	jiàojiǔ	NP.	naturally fermented alcoholic beverages; U2L3
交流	jiāoliú	V/N.	to exchange, exchange; U1L2
交通	jiāotōng	N.	transportation; U2L1
交易团	jiāoyìtuán	N.	the trade delegation; U3L1
加强	jiāqiáng	V.	to strengthen; U1L2
加油	jiāyóu	V.	to cheer for; go, team! (lit. "step on the gas"); U4L1
基本功	jīběngōng	N.	basic skill(s), the essential technique(s); U3L4
基本结构	jīběnjiégòu	NP.	basic structure; U4L2
基地	jīdì	N.	base; source; U2L2
届	jiè	Classifier.	session; U3L1
结合	jiéhé	V.	to combine; U2L3
节目	jiémù	N.	program (TV); U1L1
接洽	jiēqià	V.	to contact, make arrangement; U4L3
节日	jiérì	N.	holidays, festival; U3L1
届时	jièshí	Adv.	at the appointed hour; when the time comes, at that time; U4L2
街市	jiēshì	V.	street fair; U2L4
节选	jiéxuǎn	N.	excerpt; U3L1
结业	jiéyè	N.	graduation; U2L4
杰作	jiézuò	N.	outstanding work; U3L3
机构	jīgòu	N.	institution; organization; administrative organization; U2L3
集锦	jíjǐn	N.	collection of outstanding examples; U4L3

吉林省	jílínshéng	Place N.	Jilin Province; U2L2
記錄	jìlù	N.	record; U2L1
錦	jǐn	N.	a rich fabric with raised designs woven or embroidered into it; U3L4
金杯	jīnbēi	N.	gold cup; U3L1
精	jīng	Adj.	skillful, accurate; U4L3
境地	jìngdì	N.	situation; predicament; plight; U3L2
警方	jǐngfāng	N.	the police (the police authorities); U1L3
經過	jīngguò	N.	process; expereinces from beginning to end, whole course of events; U3L1
經久	jīngjiǔ	Adj.	durable, long-lasting; U3L4
經理	jīnglǐ	N.	manager; U2L4
精品	jīngpǐn	N.	choice works (of artistic creation), "representative" works for highest quality; U3L3
敬獻	jìngxiàn	V.	to dedicate to; U3L4
精心	jīngxīn	Adv.	with the best care, painstakingly, meticulously; U3L2
經驗	jīngyàn	N.	experience; U3L2
經營	jīngyíng	V.	to manage; U2L3
金牌	jīnpái	N.	gold medal; U4L1
浸泡	jìnpào	V.	to soak; U3L4
金山嶺	jīnshānlǐng	Place N.	Mount Jinshan; U4L3
金獅獎	jīnshījiǎng	N.	Golden Lion Award; U3L1
金石篆刻	jīnshízhuànkè	NP.	metal and stone inscriptions, inscriptions on ancient bronzes and stone tablets; U3L3
吉諾爾	jínuòěr	Proper.N.	the name of a company; U2L2
進展	jìnzhǎn	N.	progress; U1L4
技巧	jìqiǎo	N.	technique(s), skill(s); U2L4
躋身	jīshēn	VO.	to be ranked among, to be placed in; U3L3
技術	jìshù	N.	technology; technique; U1L1
集體工業	jítǐgōngyè	NP.	collectively-owned industries; U2L2
集團	jítuán	N.	group; U1L2
就	jiu	Prep.	on, about, with regard to (certain issues); U1L4
就讀於	jiùdúyú	VP.	to go to school at; U3L4
舊聞	jiuwén	N.	old news, out-of-date news;

198

吉林省	jílínshěng	*Place N.*	Jilin Province; U2L2
记录	jìlù	*N.*	record; U2L1
锦	jǐn	*N.*	a rich fabric with raised designs woven or embroidered into it; U3L4
金杯	jīnbēi	*N.*	gold cup; U3L1
精	jīng	*Adj.*	skillful, accurate; U4L3
境地	jìngdì	*N.*	situation; predicament; plight; U3L2
警方	jǐngfāng	*N.*	the police (the police authorities); U1L3
经过	jīngguò	*N.*	process; expereinces from beginning to end, whole course of events; U3L1
经久	jīngjiǔ	*Adj.*	durable, long-lasting; U3L4
经理	jīnglǐ	*N.*	manager; U2L4
精品	jīngpǐn	*N.*	choice works (of artistic creation), "representative" works for highest quality; U3L3
敬献	jìngxiàn	*V.*	to dedicate to; U3L4
精心	jīngxīn	*Adv.*	with the best care, painstakingly, meticulously; U3L2
经验	jīngyàn	*N.*	experience; U3L2
经营	jīngyíng	*V.*	to manage; U2L3
金牌	jīnpái	*N.*	gold medal; U4L1
浸泡	jìnpào	*V.*	to soak; U3L4
金山岭	jīnshānlǐng	*Place N.*	Mount Jinshan; U4L3
金狮奖	jīnshījiǎng	*N.*	Golden Lion Award; U3L1
金石篆刻	jīnshízhuànkè	*NP.*	metal and stone inscriptions, inscriptions on ancient bronzes and stone tablets; U3L3
吉诺尔	jínuòěr	*Proper.N.*	the name of a company; U2L2
进展	jìnzhǎn	*N.*	progress; U1L4
技巧	jìqiǎo	*N.*	technique(s), skill(s); U2L4
跻身	jīshēn	*VO.*	to be ranked among, to be placed in; U3L3
技术	jìshù	*N.*	technology; technique; U1L1
集体工业	jítǐgōngyè	*NP.*	collectively-owned industries; U2L2
集团	jítuán	*N.*	group; U1L2
就	jiù	*Prep.*	on, about, with regard to (certain issues); U1L4
就读于	jiùdúyú	*VP.*	to go to school at; U3L4
旧闻	jiùwén	*N.*	old news, out-of-date news;

			U1L1
揪住	jīuzhù	V.	to grab firmly, to take a firm grip on, to seize tightly; U1L1
吉祥物	jíxiángwù	N.	mascot; U3L2
記者	jìzhě	N.	reporter, journalist,; U1L2
集中	jízhōng	Adv.	collectively, typically; U4L2
集中資金	jízhōngzījīn	VO.	to pool funds, to amass capital; U2L2
據	jù	Prep.	according to; U1L4
居	jū	V.	排在; U4L1
絹花	juànhuā	N.	silk flowers; U2L3
舉辦	jǔbàn	V.	to conduct, to put on or to hold (an exhibition), to give (a concert); to sponsor＝主辦; U2L4
據稱	jùchēng	VP.	it is said＝據說; U2L1
決出	juéchū	V.	as decided by the outcome of a competition; U4L1
決賽	juésài	N.	final contest or match, finals, deciding match; U4L2
角逐	juézhú	V.	to compete for, to vie for; U3L1
拒絕	jùjué	V/N.	to refuse; refusal; U1L1
軍事行動	jūnshìxíngdòng	NP.	military action (s); U1L3
具體	jùtǐ	Adj.	in detail, specific, concrete, detailed; U1L4
舉行	jǔxíng	V.	to hold; U1L4
舉重	jǔzhòng	N.	weight-lifting; U4L2
巨作	jùzuò	Abbrev.	magnumopus, monumental creation, landmark work＝巨大的作品; U3L4
開發	kāifā	V.	to develop; to open up; U1L1
開放	kāifàng	V/Adj.	to open; to be open (unrestricted); U2L2
開發區	kāifāqū	N.	(the) development zone; a district or a region slated for concentrated industrial, commercial and/or agribusiness development; U1L1
開幕式	kāimùshì	N.	the opening ceremony; U3L1
開闢	kāipì	V.	to open up; to start; to usher in; U2L1
開設	kāishè	V.	to provide; U2L1
凱旋	kǎixuán	V.	triumphant return; returning in triumph; U1L1

U1L1

揪住	jiūzhù	V.	to grab firmly, to take a firm grip on, to seize tightly; U1L1
吉祥物	jíxiángwù	N.	mascot; U3L2
记者	jìzhě	N.	reporter, journalist,; U1L2
集中	jízhōng	Adv.	collectively, typically; U4L2
集中资金	jízhōngzījīn	VO.	to pool funds, to amass capital; U2L2
据	jù	Prep.	according to; U1L4
居	jú	V.	排在; U4L1
绢花	juànhuā	N.	silk flowers; U2L3
举办	jǔbàn	V.	to conduct, to put on or to hold (an exhibition), to give (a concert); to sponsor = 主办; U2L4
据称	jùchēng	VP.	it is said = 据说; U2L1
决出	juéchū	V.	as decided by the outcome of a competition; U4L1
决赛	juésài	N.	final contest or match, finals, deciding match; U4L2
角逐	juézhú	V.	to compete for, to vie for; U3L1
拒绝	jùjué	V/N.	to refuse; refusal; U1L1
军事行动	jūnshìxíngdòng	NP.	military action (s); U1L3
具体	jùtǐ	Adj.	in detail, specific, concrete, detailed; U1L4
举行	jǔxíng	V.	to hold; U1L4
举重	jǔzhòng	N.	weight-lifting; U4L2
巨作	jùzuò	Abbrev.	magnum opus, monumental creation, landmark work = 巨大的作品; U3L4
开发	kāifā	V.	to develop; to open up; U1L1
开放	kāifàng	V/Adj.	to open; to be open (unrestricted); U2L2
开发区	kāifāqū	N.	(the) development zone; a district or a region slated for concentrated industrial, commercial and/or agribusiness development; U1L1
开幕式	kāimùshì	N.	the opening ceremony; U3L1
开辟	kāipì	V.	to open up; to start; to usher in; U2L1
开设	kāishè	V.	to provide; U2L1
凯旋	kǎixuán	V.	triumphant return; returning in triumph; U1L1

考察	kǎochá	N.	investigation, inspection; U2L4
可愛	kěài	Adj.	cute; U3L2
科技成果	kējìchéngguǒ	NP.	the fruits (achievements) of science and technology; U2L4
科技文化	kējìwénhuà	NP.	science and technology, "scientific and technological literacy"; U2L4
可惜	kěxì	Adj.	it is a pity that; U3L3
控制	kòngzhì	V/N.	to control; control; U2L4
空中禁區	kōngzhōngjìnqū	NP.	no-fly zone; restricted airspace; U1L1
空中小姐	kōngzhōngxiǎojiě	N.	stewardess, female flight attendant; U2L1
跨度	kuàdù	N.	gap; U4L3
跨國經營	kuàguójīngyíng	VP.	to manage transnationally; U2L3
苦心揣摩	kǔxīnchuǎimó	Idiom.	(here) to painstakingly progress through trial and error; U3L4
來訪	láifǎng	VP.	to visit, to pay a visit to; to come and visit; U1L2
來歷	láilì	N.	origin, background, past history; U4L2
賴內爾．庫斯查爾	làinèiěrkùsīcháěr	Personal N.	the name of a Swedish athlete; U4L1
拉開	lākāi	V.	to pull open (curtain, drawer, etc.), to raise (curtain); U2L4
藍本	lánběn	N.	the original version, chief source (upon which later work was based); U3L4
蘭開夏	lánkāixià	Place N.	Lancashire (nothern England shire); U2L4
欄目	lánmù	N.	column; U4L3
籃球	lánqíu	N.	basketball; U4L2
累累	lěilěi	Adj.	plenty, many; U4L2
冷門	lěngmén	N.	unexpected result; dark horse; U4L2
聯播	liánbō	N.	broadcast over a network; i.e., national news broadcast hookup; U1L1
晾乾	liànggàn	V.	to dry by airing, to hang out to dry, to dry in the sun; U3L4
諒解	liàngjiě	N.	understanding; U1L4
聯合	liánhé	Adj/Adv/V.	united; jointly; to unite; (here) United Airlines; U2L1

考察	kǎochá	N.	investigation, inspection; U2L4
可爱	kěài	Adj.	cute; U3L2
科技成果	kējìchéngguǒ	NP.	the fruits (achievements) of science and technology; U2L4
科技文化	kējìwénhuà	NP.	science and technology, "scientific and technological literacy"; U2L4
可惜	kěxī	Adj.	it is a pity that; U3L3
控制	kòngzhì	V/N.	to control; control; U2L4
空中禁区	kōngzhōngjìnqū	NP.	no fly zone; restricted airspace; U1L1
空中小姐	kōngzhōngxiǎojiě	N.	stewardess, female flight attendant; U2L1
跨度	kuàdù	N.	gap; U4L3
跨国经营	kuàguójīngyíng	VP.	to manage transnationally; U2L3
苦心揣摩	kǔxīnchuǎimó	Idiom.	(here) to painstakingly progress through trial and error; U3L4
来访	láifǎng	VP.	to visit, to pay a visit to; to come and visit; U1L2
来历	láilì	N.	origin, background, past history; U4L2
赖内尔·库斯查尔	làinèiěrkùsīcháěr	Personal N.	the name of a Swedish athlete; U4L1
拉开	lākāi	V.	to pull open (curtain, drawer, etc.), to raise (curtain); U2L4
蓝本	lánběn	N.	the original version, chief source (upon which later work was based); U3L4
兰开夏	lánkāixià	Place N.	Lancashire (nothern England shire); U2L4
栏目	lánmù	N.	column; U4L3
篮球	lánqiú	N.	basketball; U4L2
累累	léiléi	Adj.	plenty, many; U4L2
冷门	léngmén	N.	unexpected result; dark horse; U4L2
联播	liánbō	N.	broadcast over a network; i.e., national news broadcast hookup; U1L1
晾干	liànggān	V.	to dry by airing, to hang out to dry, to dry in the sun; U3L4
谅解	liàngjiě	N.	understanding; U1L4
联合	liánhé	Adj/Adv/V.	united; jointly; to unite; (here) United Airlines; U2L1

聯合國	liánhéguó	N.	the United Nations; U1L3
聯合會	liánhéhuì	N.	federation; U2L4
聯合聲明	liánhéshēngmíng	NP.	joint communique; U1L4
了不起	liǎobùqǐ	Idiom.	great; U4L1
歷程	lìchéng	N.	the course of, the process of; U3L3
歷代	lìdài	N.	successive dynasties; down through the ages, throughout the decades; U3L4
列	liè	N.	rank (s); U3L3
列出	lièchū	V.	to specify, to name, to list as; U3L2
力量	lìliàng	N.	force; U2L1
理論	lǐlùn	N.	theory, theories; U2L4
凌晨	língchén	N.	early morning, before dawn; U3L2
領導人	lǐngdǎorén	N.	leaders; U3L3
領獎台	lǐngjiǎngtái	N.	the awards platform or podium; U4L2
領空	lǐngkōng	N.	territorial airspace (i.e., airspace over sovereign territory); U1L1
零售	língshòu	N.	retail; U2L4
領袖	lǐngxiù	N.	leader; U3L3
林莉	línlì	Personal N.	Lin Li, the name of a Chinese swimmer; U4L2
淋漓盡致	línlíjìnzhì	Idiom.	thoroughly, most vividly; to greatest effect; U3L4
李鵬	lǐpéng	Personal N.	Li Peng, Chinese Premier; U1L1
歷史最高水平	lìshǐzuìgāoshuǐpíng	NP.	record high, all time high; U1L1
立體感	lìtǐgǎn	N.	the sense of three-dimensional depth; U3L4
留級	liújí	VO.	to be held back a year, to fail to advance to the next grade; U2L3
六級大風	liùjídàfēng	NP.	a force six wind; U4L3
理由	lǐyóu	N.	reason; U2L3
隆重	lóngzhòng	Adj/Adv.	impressive, impressive and solemn, ceremonious; ceremoniously, solemnly; U3L3
露出馬腳	lòuchūmǎjiǎo	VO.	to let the cat out of the bag; to give oneself away; U1L2
樓台亭閣	lóutáitínggé	NP.	buildings and pavilions (implicitly two storied); U3L4
璐璐	lùlu	Personal N.	personal name or pet name;

联合国	liánhéguó	N.	the United Nations; U1L3
联合会	liánhéhuì	N.	federation; U2L4
联合声明	liánhéshēngmíng	NP.	joint communique; U1L4
了不起	liǎobùqǐ	Idiom.	great; U4L1
历程	lìchéng	N.	the course of, the process of; U3L3
历代	lìdài	N.	successive dynasties; down through the ages, throughout the decades; U3L4
列	liè	N.	rank (s); U3L3
列出	lièchū	V.	to specify, to name, to list as; U3L2
力量	lìliàng	N.	force; U2L1
理论	lǐlùn	N.	theory, theories; U2L4
凌晨	língchén	N.	early morning, before dawn; U3L2
领导人	lǐngdǎorén	N.	leaders; U3L3
领奖台	lǐngjiǎngtái	N.	the awards platform or podium; U4L2
领空	lǐngkōng	N.	territorial airspace (i.e., airspace over sovereign territory); U1L1
零售	língshòu	N.	retail; U2L4
领袖	lǐngxiù	N.	leader; U3L3
林莉	línlì	Personal N.	Lin Li, the name of a Chinese swimmer; U4L2
淋漓尽致	línlíjìnzhì	Idiom.	thoroughly, most vividly; to greatest effect; U3L4
李鹏	lǐpéng	Personal N.	Li Peng, Chinese Premier; U1L1
历史最高水平	lìshǐzuìgāoshuǐpíng	NP.	record high, all time high; U1L1
立体感	lìtǐgǎn	N.	the sense of three-dimensional depth; U3L4
留级	liújí	VO.	to be held back a year, to fail to advance to the next grade; U2L3
六级大风	liùjídàfēng	NP.	a force six wind; U4L3
理由	lǐyóu	N.	reason; U2L3
隆重	lóngzhòng	Adj/Adv.	impressive, impressive and solemn, ceremonious; ceremoniously, solemnly; U3L3
露出马脚	lòuchūmǎjiǎo	VO.	to let the cat out of the bag; to give oneself away; U1L2
楼台亭阁	lóutáitínggé	NP.	buildings and pavilions (implicitly two storied); U3L4
璐璐	lùlu	Personal N.	personal name or pet name;

			U3L2
縷縷青絲	lǚlǚqīngsī	NP.	many tresses of black hair (long black locks of women's hair); U3L4
《綠梅》	lǜméi	N.	Green Plum Blossom, the name of the art work; U3L3
輪	lún	Classifier.	the/a round (of talks, sports); U1L4
羅中立	luózhōnglì	Personal N.	Luo Zhongli, a well known Sichuanese oil painter, 1950-; U3L3
麥若彬	màiruòbīn	Personal N.	Mai Ruobin; U1L4
馬克	mǎkè	N.	the Deutsche Mark, the German Mark; U1L1
馬拉松	mǎlāsōng	N.	Marathon; U4L1
慢動作	màndòngzuò	NP.	slow motion; U4L3
曼谷	màngǔ	Place N.	Bangkok; U2L1
滿足於	mǎnzúyú	VP.	to be satisfied with; U3L4
貓	māo	N.	cat; U3L2
貿易	màoyì	N.	trade; commerce; U2L4
馬失前蹄	mǎshīqiántí	Idiom.	the horse lost its footing; i.e., to suffer an unexpected reversal; U4L2
馬英傑	mǎyīngjié	Personal N.	Ma Yingjie, the name of a bowling star from Taiwan; U4L2
枚	méi	Classifier.	classifier for medals＝塊; U4L1
美觀	měiguān	Adj.	to be attractive; good looking; U2L2
美國航空公司	měiguóhángkōnggōngsī	NP.	American Airlines (AA); U2L1
美術	měishù	N.	fine arts (as fields of study); U3L3
美術館	měishùguǎn	N.	Art Center, Musem of Fine Arts; U3L3
美元	měiyuán	N.	U.S. dollar; U1L1
蒙古族	měnggǔzú	N.	Mongolian nationality; U3L3
蒙漢	ménghàn	NP.	Mongolian and Han; U3L3
面積	miànji	N.	area, floor space; surface area; U3L1
面臨	miànlín	V.	to be faced with, to be up against; U3L2
描寫	miáoxiě	V.	to describe; to depict; U3L1
滅絕	mièjué	N/V.	extinction; to become extinct; U3L2
秘密	mìmì	Adj.	secret; U1L3

			U3L2
缕缕青丝	lǚlǚqīngsī	NP.	many tresses of black hair (long black locks of women's hair); U3L4
《绿梅》	lǜméi	N.	Green Plum Blossom, the name of the art work; U3L3
轮	lún	Classifier.	the/a round (of talks, sports); U1L4
罗中立	luózhōnglì	Personal N.	Luo Zhongli, a well known Sichuanese oil painter, 1950-; U3L3
麦若彬	màiruòbīn	Personal N.	Mai Ruobin; U1L4
马克	mǎkè	N.	the Deutsche Mark, the German Mark; U1L1
马拉松	mǎlāsōng	N.	Marathon; U4L1
慢动作	màndòngzuò	NP.	slow motion; U4L3
曼谷	màngǔ	Place N.	Bangkok; U2L1
满足于	mǎnzúyú	VP.	to be satisfied with; U3L4
猫	māo	N.	cat; U3L2
贸易	màoyì	N.	trade; commerce; U2L4
马失前蹄	mǎshíqiántí	Idiom.	the horse lost its footing; i.e., to suffer an unexpected reversal; U4L2
马英杰	mǎyīngjié	Personal N.	Ma Yingjie, the name of a bowling star from Taiwan; U4L2
枚	méi	Classifier.	classifier for medals = 块; U4L1
美观	měiguān	Adj.	to be attractive; good looking; U2L2
美国航空公司	měiguóhángkōnggōngsī	NP.	American Airlines (AA); U2L1
美术	měishù	N.	fine arts (as fields of study); U3L3
美术馆	měishùguǎn	N.	Art Center, Musem of Fine Arts; U3L3
美元	měiyuán	N.	U.S. dollar; U1L1
蒙古族	ménggǔzú	N.	Mongolian nationality; U3L3
蒙汉	ménghàn	NP.	Mongolian and Han; U3L3
面积	miànjī	N.	area, floor space; surface area; U3L1
面临	miànlín	V.	to be faced with, to be up against; U3L2
描写	miáoxiě	V.	to describe; to depict; U3L1
灭绝	mièjué	N/V.	extinction; to become extinct; U3L2
秘密	mìmì	Adj.	secret; U1L3

名將	míngjiàng	N.	famous star; U4L2
民間	mínjiān	N.	folk; U3L3
民間美術	mínjiānméishù	NP.	folk art; U3L3
民族	mínzú	N.	nationality; U3L3
秘書長	mìshūzhǎng	N.	the secretary-general; head of the secretariat; U1L2
模式	móshì	N.	the pattern; U3L3
莫斯科	mòsīkē	Place N.	Moscow; U2L1
摩托車	mótuōchē	N.	motorcycle; U4L3
《牡丹》	múdān	N.	peony, the name of a painting; U3L3
目的	mùdì	N.	purpose, goal, aim; U1L1
牧羊女	mùyángnǚ	N.	herd woman; U3L3
乃至	nǎizhì	Conj.	and (up to; including, to the extent of)＝以至; U1L2
難產	nánchǎn	N.	difficult labor; U3L2
內容	nèiróng	N.	content; U1L1
《紐約時報》	niǔyuēshíbào	N.	New York Times; U1L3
諾貝爾	nuòbèiěr	Personal N.	Alfred Bernhard Nobel (1833-1896), Swedish inventor of dynamite and other explosives, founder and legator of the Nobel Prizes; U3L4
排練	páiliàn	V.	to rehearse (play, performance, etc.); U3L1
排球	páiqiú	N.	volleyball; U4L1
排在	páizài	VP.	to be ranked at; U4L1
攀登	pāndēng	V.	to climb, to scale (a height, a mountain); U1L4
培訓	péixùn	V.	to train; U2L4
片斷	piànduàn	N.	excerpts; U4L3
平方米	píngfāngmǐ	N.	square meter; U3L1
評價	píngjià	V/N.	to evaluate; evaluation; U3L4
平靜地	píngjìngde	Adv.	peacefully; calmly; U1L3
乒乓球	pīngpāngqiú	N.	table tennis; U4L1
平穩	píngwěn	Adj.	smooth, stable, smooth and stable; U1L4
品種	pǐnzhǒng	N.	type, design, variety; breed(s), strain(s); U3L1
批准	pīzhǔn	N/V.	approval; to approve; U2L3
破壞	pòhuài	V.	to break; to undermine; U1L3
浦東	pǔdōng	Place N.	district east of Huang Pu River in Shanghai (an important special

名将	míngjiàng	N.	famous star; U4L2
民间	mínjiān	N.	folk; U3L3
民间美术	mínjiānměishù	NP.	folk art; U3L3
民族	mínzú	N.	nationality; U3L3
秘书长	mìshūzhǎng	N.	the secretary-general; head of the secretariat; U1L2
模式	móshì	N.	the pattern; U3L3
莫斯科	mòsīkē	Place N.	Moscow; U2L1
摩托车	mótuóchē	N.	motorcycle; U4L3
《牡丹》	mǔdān	N.	peony, the name of a painting; U3L3
目的	mùdì	N.	purpose, goal, aim; U1L1
牧羊女	mùyángnǚ	N.	herd woman; U3L3
乃至	nǎizhì	Conj.	and (up to; including, to the extent of) = 以至; U1L2
难产	nánchǎn	N.	difficult labor; U3L2
内容	nèiróng	N.	content; U1L1
《纽约时报》	niǔyuēshíbào	N.	New York Times; U1L3
诺贝尔	nuòbèiěr	Personal N.	Alfred Bernhard Nobel (1833-1896), Swedish inventor of dynamite and other explosives, founder and legator of the Nobel Prizes; U3L4
排练	páiliàn	V.	to rehearse (play, performance, etc.); U3L1
排球	páiqiú	N.	volleyball; U4L1
排在	páizài	VP.	to be ranked at; U4L1
攀登	pāndēng	V.	to climb, to scale (a height, a mountain); U1L4
培训	péixùn	V.	to train; U2L4
片断	piànduàn	N.	excerpts; U4L3
平方米	píngfāngmǐ	N.	square meter; U3L1
评价	píngjià	V/N.	to evaluate; evaluation; U3L4
平静地	píngjìngde	Adv.	peacefully; calmly; U1L3
乒乓球	pīngpāngqiú	N.	table tennis; U4L1
平稳	píngwěn	Adj.	smooth, stable, smooth and stable; U1L4
品种	pǐnzhǒng	N.	type, design, variety; breed(s), strain(s); U3L1
批准	pīzhǔn	N/V.	approval; to approve; U2L3
破坏	pòhuài	V.	to break; to undermine; U1L3
浦东	pǔdōng	Place N.	district east of Huang Pu River in Shanghai (an important special

			enterprise zone); U2L2
恰	qià	*Adv.*	just; right; U3L2
強調	qiángdiào	*V.*	to emphasize; U1L4
強化	qiánghuà	*V.*	to strengthen; U2L2
強勁	qiángjìn	*Adj.*	strong; U4L1
前進	qiánjìn	*N.*	progress; U1L4
簽名	qiānmíng	*VO.*	to sign (one's signature); U1L3
前往	qiánwǎng	*V.*	to proceed to, to go to, to head out for (place, event); U4L2
前原仁美	qiányuánrénměi	*Personal N.*	the name of a Japanese medley swimmer; U4L2
洽談	qiàtán	*V.*	to hold talks, to have consultation, to talk about (business, trade, commerce); U2L4
洽談會	qiàtánhuì	*N.*	talks (often business talks or informal negotiations); U2L2
齊白石	qíbáishí	*Personal N.*	Qi Baishi, great ink painter, 1863-1957; U3L3
期待	qídài	*V.*	to expect, to anticipate; to look forward to, to await; U1L4
啟德機場	qǐdéjīcháng	*NP.*	Kaitak Airport (in Hong Kong); U2L1
輕而易舉	qīngéryìjǔ	*Idiom*	without effort, easily; U1L4
輕工業	qīnggóngyè	*NP.*	light industry; U2L2
青年團	qīngniántuán	*N.*	Youth League; U2L4
輕傷	qīngshāng	*NP.*	light wound; U4L3
清新明麗	qīngxīnmínglì	*Idiom.*	to be fresh and (luminously) beautiful; U3L4
輕重工業	qīngzhònggōngyè	*NP.*	light and heavy industry; U2L2
起速	qǐsù	*VP.*	to accelerate, to start to accelerate; U4L3
秋菊	qiūjú	*Personal N.*	personal name, "Autumn Chrysanthemum(s)"; U3L1
企業	qǐyè	*N.*	enterprise, business; U2L2
企業界	qǐyèjiè	*N.*	business circles, entrepreneurial circles; U2L4
汽油	qìyóu	*N.*	gas; U4L3
奇中之奇	qízhōngzhíqí	*Idiom.*	the strangest of the strange; U3L4
區	qū	*N.*	area; district; zone; U1L1
全炳寬	quánbǐngkuān	*Personal N.*	the name of a South Korean weight-lifter; U4L2

			enterprise zone); U2L2
恰	qià	Adv.	just; right; U3L2
强调	qiángdiào	V.	to emphasize; U1L4
强化	qiánghuà	V.	to strengthen; U2L2
强劲	qiángjìn	Adj.	strong; U4L1
前进	qiánjìn	N.	progress; U1L4
签名	qiānmíng	VO.	to sign (one's signature); U1L3
前往	qiánwǎng	V.	to proceed to, to go to, to head out for (place, event); U4L2
前原仁美	qiányuánrénměi	Personal N.	the name of a Japanese medley swimmer; U4L2
洽谈	qiàtán	V.	to hold talks, to have consultation, to talk about (business, trade, commerce); U2L4
洽谈会	qiàtánhuì	N.	talks (often business talks or informal negotiations); U2L2
齐白石	qíbáishí	Personal N.	Qi Baishi, great ink painter, 1863-1957; U3L3
期待	qīdài	V.	to expect, to anticipate; to look forward to, to await; U1L4
启德机场	qǐdéjīchǎng	NP.	Kaitak Airport (in Hong Kong); U2L1
轻而易举	qīngéryìjǔ	Idiom.	without effort, easily; U1L4
轻工业	qīnggōngyè	NP.	light industry; U2L2
青年团	qīngniántuán	N.	Youth League; U2L4
轻伤	qīngsháng	NP.	light wound; U4L3
清新明丽	qīngxīnmínglì	Idiom.	to be fresh and (luminously) beautiful; U3L4
轻重工业	qīngzhònggōngyè	NP.	light and heavy industry; U2L2
起速	qǐsù	VP.	to accelerate, to start to accelerate; U4L3
秋菊	qiūjú	Personal N.	personal name, "Autumn Chrysanthemum(s)"; U3L1
企业	qǐyè	N.	enterprise, business; U2L2
企业界	qǐyèjiè	N.	business circles, entrepreneurial circles; U2L4
汽油	qìyóu	N.	gas; U4L3
奇中之奇	qízhōngzhīqí	Idiom.	the strangest of the strange; U3L4
区	qū	N.	area; district; zone; U1L1
全炳宽	quánbǐngkuān	Personal N.	the name of a South Korean weight-lifter; U4L2

全民工業	quánmíngōngyè	NP.	industries owned and operated by the State, State Industry; U2L2
取得	qǔdé	V.	to achieve; to obtain; U1L1
缺口	quēkǒu	N.	breach, gap; U4L3
取名	qǔmíng	VO.	to name, to choose a name for; U3L2
熱烈	rèliè	Adj/Adv.	warm, warmly, ardent; U1L2
人次	réncì	Classifier.	the sum of total people; U2L1
人工	réngōng	Adj/Adv.	artificial; artificially; U3L2
人民幣	rénmínbì	N.	Chinese Yuan (dollar), RMB; U1L1
任務	rènwù	N.	task, mission; U1L4
人像	rénxiàng	N.	portrait; U3L4
熱情	rèqíng	Adj.	warm, enthusiastic; U2L3
熱情洋溢	rèqíngyángyì	Idiom.	with enthusiasm and warmth; U3L4
日前	rìqián	N.	at present; now; U2L2
日用品	rìyòngpǐn	N.	articles of daily use; U2L2
榮獲	rónghuò	V.	to have the honor of winning, to be awarded (the prize, the distinction of); U3L1
入股	rùgǔ	VO.	to buy a share; to become a share holder; U2L3
瑞典	ruìdiǎn	Place N.	Sweden; U4L1
入口處	rùkǒuchù	NP.	entrance; U4L1
賽場	sàichǎng	N.	court, site of contest (here: bowling alley); U4L2
薩翁	sàwēng	N.	personal name: Saimlech, head of International Olympic Committee＝薩馬蘭奇; U3L2
色彩斑斕	sècǎibānlàn	Idiom.	richly colored, full of many rich shades and hues; U3L4
色彩繽紛	sècǎibīnfēn	Idiom.	extremely colorful, all the colors of the rainbow; U2L3
傻	shǎ	Adj.	stupid; U2L4
刹車	shāchē	VO.	to brake, to put on the brakes of a vehicle; U4L3
商定	shāngdìng	V.	to agree upon after consultation; U1L4
商品	shāngpǐn	N.	commodity; goods; U2L3
商人	shāngrén	N.	businessman; U2L4
商社	shāngshè	NP.	trading firm or company, shop, store; U2L3

全民工业	quánmíngōngyè	NP.	industries owned and operated by the State, State Industry; U2L2
取得	qǔdé	V.	to achieve; to obtain; U1L1
缺口	quēkǒu	N.	breach, gap; U4L3
取名	qǔmíng	VO.	to name, to choose a name for; U3L2
热烈	rèliè	Adj/Adv.	warm, warmly, ardent; U1L2
人次	réncì	Classifier.	the sum of total people; U2L1
人工	réngōng	Adj/Adv.	artificial; artificially; U3L2
人民币	rénmínbì	N.	Chinese Yuan (dollar), RMB; U1L1
任务	rènwù	N.	task, mission; U1L4
人像	rénxiàng	N.	portrait; U3L4
热情	rèqíng	Adj.	warm, enthusiastic; U2L3
热情洋溢	rèqíngyángyì	Idiom.	with enthusiasm and warmth; U3L4
日前	rìqián	N.	at present; now; U2L2
日用品	rìyòngpǐn	N.	articles of daily use; U2L2
荣获	rónghuò	V.	to have the honor of winning, to be awarded (the prize, the distinction of); U3L1
入股	rùgǔ	VO.	to buy a share; to become a share holder; U2L3
瑞典	ruìdiǎn	Place N.	Sweden; U4L1
入口处	rùkǒuchù	NP.	entrance; U4L1
赛场	sàichǎng	N.	court, site of contest (here: bowling alley); U4L2
萨翁	sàwēng	N.	personal name: Saimlech, head of International Olympic Committee = 萨马兰奇; U3L2
色彩斑斓	sècǎibānlàn	Idiom.	richly colored, full of many rich shades and hues; U3L4
色彩缤纷	sècǎibīnfēn	Idiom.	extremely colorful, all the colors of the rainbow; U2L3
傻	shǎ	Adj.	stupid; U2L4
刹车	shāchē	VO.	to brake, to put on the brakes of a vehicle; U4L3
商定	shāngdìng	V.	to agree upon after consultation; U1L4
商品	shāngpǐn	N.	commodity; goods; U2L3
商人	shāngrén	N.	businessman; U2L4
商社	shāngshè	NP.	trading firm or company, shop, store; U2L3

商學院	shāngxuéyuàn	N.	business school; U2L4
商業部門	shāngyèbùmén	NP.	the commerce department; U2L3
上映	shàngyìng	V.	to screen (a film), to be shown (in a cinema); U3L1
上院議長	shàngyuànyìzhǎng	Title/rank.	the leader of the upper house (of a congress, parliament); U1L1
殺傷	shāshāng	Adj/V.	to kill and wound; to inflict severe casualities (including death) upon; U1L3
沙特阿拉伯	shātèālābó	Place N.	Saudi Arabia; U2L2
設點	shèdiǎn	VO.	to select a spot, set something up; U2L4
省會	shěnghuì	N.	capital city of a province; U3L1
盛會	shènghuì	N.	a grand meeting; a grand competition or tournament; U3L1
聲明	shēngmíng	V/N.	to announce, to declare; announcement, declaration; U1L3
生涯	shēngyá	N.	career; U3L4
盛譽	shèngyù	N.	great fame; U4L3
神奇	shénqí	Adj.	wondrous, amazing, magical, miraculous; U3L4
涉外	shèwài	Abbrev.	involving foreign affairs or foreign nationals; U2L3
設有	shèyǒu	V.	to include within it, incorporate, to have established within it...; U3L3
攝製	shèzhì	V.	to film, to produce (a film), to make (a movie); U3L1
市	shì	N.	city; U2L4
拾	shí	V.	to pick up (from ground/floor); U1L1
市場	shìchǎng	N.	market; U2L2
實地	shídì	N.	on the spot, on site; U2L4
施工	shīgōng	VO.	to be under construction; U4L3
事故	shìgù	N.	accident; U2L1
世紀	shìjì	N.	century; U3L4
實踐	shíjiàn	N/V.	practice; to put into practice; U2L4
世界紀錄	shìjièjìlù	NP.	the world record; U4L1
實際需要	shíjìxūyào	NP.	actual needs, practical needs; U2L4
實力	shílì	N.	actual strength, real power;

商学院	shāngxuéyuàn	N.	business school; U2L4
商业部门	shāngyèbùmén	NP.	the commerce department; U2L3
上映	shàngyìng	V.	to screen (a film), to be shown (in a cinema); U3L1
上院议长	shàngyuànyìzhǎng	Title/rank .	the leader of the upper house (of a congress, parliament); U1L1
杀伤	shāshāng	Adj/V.	to kill and wound; to inflict severe casualities (including death) upon; U1L3
沙特阿拉伯	shātèālabó	Place N.	Saudi Arabia; U2L2
设点	shèdiǎn	VO.	to select a spot, set something up; U2L4
省会	shěnghuì	N.	capital city of a province; U3L1
盛会	shènghuì	N.	a grand meeting; a grand competition or tournament; U3L1
声明	shēngmíng	V/N.	to announce, to declare; announcement, declaration; U1L3
生涯	shēngyá	N.	career; U3L4
盛誉	shèngyù	N.	great fame; U4L3
神奇	shénqí	Adj.	wondrous, amazing, magical, miraculous; U3L4
涉外	shèwài	Abbrev.	involving foreign affairs or foreign nationals; U2L3
设有	shèyǒu	V.	to include within it, incorporate, to have established within it...; U3L3
摄制	shèzhì	V.	to film, to produce (a film), to make (a movie); U3L1
市	shì	N.	city; U2L4
拾	shí	V.	to pick up (from ground/floor); U1L1
市场	shìchǎng	N.	market; U2L2
实地	shídì	N.	on the spot, on site; U2L4
施工	shīgōng	VO.	to be under construction; U4L3
事故	shìgù	N.	accident; U2L1
世纪	shìjì	N.	century; U3L4
实践	shíjiàn	N/V.	practice; to put into practice; U2L4
世界纪录	shìjièjìlù	NP.	the world record; U4L1
实际需要	shíjìxūyào	NP.	actual needs, practical needs; U2L4
实力	shílì	N.	actual strength, real power;

206

			U4L1
市民	shìmín	*N.*	residents (of a city), townspeople; U2L4
使命	shǐmìng	*N.*	mission; U1L3
時期	shíqí	*N.*	period; U4L2
士氣	shìqì	*N.*	morale; U4L3
師生	shīshēng	*Abbrev.*	teachers and students＝老師和學生; U2L4
實施	shíshǐ	*V.*	to implement, to carry out, to put into effect; U2L4
石鐵音	shítiěyīn	*Personal N.*	Shi Tieyin; U4L1
實現	shíxiàn	*V.*	to achieve, to bring about, to realize (a victory or goal); U4L2
試驗隊	shìyànduì	*N.*	"test crew"; U1L1
失主	shīzhǔ	*N.*	person who lost the thing (or something); U1L1
首班	shǒubān	*NP.*	the first flight; U2L1
收藏	shōucáng	*V.*	to collect (works of art); U3L3
首次	shǒucì	*N.*	first time; U1L2
首都各界	shǒudūgèjiè	*NP.*	people from all walks of life in the capital city (北京); U1L1
守護	shǒuhù	*V.*	to be keeping watch over, to be on (sentry) duty; U3L2
首屆	shǒujiè	*N.*	the first session of; U2L2
首位	shǒuwèi	*N.*	top ranked, first position＝第一位; U4L1
首先	shǒuxiān	*Adv.*	first of all; firstly; U2L3
手續	shǒuxù	*N.*	procedure; U2L3
率團	shuàituán	*VO.*	to lead a delegation; U1L2
雙方	shuāngfāng	*NP.*	both sides; U1L4
書法	shūfǎ	*N.*	calligraphy (usually brush writing with Chinese brush pen and ink); U3L3
書畫	shūhuà	*NP.*	paintings and calligraphy; U3L3
水彩畫	shuǐcǎihuà	*N.*	watercolor painting(s); U3L4
順利	shùnlì	*Adv/Adj.*	smoothly; smooth; U2L1
碩果	shuòguǒ	*N.*	great achievement, impressive fruits of success; U4L2
術語	shùyǔ	*N.*	term, jargon; U2L3
屬於	shǔyú	*V.*	belong to; U4L2
絲	sī	*N.*	silk fibers; U3L4
絲綢錦緞	sīchóujǐnduàn	*NP.*	silks and brocades; U3L4
斯米多維奇	sīmǐduōwéiqí	*Personal N.*	the name of a person; U1L3

			U4L1
市民	shìmín	N.	residents (of a city), townspeople; U2L4
使命	shǐmìng	N.	mission; U1L3
时期	shíqī	N.	period; U4L2
士气	shìqì	N.	morale; U4L3
师生	shīshēng	Abbrev.	teachers and students = 老师和学生; U2L4
实施	shíshǐ	V.	to implement, to carry out, to put into effect; U2L4
石铁音	shítiěyīn	Personal N.	Shi Tieyin; U4L1
实现	shíxiàn	V.	to achieve, to bring about, to realize (a victory or goal); U4L2
试验队	shìyànduì	N.	"test crew"; U1L1
失主	shīzhǔ	N.	person who lost the thing (or something); U1L1
首班	shǒubān	NP.	the first flight; U2L1
收藏	shōucáng	V.	to collect (works of art); U3L3
首次	shǒucì	N.	first time; U1L2
首都各界	shǒudūgèjiè	NP.	people from all walks of life in the capital city (北京); U1L1
守护	shǒuhù	V.	to be keeping watch over, to be on (sentry) duty; U3L2
首届	shǒujiè	N.	the first session of; U2L2
首位	shǒuwèi	N.	top ranked, first position = 第一位; U4L1
首先	shǒuxiān	Adv.	first of all; firstly; U2L3
手续	shǒuxù	N.	procedure; U2L3
率团	shuàituán	VO.	to lead a delegation; U1L2
双方	shuāngfāng	NP.	both sides; U1L4
书法	shūfǎ	N.	calligraphy (usually brush writing with Chinese brush pen and ink); U3L3
书画	shūhuà	NP.	paintings and calligraphy; U3L3
水彩画	shuǐcǎihuà	N.	watercolor painting(s); U3L4
顺利	shùnlì	Adv/Adj.	smoothly; smooth; U2L1
硕果	shuòguǒ	N.	great achievement, impressive fruits of success; U4L2
术语	shùyǔ	N.	term, jargon; U2L3
属于	shǔyú	V.	belong to; U4L2
丝	sī	N.	silk fibers; U3L4
丝绸锦缎	sīchóujǐnduàn	NP.	silks and brocades; U3L4
斯米多维奇	sīmǐduōwéiqí	Personal N.	the name of a person; U1L3

絲線	sīxiàn	N.	silk thread; U3L4
飼養	sìyǎng	V.	to feed; to raise; U3L2
飼養員	sìyǎngyuán	N.	animal keeper; U3L2
宋德敏	sòngdémǐn	Personal N.	Song Demin, high ranking member of CCP and an important Chinese government official; U1L2
速度	sùdù	N.	speed, rate of speed, velocity; U1L3
蘇哈托	sūhātuō	Personal N.	Suharto, the president of Indonisia; U1L2
素描	sùmiáo	N/V.	sketch; to sketch; U3L4
縮寫	suōxiě	V.	to reduce, to shrink; U2L2
所需	suǒxū	Abbrev.	what is needed; U2L3
蘇蘇	sūsu	Personal N.	personal name or pet name; U3L2
蘇州	sūzhōu	Place N.	Suzhou, an old, scenic city located in Jiangsu Province; U3L3
泰國	tàiguó	Place N.	Thailand; U1L1
套語	tàoyǔ	N.	set phrase, fixed expressions; U1L1
特點	tèdiǎn	N.	characteristic; U2L1
特赫奧	tèhèào	Personal N.	the name of a Dutch athlete; U4L1
特技	tèjì	N.	stunts, tricks; stunts and special effects (in movies, photography, TV production); U4L3
特技王	tèjìwáng	NP.	the king of stunts; U4L3
特展	tèzhǎn	N.	a special exhibition; U3L3
特徵	tèzhēng	N.	characteristic, trait, distinguishing feature; U2L2
田徑	tiánjìng	N.	track and field; U4L1
天氣預報	tiānqìyùbào	NP.	weather broadcasting; U4L3
天然色澤	tiānránsèzé	NP.	natural color and sheen; U3L4
跳高	tiàogāo	N.	high jump; U4L2
跳遠	tiàoyuǎn	N.	long jump; U4L2
體操	tǐcāo	N.	gymnastics; U4L2
題辭	tící	VO.	to inscribe, to write a few words of commemoration; U3L3
鐵飯碗	tiěfànwǎn	N.	"the iron rice bowl" (refers to a job which one can not lose); U2L4

丝线	sīxiàn	N.	silk thread; U3L4
饲养	sìyǎng	V.	to feed; to raise; U3L2
饲养员	sìyǎngyuán	N.	animal keeper; U3L2
宋德敏	sòngdémǐn	Personal N.	Song Demin, high ranking member of CCP and an important Chinese government official; U1L2
速度	sùdù	N.	speed, rate of speed, velocity; U1L3
苏哈托	sūhátuō	Personal N.	Suharto, the president of Indonisia; U1L2
素描	sùmiáo	N/V.	sketch; to sketch; U3L4
缩写	suōxiě	V.	to reduce, to shrink; U2L2
所需	suóxū	Abbrev.	what is needed; U2L3
苏苏	sūsu	Personal N.	personal name or pet name; U3L2
苏州	sūzhōu	Place N.	Suzhou, an old, scenic city located in Jiangsu Province; U3L3
泰国	tàiguó	Place N.	Thailand; U1L1
套语	tàoyǔ	N.	set phrase, fixed expressions; U1L1
特点	tèdiǎn	N.	characteristic; U2L1
特赫奥	tèhèào	Personal N.	the name of a Dutch athlete; U4L1
特技	tèjì	N.	stunts, tricks; stunts and special effects (in movies, photography, TV production); U4L3
特技王	tèjìwáng	NP.	the king of stunts; U4L3
特展	tèzhǎn	N.	a special exhibition; U3L3
特征	tèzhēng	N.	characteristic, trait, distinguishing feature; U2L2
田径	tiánjìng	N.	track and field; U4L1
天气预报	tiānqìyùbào	NP.	weather broadcasting; U4L3
天然色泽	tiānránsèzé	NP.	natural color and sheen; U3L4
跳高	tiàogāo	N.	high jump; U4L2
跳远	tiàoyuán	N.	long jump; U4L2
体操	tǐcāo	N.	gymnastics; U4L2
题辞	tící	VO.	to inscribe, to write a few words of commemoration; U3L3
铁饭碗	tiěfànwǎn	N.	"the iron rice bowl" (refers to a job which one can not lose); U2L4

鐵管	tiěguǎn	N.	iron pipe; U4L3
提供	tígōng	V.	to provide; to supply; U2L2
停車場	tíngchēchǎng	N.	parking spot, parking lot; U4L1
停留	tíngliú	V.	to stop over (at); U2L1
聽取	tīngqǔ	V.	listen carefully; U2L4
體壇	tǐtán	N.	the field of sports, sports world, realm of athletics; U4L2
體壇縱橫	tǐtánzōnghéng	N.	sports review; U4L3
體委	tǐwěi	Abbrev.	sports committee＝中國體育委員會; U3L2
提要	tíyào	N.	highlight, synopsis, summary of main points; U1L1
體育	tǐyù	N.	sports; physical training, physical education; U4L1
體制	tǐzhì	N.	(political/economic) form(s), system; U1L4
體重	tǐzhòng	N.	weight; U3L2
同步	tóngbù	Adj.	synchronous, simultaneous, synchronic; U2L2
通航	tōngháng	VO.	to be in service; U2L1
銅牌	tóngpái	N.	bronze medal; U4L1
同期	tóngqī	N.	(in) the same period, (at) the same time, during the corresponding period; U2L2
通用設備	tōngyòngshèbèi	NP.	general equipment; U2L3
頭	tóu	Classifier.	head, the classifier for animals; U3L2
透露	tòulù	V.	to divulge; to leak out; to reveal; U1L3
投資	tóuzī	VO/N.	to invest; investment; U1L1
團體	tuántǐ	N.	team; U4L2
團體賽	tuántǐsài	N.	team competition; U4L2
推向	tuīxiàng	V.	to promote, to introduce into, to propel into; U2L4
推銷	tuīxiāo	V.	to promote (a product); U2L4
突破	tūpò	V/N.	to break through, to surpass, to break (a record); a breakthrough; U2L2
瓦霍諾	wǎhuònuò	Personal N.	personal name; U1L2
外方	wàifāng	N.	the foreign side; U2L3
外交部	wàijiāobù	N.	Foreign Ministry, Department (or Ministry of External Affairs [in USA＝Department of State]);

铁管	tiěguǎn	N.	iron pipe; U4L3
提供	tígōng	V.	to provide; to supply; U2L2
停车场	tíngchēchǎng	N.	parking spot, parking lot; U4L1
停留	tíngliú	V.	to stop over (at); U2L1
听取	tīngqǔ	V.	listen carefully; U2L4
体坛	tǐtán	N.	the field of sports, sports world, realm of athletics; U4L2
体坛纵横	tǐtánzònghéng	N.	sports review; U4L3
体委	tǐwěi	Abbrev.	sports committee = 中国体育委员会; U3L2
提要	tíyào	N.	highlight, synopsis, summary of main points; U1L1
体育	tǐyù	N.	sports; physical training, physical education; U4L1
体制	tǐzhì	N.	(political/economic) form(s), system; U1L4
体重	tǐzhòng	N.	weight; U3L2
同步	tóngbù	Adj.	synchronous, simultaneous, synchronic; U2L2
通航	tōngháng	VO.	to be in service; U2L1
铜牌	tóngpái	N.	bronze medal; U4L1
同期	tóngqī	N.	(in) the same period, (at) the same time, during the corresponding period; U2L2
通用设备	tōngyòngshèbèi	NP.	general equipment; U2L3
头	tóu	Classifier.	head, the classifier for animals; U3L2
透露	tòulù	V.	to divulge; to leak out; to reveal; U1L3
投资	tóuzī	VO/N.	to invest; investment; U1L1
团体	tuántǐ	N.	team; U4L2
团体赛	tuántǐsài	N.	team competition; U4L2
推向	tuīxiàng	V.	to promote, to introduce into, to propel into; U2L4
推销	tuīxiāo	V.	to promote (a product); U2L4
突破	tūpò	V/N.	to break through, to surpass, to break (a record); a breakthrough; U2L2
瓦霍诺	wǎhuònuò	Personal N.	personal name; U1L2
外方	wàifāng	N.	the foreign side; U2L3
外交部	wàijiāobù	N.	Foreign Ministry, Department (or Ministry of External Affairs [in USA=Department of State]);

			U1L3
外交家	wàijiāojiā	N.	diplomat; U3L4
外商	wàishāng	Abbrev.	外國商人 foreign business people; U1L1
王大力	wángdàlì	Personal N.	Wang Dali, the name of a Chinese swimmer; U4L2
往來	wánglái	V/N.	to have dealings with each other; exchange; U1L2
王室成員	wángshìchéngyuán	NP.	members of the royal family, royalty; U3L4
萬里	wànlǐ	Personal N.	Wan Li, an important Chinese government official; U1L1
頑強毅力	wánqiángyìlì	Idiom.	strong will; U4L1
維持	wéichí	V.	to maintain; U1L4
維妙維肖	wéimiàowéixiào	Idiom.	remarkably true to life; U3L4
帷幕	wéimù	N.	curtain(s); U2L4
威尼斯	wēinísī	Place N.	Venice; U3L1
為期	wéiqī	VO.	to be in effect, to last for (a certain period of time), to be completed by such and such a date; U1L4
喂養	wèiyǎng	V.	to raise; to feed＝飼養; U3L2
唯一	wéiyī	Adv.	only; U2L3
位於	wèiyú	V.	to be located at/in; U2L2
未中	wèizhòng	V.	fail to hit/score (the goal, the target, basket, etc.); U4L2
穩定	wěndìng	N/Adj/V.	stability; stable, firm; to stabilize; U1L2
文房四寶	wénfángsìbǎo	NP.	the four precious things in a Chinese study (紙 paper, 墨 ink, 筆 brushes, 硯 inkstone, inkslab for grinding and mixing ink); U3L3
問候	wènhòu	N/V.	greetings; to send one's best wishes to; U1L2
文化宮	wénhuàgōng	N.	the cultural palace; U3L3
溫州	wēnzhōu	Place N.	major coastal city, cultural center in southern Zhejiang province, China; U3L4
吳昌碩	wúchāngshuò	Personal N.	Wu Changshuo, great ink painter, 1844-1927; U3L3
烏爾提杯	wūěrtíbēi	N.	the Ugarti Cup; U3L1
武器	wǔqì	N.	weapon; U1L3
伍紹祖	wǔshàozǔ	Personal N.	the name of a person; U3L2

			U1L3
外交家	wàijiāojiā	N.	diplomat; U3L4
外商	wàishāng	Abbrev.	外国商人 foreign business people; U1L1
王大力	wángdàlì	Personal N.	Wang Dali, the name of a Chinese swimmer; U4L2
往来	wánglái	V/N.	to have dealings with each other; exchange; U1L2
王室成员	wángshìchéngyuán	NP.	members of the royal family, royalty; U3L4
万里	wànlǐ	Personal N.	Wan Li, an important Chinese government official; U1L1
顽强毅力	wánqiángyìlì	Idiom.	strong will; U4L1
维持	wéi chí	V.	to maintain; U1L4
维妙维肖	wéimiàowéixiāo	Idiom.	remarkably true to life; U3L4
帷幕	wéimù	N.	curtain(s); U2L4
威尼斯	wēinísī	Place N.	Venice; U3L1
为期	wéiqī	VO.	to be in effect, to last for (a certain period of time), to be completed by such and such a date; U1L4
喂养	wèiyǎng	V.	to raise; to feed = 饲养; U3L2
唯一	wéiyī	Adv.	only; U2L3
位于	wèiyú	V.	to be located at/in; U2L2
未中	wèizhòng	V.	fail to hit/score (the goal, the target, basket, etc.); U4L2
稳定	wěndìng	N/Adj/V.	stability; stable, firm; to stabilize; U1L2
文房四宝	wénfángsìbǎo	NP.	the four precious things in a Chinese study (纸 paper, 墨 ink, 笔 brushes, 砚 inkstone, inkslab for grinding and mixing ink); U3L3
问候	wènhòu	N/V.	greetings; to send one's best wishes to; U1L2
文化宫	wénhuàgōng	N.	the cultural palace; U3L3
温州	wēnzhōu	Place N.	major coastal city, cultural center in southern Zhejiang province, China; U3L4
吴昌硕	wúchāngshuò	Personal N.	Wu Changshuo, great ink painter, 1844-1927; U3L3
乌尔提杯	wūěrtíbēi	N.	the Ugarti Cup; U3L1
武器	wǔqì	N.	weapon; U1L3
伍绍祖	wǔshàozǔ	Personal N.	the name of a person; U3L2

無疑	wúyí	Adv.	doubtless; U4L3
夏季	xiàjì	N.	summer season; summer; U4L2
縣	xiàn	N.	county; U2L4
項	xiàng	Classifier.	event (s), classifier for athletic contests; U4L1
相處	xiāngchǔ	V.	get along with; U1L2
相得益彰	xiāngdéyìzhāng	Idiom.	each setting off (complementing) the other to best advantage; U3L3
項目	xiàngmù	N.	item(s); U2L3
詳細	xiángxì	Adv/Adj.	in detail, detailed; U1L1
享有	xiǎngyǒu	V.	to enjoy (fame, rights, prestige); U4L3
象徵	xiàngzhēng	N/V.	symbol; to symbolize; U3L2
鮮花	xiānhuā	N.	fresh flower; U4L3
銜接	xiánjiē	V.	to connect, to link up with, to dovetail with; U1L4
小麥	xiǎomài	N.	wheat; U2L3
銷售	xiāoshòu	N/V.	sale; to sell, to market; U2L2
銷售額	xiāoshòué	N.	total sales of ...; volume of sales or sales quota; U2L2
肖像	xiāoxiàng	N.	portrait (painted or drawn), portraiture; U3L4
小組	xiǎozǔ	N.	team, small group; U1L3
西北	xībéi	N.	northwest; (here) Northest Airlines; U2L1
洗滌	xǐdí	V.	to wash; to cleanse; U3L4
洩露	xièlù	V.	to divulge, to leak out, to reveal (a secret); U1L4
希爾頓飯店	xīěrdùnfàndiàn	NP.	Hilton Hotel; U1L3
協議	xiéyì	N.	agreement; U1L4
寫字檯	xiézìtái	N.	desk; U2L2
型	xíng	N.	model, type; U2L2
行動	xíngdòng	N.	action; U1L3
行人	xíngrén	N.	pedestrian; U3L1
形式	xíngshì	N.	form, style; U1L1
形象	xíngxiàng	N.	appearance; image; form; U2L2
形象逼真	xíngxiàngbīzhēn	VP.	image (s) is /are true to life, lifelike in shape and form; U3L4
新華社	xīnhuáshè	N.	Xin Hua News Agency; U1L2
新建的	xīnjiànde	Adj.	newly established; U2L3
新奇	xīnqí	Adj.	novel; strange; U3L2
欣然	xīnrán	Adv.	gladly; happily; U3L2

无疑	wúyí	Adv.	doubtless; U4L3
夏季	xiàjì	N.	summer season; summer; U4L2
县	xiàn	N.	county; U2L4
项	xiàng	Classifier.	event (s), classifier for athletic contests; U4L1
相处	xiāngchǔ	V.	get along with; U1L2
相得益彰	xiāngdéyìzhāng	Idiom.	each setting off (complementing) the other to best advantage; U3L3
项目	xiàngmù	N.	item(s); U2L3
详细	xiángxì	Adv/Adj.	in detail, detailed; U1L1
享有	xiǎngyǒu	V.	to enjoy (fame, rights, prestige); U4L3
象征	xiàngzhēng	N/V.	symbol; to symbolize; U3L2
鲜花	xiānhuā	N.	fresh flower; U4L3
衔接	xiánjiē	V.	to connect, to link up with, to dovetail with; U1L4
小麦	xiǎomài	N.	wheat; U2L3
销售	xiāoshòu	N/V.	sale; to sell, to market; U2L2
销售额	xiāoshòué	N.	total sales of ...; volume of sales or sales quota; U2L2
肖像	xiàoxiàng	N.	portrait (painted or drawn), portraiture; U3L4
小组	xiǎozǔ	N.	team, small group; U1L3
西北	xǐběi	N.	northwest; (here) Northest Airlines; U2L1
洗涤	xǐdí	V.	to wash; to cleanse; U3L4
泄露	xièlù	V.	to divulge, to leak out, to reveal (a secret); U1L4
希尔顿饭店	xīěrdùnfàndiàn	NP.	Hilton Hotel; U1L3
协议	xiéyì	N.	agreement; U1L4
写字台	xiězìtái	N.	desk; U2L2
型	xíng	N.	model, type; U2L2
行动	xíngdòng	N.	action; U1L3
行人	xíngrén	N.	pedestrian; U3L1
形式	xíngshì	N.	form, style; U1L1
形象	xíngxiàng	N.	appearance; image; form; U2L2
形象逼真	xíngxiàngbīzhēn	VP.	image (s) is /are true to life, lifelike in shape and form; U3L4
新华社	xǐnhuáshè	N.	Xin Hua News Agency; U1L2
新建的	xīnjiànde	Adj.	newly established; U2L3
新奇	xīnqí	Adj.	novel; strange; U3L2
欣然	xīnrán	Adv.	gladly; happily; U3L2

新聞	xīnwén	N.	news; U1L1
新聞記者	xīnwénjìzhě	N.	journalist, reporter, news reporter; U4L2
新聞媒介	xīnwénméijiè	N.	the news media; U1L3
信息	xìnxī	N.	information; U3L1
新作	xīnzuò	Abbrev.	new works=新的作品; U3L1
熊	xióng	N.	bear; U3L3
雄性	xióngxìng	N/A.	male gender; male; U3L2
喜慶	xǐqìng	N/Adj.	happy event; joyous; jubilant; U3L2
稀少	xīshǎo	Adj.	rare; scarce; U3L2
西斯科‧豪特爾	xīsīkēháotèěr	Personal N.	the name of an American athlete; U4L1
系統	xìtǒng	N.	system; U2L2
吸引	xīyǐn	V.	to attract; U2L4
稀有	xīyǒu	Adj.	rare; scarce; U3L2
宣告	xuāngào	V/N.	to announce; announcement; U3L2
選舉	xuǎnjǔ	V/N.	to hold an election, to elect; election; U1L4
選手	xuǎnshǒu	N.	contestant; player; U4L1
學生聯合會	xuéshēngliánhéhuì	N.	student federation; U2L4
學術	xuéshù	Adj.	academic; U3L3
序幕	xùmù	N.	prelude, "inaugural curtain", opening; U2L4
尋找	xúnzhǎo	V.	to look for, to search for; U1L3
栩栩如生	xúxúrúshēng	Idiom.	striking and lifelike; U3L4
亞軍	yàjūn	N.	runner-up, 2nd place; U4L2
楊斌	yángbīn	Personal N.	Yang Bin, the name of a Chinese weight-lifter; U4L2
楊東海	yángdōnghǎi	Personal N.	Yang Donghai, a well known artist; U3L3
嚴格	yángé	Adj.	strict; U2L2
楊尚昆	yángshàngkūn	Personal N.	Yang Shangkun, a very senior Chinese military and government official; U1L1
楊毅	yángyì	Personal N.	Yang Yi; U4L1
嚴謹	yánjǐn	Adj.	tight and well-knit; rigorous, strict (approach to learning, research, etc.); U3L4
嚴守	yánshǒu	VP.	to strictly observe or follow; U1L4
演藝界	yǎnyìjiè	NP.	the show business; U4L3

新闻	xīnwén	N.	news; U1L1
新闻记者	xīnwénjìzhě	N.	journalist, reporter, news reporter; U4L2
新闻媒介	xīnwénméijiè	N.	the news media; U1L3
信息	xìnxī	N.	information; U3L1
新作	xīnzuò	Abbrev.	new works = 新的作品; U3L1
熊	xióng	N.	bear; U3L3
雄性	xióngxìng	N/A.	male gender; male; U3L2
喜庆	xǐqìng	N/Adj.	happy event; joyous; jubilant; U3L2
稀少	xīshǎo	Adj.	rare; scarce; U3L2
西斯科·豪特尔	xīsīkēháotèěr	Personal N.	the name of an American athlete; U4L1
系统	xìtǒng	N.	system; U2L2
吸引	xīyǐn	V.	to attract; U2L4
稀有	xīyǒu	Adj.	rare; scarce; U3L2
宣告	xuāngào	V/N.	to announce; announcement; U3L2
选举	xuǎnjǔ	V/N.	to hold an election, to elect; election; U1L4
选手	xuǎnshǒu	N.	contestant; player; U4L1
学生联合会	xuéshēngliánhéhuì	N.	student federation; U2L4
学术	xuéshù	Adj.	academic; U3L3
序幕	xùmù	N.	prelude, "inaugural curtain", opening; U2L4
寻找	xúnzhǎo	V.	to look for, to search for; U1L3
栩栩如生	xúxǔrúshēng	Idiom.	striking and lifelike; U3L4
亚军	yàjūn	N.	runner-up, 2nd place; U4L2
杨斌	yángbīn	Personal N.	Yang Bin, the name of a Chinese weight-lifter; U4L2
杨东海	yángdōnghǎi	Personal N.	Yang Donghai, a well known artist; U3L3
严格	yángé	Adj.	strict; U2L2
杨尚昆	yángshàngkūn	Personal N.	Yang Shangkun, a very senior Chinese military and government official; U1L1
杨毅	yángyì	Personal N.	Yang Yi; U4L1
严谨	yánjǐn	Adj.	tight and well-knit; rigorous, strict (approach to learning, research, etc.); U3L4
严守	yánshǒu	VP.	to strictly observe or follow; U1L4
演艺界	yǎnyìjiè	NP.	the show business; U4L3

演員	yǎnyuán	N.	actor or actress; U3L1
邀請	yāoqǐng	V.	to invite; U1L2
要人	yàorén	N.	important people, VIP; U1L2
鴨溪	yāxī	Place N.	Duck Creek; U2L3
亞洲	yàzhóu	Place N.	Asia; U1L2
野外	yěwài	N.	in the wild; U3L2
伊	yī	Abbrev.	Iraq= 伊拉克; U1L3
以便	yǐbiàn	Prep.	so that, for the sake of, in order to; U1L2
已故	yǐgù	Adj.	late (refer to someone who has passed away); U3L3
一貫	yīguàn	Adv.	all along; U1L4
遺憾	yíhàn	V./N.	to regret; regret; U3L1
異乎尋常	yìhūxúncháng	Idiom.	extraordinary; very unusual; U1L3
一級	yījí	N.	of the first rank; grade one (here: of top priority); U3L2
移交	yíjiāo	V.	to hand over; to turn over; to transfer; U2L1
伊拉克	yīlākè	Place N.	Iraq; U1L1
毅力	yìlì	N.	persistence, will power, stamina; U1L4
銀杯	yínbēi	N.	silver cup; U3L1
引導	yǐndǎo	V.	to guide, to draw into; U2L4
印度尼西亞	yìndùníxīyà	Place N.	Indonesia; U1L1
應	yìng	Prep.	in response to; U1L2
贏得	yíngdé	V.	to win; U4L3
迎來	yínglái	V.	to welcome; to meet; U3L3
銀河	yínhé	N.	the Milky Way; U2L3
印尼	yìnní	Abbrev.	Indonesia＝印度尼西亞; U1L2
銀牌	yínpái	N.	silver medal; U4L1
引起	yǐnqǐ	V.	to arouse; U3L2
飲水	yǐnshuǐ	VO.	to drink water＝喝水; U3L3
翌日	yìrì	N.	＝第二天; U2L1
藝術	yìshù	N.	art, the arts; U3L1
一胎	yìtāi	N.	one litter of; U3L2
一條龍	yìtiáolóng	N.	a series of (a continuous process), an uninterrupted run of a series; U2L3
一行	yìxíng	N.	and accompanying party, and his/her group; U1L2
以至	yǐ zhì	Conj.	and (up to; including, to the

演员	yǎnyuán	N.	actor or actress; U3L1
邀请	yāoqǐng	V.	to invite; U1L2
要人	yàorén	N.	important people, VIP; U1L2
鸭溪	yāxī	Place N.	Duck Creek; U2L3
亚洲	yàzhōu	Place N.	Asia; U1L2
野外	yěwài	N.	in the wild; U3L2
伊	yī	Abbrev.	Iraq= 伊拉克; U1L3
以便	yǐbiàn	Prep.	so that, for the sake of, in order to; U1L2
已故	yǐgù	Adj.	late (refer to someone who has passed away); U3L3
一贯	yíguàn	Adv.	all along; U1L4
遗憾	yíhàn	V/N.	to regret; regret; U3L1
异乎寻常	yìhūxúncháng	Idiom.	extraordinary; very unusual; U1L3
一级	yìjí	N.	of the first rank; grade one (here: of top priority); U3L2
移交	yíjiāo	V.	to hand over; to turn over; to transfer; U2L1
伊拉克	yìlākè	Place N.	Iraq; U1L1
毅力	yìlì	N.	persistence, will power, stamina; U1L4
银杯	yínbēi	N.	silver cup; U3L1
引导	yǐndǎo	V.	to guide, to draw into; U2L4
印度尼西亚	yìndùníxīyà	Place N.	Indonesia; U1L1
应	yìng	Prep.	in response to; U1L2
赢得	yíngdé	V.	to win; U4L3
迎来	yínglái	V.	to welcome; to meet; U3L3
银河	yínhé	N.	the Milky Way; U2L3
印尼	yìnní	Abbrev.	Indonesia = 印度尼西亚; U1L2
银牌	yínpái	N.	silver medal; U4L1
引起	yǐnqǐ	V.	to arouse; U3L2
饮水	yǐnshuǐ	VO.	to drink water = 喝水; U3L3
翌日	yìrì	N.	= 第二天; U2L1
艺术	yìshù	N.	art, the arts; U3L1
一胎	yītāi	N.	one litter of; U3L2
一条龙	yìtiáolóng	N.	a series of (a continuous process), an uninterrupted run of a series; U2L3
一行	yìxíng	N.	and accompanying party, and his/her group; U1L2
以至	yǐzhì	Conj.	and (up to; including, to the

			extent of)＝乃至; U1L2
用戶	yònghù	N.	customers, consumers, users; U2L3
擁有	yǒngyǒu	V.	to possess; U3L3
有功	yǒugōng	VO.	to have made contributions to, to have rendered service to, commendable, noteworthy; U3L2
有關	yǒuguān	Prep.	related; concerning; relevant to; U3L1
有關各方	yǒuguāngèfāng	NP.	the concerned parties; U2L1
右肩	yòujiān	N.	the right shoulder; U4L3
有權	yǒuquán	VO.	to have a right (to do ...); U1L3
優勢	yōushì	N.	dominant position, favorable position; U4L2
有限公司	yǒuxiàngōngsī	NP.	limited company-Co., ltd.; U2L3
有益（於）	yǒuyì	Adj.	to be beneficial (to); to be advantageous (to); U1L3
游泳	yóuyǒng	V/N.	to swim; swimming; U4L1
游泳池	yóuyǒngchí	N.	swimming pool; U4L2
有針對性地	yǒuzhēnduìxìngde	Adv.	purposefully, with a focused goal; U2L4
有助（於）	yǒuzhù	Adj.	to be helpful; U1L3
於	yú	Prep.	to; U1L3
原訂計劃	yuándìngjìhuà	NP.	original plan; U1L3
緣何	yuánhé	QW.	why; U1L1
園林	yuánlín	N.	garden; U3L3
圓滿	yuánmǎn	Adv.	successfully, satisfactorily; U3L1
遇到	yùdào	V.	to encounter, to run into, to come across; U1L3
閱讀	yuèdú	N/V.	reading; to read; U1L3
預計	yùjì	V.	to estimate; U4L2
運動員	yùndòngyuán	N.	athlete; U4L1
運送	yùnsòng	V.	to transport; to ship; U2L1
運用	yùnyòng	V.	to utilize; to make use of; U2L4
運作	yùnzuò	N.	operation(s), procedures (business, manufacturing); U2L4
喻為	yùwéi	VP.	to be referred to as, to be likened to; U3L3
譽為	yùwéi	VP.	to be renowned as famous for; to be noted for, to be praised as; U3L4
在其	zàiqí	Prep P.	at its, on its; U1L1

			extent of) = 乃至; U1L2
用户	yònghù	N.	customers, consumers, users; U2L3
拥有	yōngyǒu	V.	to possess; U3L3
有功	yǒugōng	VO.	to have made contributions to, to have rendered service to, commendable, noteworthy; U3L2
有关	yǒuguān	Prep.	related; concerning; relevant to; U3L1
有关各方	yǒuguāngèfāng	NP.	the concerned parties; U2L1
右肩	yòujiān	N.	the right shoulder; U4L3
有权	yǒuquán	VO.	to have a right (to do ...); U1L3
优势	yōushì	N.	dominant position, favorable position; U4L2
有限公司	yǒuxiàngōngsī	NP.	limited company-Co., ltd.; U2L3
有益（于）	yǒuyì	Adj.	to be beneficial (to); to be advantageous (to); U1L3
游泳	yóuyǒng	V/N.	to swim; swimming; U4L1
游泳池	yóuyǒngchí	N.	swimming pool; U4L2
有针对性地	yǒuzhēnduìxìngde	Adv.	purposefully, with a focused goal; U2L4
有助（于）	yǒuzhù	Adj.	to be helpful; U1L3
于	yú	Prep.	to; U1L3
原订计划	yuándìngjìhuà	NP.	original plan; U1L3
缘何	yuánhé	QW.	why; U1L1
园林	yuánlín	N.	garden; U3L3
圆满	yuánmǎn	Adv.	successfully, satisfactorily; U3L1
遇到	yùdào	V.	to encounter, to run into, to come across; U1L3
阅读	yuèdú	N/V.	reading; to read; U1L3
预计	yùjì	V.	to estimate; U4L2
运动员	yùndòngyuán	N.	athlete; U4L1
运送	yùnsòng	V.	to transport; to ship; U2L1
运用	yùnyòng	V.	to utilize; to make use of; U2L4
运作	yùnzuò	N.	operation(s), procedures (business, manufacturing); U2L4
喻为	yùwéi	VP.	to be referred to as, to be likened to; U3L3
誉为	yùwéi	VP.	to be renowned as famous for; to be noted for, to be praised as; U3L4
在其	zàiqí	Prep P.	at its, on its; U1L1

讚賞	zànshǎng	V/N.	to praise and appreciate; praise and appreciation, appreciation; U2L3
贊同	zàntóng	V/N.	to agree, to approve of; agreement; U1L4
增進	zēngjìn	V.	to promote, to enhance; U1L2
增長	zēngzhǎng	V.	to increase; U2L2
摘取	zhāiqǔ	V.	to pick up; to take, to capture (prize, award); U4L2
漲到	zhǎngdào	V.	to go up to, to rise; U1L1
張小玲	zhāngxiǎolíng	Personal N.	Zhang Xiaoling; U4L1
張藝謀	zhāngyìmóu	Personal N.	personal name: a famous Chinese film director, directed "Red Sorghum", "Judou", "Raise the Red Lantern", etc.; U3L1
展覽	zhǎnlǎn	N/V.	exhibition; to exhbit; U3L3
戰勝	zhànshèng	V.	to overcome; U4L1
展示	zhǎnshì	V.	to demonstrate; to show; U4L1
展映	zhǎnyìng	V.	to exhibit, to show (a film); U3L1
照顧	zhàogù	V.	to take care of; look after; U4L1
珍藏	zhēncáng	V.	to collect (valuable, rare object); U3L3
針法	zhēnfǎ	N.	needle work; U3L4
政策	zhèngcè	N.	policy; U1L2
政黨	zhèngdǎng	N.	political party; U1L2
證據	zhèngjù	N.	evidence; proof of; testimony; U1L3
正面	zhèngmiàn	N.	the front; U4L3
正式	zhèngshì	Adj.	formal; U1L4
整體結構	zhěngtǐjiégòu	NP.	the overall pattern, the overall framework; U3L3
政協	zhèngxié	Abbrev.	the Chinese People's Political Consultative Conference; U1L2
徵兆	zhēngzhào	N.	omen, portent, sign; U4L3
珍品	zhēnpǐn	N.	treasures, master works; U3L3
真實性	zhēnshíxìng	N.	truthfulness; U2L1
箴言	zhēnyán	N.	admonition; a type of didactic literary composition; U3L3
折起來	zhéqǐlái	V.	to fold up, to fold together; U2L2
指	zhǐ	V.	to refer to; U2L3
值班	zhíbān	VO.	to be on duty; U3L2
製成	zhìchéng	V.	to make (into); to finish; U3L4

赞赏	zànshǎng	V.N.	to praise and appreciate; praise and appreciation, appreciation; U2L3
赞同	zàntóng	V/N.	to agree, to approve of; agreement; U1L4
增进	zēngjìn	V.	to promote, to enhance; U1L2
增长	zēngzhǎng	V.	to increase; U2L2
摘取	zhāiqǔ	V.	to pick up; to take, to capture (prize, award); U4L2
涨到	zhǎngdào	V.	to go up to, to rise; U1L1
张小玲	zhàngxiǎolíng	Personal N.	Zhang Xiaoling; U4L1
张艺谋	zhāngyìmóu	Personal N.	personal name: a famous Chinese film director, directed "Red Sorghum", "Judou", "Raise the Red Lantern", etc.; U3L1
展览	zhǎnlǎn	N/V.	exhibition; to exhbit; U3L3
战胜	zhànshèng	V.	to overcome; U4L1
展示	zhǎnshì	V.	to demonstrate; to show; U4L1
展映	zhǎnyìng	V.	to exhibit, to show (a film); U3L1
照顾	zhàogù	V.	to take care of; look after; U4L1
珍藏	zhēncáng	V.	to collect (valuable, rare object); U3L3
针法	zhēnfǎ	N.	needle work; U3L4
政策	zhèngcè	N.	policy; U1L2
政党	zhèngdǎng	N.	political party; U1L2
证据	zhèngjù	N.	evidence; proof of; testimony; U1L3
正面	zhèngmiàn	N.	the front; U4L3
正式	zhèngshì	Adj.	formal; U1L4
整体结构	zhěngtǐjiégòu	NP.	the overall pattern, the overall framework; U3L3
政协	zhèngxié	Abbrev.	the Chinese People's Political Consultative Conference; U1L2
征兆	zhēngzhào	N.	omen, portent, sign; U4L3
珍品	zhēnpǐn	N.	treasures, master works; U3L3
真实性	zhēnshíxìng	N.	truthfulness; U2L1
箴言	zhēnyán	N.	admonition; a type of didactic literary composition; U3L3
折起来	zhéqǐlái	V.	to fold up, to fold together; U2L2
指	zhǐ	V.	to refer to; U2L3
值班	zhíbān	VO.	to be on duty; U3L2
制成	zhìchéng	V.	to make (into); to finish; U3L4

指導	zhǐdǎo	V.	to guide and supervise; U3L4
執導	zhídǎo	V.	to direct; U3L1
制度	zhìdù	N.	system; U1L4
職工	zhígōng	N.	staff member; U3L2
直航	zhíháng	NP.	direct flight, direct routing (air or sea); U2L1
致力	zhìlì	V.	to engage in, to strive for, to devote one's energies to; U1L4
質量	zhǐliàng	N.	quality; U2L2
製片廠	zhìpiānchǎng	N.	film studio; U3L1
之前/後	zhíqián/hòu	Prep.	before/after; U1L1
製作	zhìzuò	V.	to manufacture, to turn out (products), to make; U2L3
眾多	zhòngduō	Adj.	many, a large number of; U2L4
中方	zhōngfāng	N.	the China side; U2L3
重工業	zhònggōngyè	NP.	heavy industry; U2L2
中共中央	zhònggòngzhōngyāng	Abbrev.	Central Committee of the Chinese Communist Party (CCCCP)＝中國共產黨中央委員會; U1L1
中南海	zhōngnánhǎi	Place N.	Zhongnanhai, the name of the walled compound in Beijing near the Imperial Palaces in which Chinese highest officials and their families reside; U1L2
重視	zhòngshì	V.	to place emphasis on, to take seriously, to devote much attenttion to, to value, to attach importance to; U3L3
中外合資	zhōngwàihézī	Idiom.	joint venture between China and a foreign country; U2L2
中央	zhōngyāng	Adj/N.	central; the center, central committee or "Party Central"; U2L4
周到	zhōudào	Adj.	attentive, considerate, paying attention to every detail, carefully worked out; U2L3
週年	zhōunián	N.	anniversary; U2L1
周學之	zhōuxuézhī	Personal N.	Zhou Xuezhi; U4L1
晝夜	zhòuyè	N.	day and night; 24 hour, round the clock; U3L2
駐	zhù	V.	to be stationed in/at; U1L4
抓舉	zhuājǔ	N.	snatch (in weight-lifting); U4L2

指导	zhǐdǎo	V.	to guide and supervise; U3L4
执导	zhídǎo	V.	to direct; U3L1
制度	zhìdù	N.	system; U1L4
职工	zhígōng	N.	staff member; U3L2
直航	zhíháng	NP.	direct flight, direct routing (air or sea); U2L1
致力	zhìlì	V.	to engage in, to strive for, to devote one's energies to; U1L4
质量	zhìliàng	N.	quality; U2L2
制片厂	zhìpiànchǎng	N.	film studio; U3L1
之前/后	zhīqián/hòu	Prep.	before/after; U1L1
制作	zhìzuò	V.	to manufacture, to turn out (products), to make; U2L3
众多	zhòngduō	Adj.	many, a large number of; U2L4
中方	zhōngfāng	N.	the China side; U2L3
重工业	zhònggōngyè	NP.	heavy industry; U2L2
中共中央	zhònggòngzhōngyāng	Abbrev.	Central Committee of the Chinese Communist Party (CCCCP) = 中国共产党中央委员会; U1L1
中南海	zhōngnánhǎi	Place N.	Zhongnanhai, the name of the walled compound in Beijing near the Imperial Palaces in which Chinese highest officials and their families reside; U1L2
重视	zhòngshì	V.	to place emphasis on, to take seriously, to devote much attenttion to, to value, to attach importance to; U3L3
中外合资	zhōngwàihézī	Idiom.	joint venture between China and a foreign country; U2L2
中央	zhōngyāng	Adj/N.	central; the center, central committee or "Party Central"; U2L4
周到	zhōudào	Adj.	attentive, considerate, paying attention to every detail, carefully worked out; U2L3
周年	zhōunián	N.	anniversary; U2L1
周学之	zhōuxuézhī	Personal N.	Zhou Xuezhi; U4L1
昼夜	zhòuyè	N.	day and night; 24 hour, round the clock; U3L2
驻	zhù	V.	to be stationed in/at; U1L4
抓举	zhuājǔ	N.	snatch (in weight-lifting); U4L2

專版	zhuānbǎn	N.	special section; U1L1
轉達	zhuǎndá	V.	to pass on to; to convey; U1L2
裝裱	zhuāngbiǎo	VP.	to mount and to frame; U3L3
壯觀	zhuàngguān	Adj.	splendid scene; U4L3
壯舉	zhuàngjǔ	N.	splendid deeds; U4L3
狀況	zhuàngkuàng	N.	state, condition, state of affairs; U2L4
莊泳	zhuāngyǒng	Personal N.	Zhuang Yong, a famous Chinese swimmer; U4L2
專家	zhuānjiā	N.	expert(s); U2L4
篆刻	zhuànkè	V/N.	to carve, seal carving; U3L3
專門	zhuānmén	V.	to specialize in; U2L3
專業	zhuānyè	N.	specialization; specialized trade; U1L2
專業性	zhuānyèxìng	Adj.	specialized; technical; U3L3
專用設備	zhuānyòngshèbèi	NP.	specialized equipment; U2L3
主辦	zhǔbàn	V.	to sponsor; U2L4
主辦單位	zhǔbàndānwèi	NP.	sponsoring institution; U4L3
註冊	zhùcè	V.	to register; U2L3
諸多	zhūduō	Adj.	many; U4L3
祝賀	zhùhè	V.	to congratulate; U1L1
駐華大使	zhùhuádàshǐ	NP.	the/an ambassador accredited to China; U1L4
矚目	zhǔmù	Adj.	amazing, remarkable, eye-opening; U1L1
準確無誤	zhǔnquèwúwù	Idiom.	accurate and precise; U4L3
主權	zhǔquán	N.	sovereignty; U2L1
助威	zhùwēi	VO.	to cheer on, to lend their moral support; U4L3
主演	zhǔyǎn	V.	to have the leading role (in a film, drama, etc.); U3L1
祝願	zhùyuàn	V.	to wish; U3L2
仔	zǐ	N.	offspring; baby; U3L2
自強	zìqiáng	VP.	to strengthen oneself; U4L1
自強不息	zìqiángbùxì	Idiom.	to make unceasing efforts to improve oneself; U4L3
自信	zìxìn	Adj/N.	self-confident; self-confidence; U4L1
自由泳	zìyóuyǒng	N.	free-style swimming; U4L2
總產量	zǒngchǎnliàng	NP.	total output; U2L2
總設計師	zǒngshèjìshǐ	NP.	the chief designer, chief architect of; U3L4
總數	zǒngshù	N.	total number; U4L1
總書記	zǒngshūjì	Title/rank.	General Secretary; U1L1

专版	zhuānbǎn	N.	special section; U1L1
转达	zhuǎndá	V.	to pass on to; to convey; U1L2
装裱	zhuāngbiǎo	VP.	to mount and to frame; U3L3
壮观	zhuàngguān	Adj.	splendid scene; U4L3
壮举	zhuàngjǔ	N.	splendid deeds; U4L3
状况	zhuàngkuàng	N.	state, condition, state of affairs; U2L4
庄泳	zhuāngyǒng	Personal N.	Zhuang Yong, a famous Chinese swimmer; U4L2
专家	zhuānjiá	N.	expert(s); U2L4
篆刻	zhuànkè	V/N.	to carve, seal carving; U3L3
专门	zhuānmén	V.	to specialize in; U2L3
专业	zhuānyè	N.	specialization; specialized trade; U1L2
专业性	zhuānyèxìng	Adj.	specialized; technical; U3L3
专用设备	zhuānyòngshèbèi	NP.	specialized equipment; U2L3
主办	zhǔbàn	V.	to sponsor; U2L4
主办单位	zhǔbàndānwèi	NP.	sponsoring institution; U4L3
注册	zhùcè	V.	to register; U2L3
诸多	zhūduō	Adj.	many; U4L3
祝贺	zhùhè	V.	to congratulate; U1L1
驻华大使	zhùhuádàshǐ	NP.	the/an ambassador accredited to China; U1L4
瞩目	zhǔmù	Adj.	amazing, remarkable, eye-opening; U1L1
准确无误	zhǔnquèwúwù	Idiom.	accurate and precise; U4L3
主权	zhǔquán	N.	sovereignty; U2L1
助威	zhùwēi	VO.	to cheer on, to lend their moral support; U4L3
主演	zhǔyǎn	V.	to have the leading role (in a film, drama, etc.); U3L1
祝愿	zhùyuàn	V.	to wish; U3L2
仔	zǐ	N.	offspring; baby; U3L2
自强	zìqiáng	VP.	to strengthen oneself; U4L1
自强不息	zìqiángbùxī	Idiom.	to make unceasing efforts to improve oneself; U4L3
自信	zìxìn	Adj/N.	self-confident; self-confidence; U4L1
自由泳	zìyóuyǒng	N.	free-style swimming; U4L2
总产量	zǒngchǎnliàng	NP.	total output; U2L2
总设计师	zǒngshèjìshǐ	NP.	the chief designer, chief architect of; U3L4
总数	zǒngshù	N.	total number; U4L1
总书记	zǒngshūjì	Title/rank.	General Secretary; U1L1

總體工程	zǒngtǐgōngchéng	NP.	the overall project; U3L1
總統	zǒngtǒng	Title/rank.	president; U1L2
總主席	zǒngzhǔxí	N.	the chairperson; U1L2
走向輝煌	zǒuxiànghuīhuáng	VO.	"Bound for Glory", "advancing towards brilliant splendor"; U3L1
鑽石	zuànshí	N.	diamond; U2L2
最佳	zuìjiā	Adj.	the best; U3L1
最具	zuìjù	V.	to possess the greatest..., the most...; U3L3
最具代表性	zuìjùdàibiǎoxìng	VO.	to be the leading example of; U3L3
最終	zuìzhōng	Adv.	finally, eventually; U1L4
作品	zuòpǐn	N.	(artistic or literary) works; U3L3
座談會	zuòtánhuì	N.	talk(s), discussion meeting, forum; U4L2
作用	zuòyòng	N.	function; role; U2L2
足球	zúqiú	N.	soccer; U4L2
組委會	zǔwěihuì	Abbrev.	executive committee＝組織委員會; U3L3
組織	zǔzhí	N/V.	organization; to organize; U1L3

总体工程	zǒngtǐgōngchéng	NP.	the overall project; U3L1
总统	zǒngtǒng	Title/rank.	president; U1L2
总主席	zǒngzhǔxí	N.	the chairperson; U1L2
走向辉煌	zóuxiànghuīhuáng	VO.	"Bound for Glory", "advancing towards brilliant splendor"; U3L1
钻石	zuànshí	N.	diamond; U2L2
最佳	zuìjiā	Adj.	the best; U3L1
最具	zuìjù	V.	to possess the greatest..., the most...; U3L3
最具代表性	zuìjùdàibiǎoxìng	VO.	to be the leading example of; U3L3
最终	zuìzhōng	Adv.	finally, eventually; U1L4
作品	zuòpǐn	N.	(artistic or literary) works; U3L3
座谈会	zuòtánhuì	N.	talk(s), discussion meeting, forum; U4L2
作用	zuòyòng	N.	function; role; U2L2
足球	zúqiú	N.	soccer; U4L2
组委会	zúwěihuì	Abbrev.	executive committee = 组织委员会; U3L3
组织	zúzhǐ	N/V.	organization; to organize; U1L3

Appendix II: Abbreviation List

Abbreviations

Abbrev.	abbreviation
Adj.	adjective
Adv.	adverb
Classifier	classifier
Idiom.	idiomatic expression
N.	noun
NP.	noun phrase
Personal N.	personal noun
Place N.	place name
Prep P.	prepositional phrase
Prep.	preposition
Title/rank	title or rank
V.	verb
VO.	verb object
VP.	verb phrase